Rebecca Wilson grew up in Forbes, New South Wales, where Kate Kelly lived in the last years of her life. Rebecca has been hearing local stories about Kate all her life, and she has been researching, painting and writing Kate's tragic story for over a decade.

www.rebeccawilsonart.com
www.instagram.com/rebeccawilsonart
www.facebook.com/rwilsonart

⁓

'Cleverly spins an untold story into a very readable yarn'
Professor Graham Seal, cultural historian

'For the first time, Kate Kelly is given the attention she deserves, and it's quite a story. Rebecca Wilson skilfully evokes the realities of the lives of the Kellys.'
Kerry Negara, documentary filmmaker

Kate KELLY

THE TRUE STORY OF
NED KELLY'S
LITTLE SISTER

REBECCA WILSON

ALLEN&UNWIN

SYDNEY·MELBOURNE·AUCKLAND·LONDON

Allen & Unwin
83 Alexander Street
Crows Nest NSW 2065
Australia
Phone: (61 2) 8425 0100
Email: info@allenandunwin.com
Web: www.allenandunwin.com

A catalogue record for this book is available from the National Library of Australia

ISBN 978 1 76087 967 9

Cover images: E.G. Tims (1878), *Kate Kelly?*, ca. 1873–1878, Australian Photographic Co., 1873, National Library of Australia; Charles Douglas Richardson, *Stringybark saplings Diamond Creek*, 1909, watercolour, 49 × 33 cm. Bayside City Council Art and Heritage Collection. Donated by the artist 1931. 0000-398

Map by John Frith, Flat Earth Mapping
Internal design by Post Pre-press Group
Set in 12/17 pt Freight Text Pro by Post Pre-press Group, Brisbane
Printed and bound in Australia by McPhersons Printing Group

10 9 8 7 6 5 4 3

The paper in this book is FSC® certified. FSC® promotes environmentally responsible, socially beneficial and economically viable management of the world's forests.

Dedicated to Dave, my family, friends and everyone who has provided their generous support, good humour and kindness. Thank you!

Contents

A Melbourne telegram states that the police are in a quandary about Kate Kelly. She has completely slipped through their fingers.

NORTHERN ARGUS, FRIDAY, 20 JUNE 1879

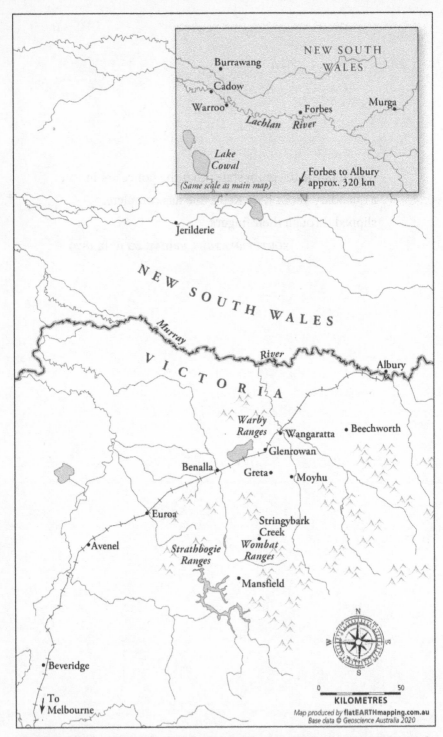

The main map shows key towns across 'Kelly country' in Victoria where Kate Kelly and the Kelly Gang were active. The inset shows the properties of Cadow, Warroo and Burrawang in New South Wales, where Kate, her friend Hugh McDougall and husband Bricky Foster worked respectively, and the town of Forbes, where Kate lived.

Preface

> *May the angels protect this young heroine bold and her*
> *name be recorded in letters of gold.*
>
> AUSTRALIAN FOLK SONG LYRIC ABOUT KATE KELLY

Every Australian knows about Ned Kelly, but quietly camouflaged in his shadow is his little sister Kate. Ned and his Kelly Gang are the best-known bushranging outlaws in Australia's history. The Kelly story continues to mesmerise and engage writers, musicians, artists and filmmakers. The legend of Ned Kelly looms large in the Australian psyche, and remains a source of controversy one hundred and forty years after Ned's execution.

Meanwhile, Kate Kelly, if remembered at all, is known mostly as the fourteen-year-old, attractive younger sister to Ned and Dan who was harassed by Constable Fitzpatrick at the Kelly homestead in April 1878 when he arrived without a warrant to supposedly arrest Dan. But there is so much more to know about Kate.

After researching her life for over a decade, I believe Kate Kelly should be remembered with admiration and compassion. This courageous and talented woman struggled to overcome enormous adversity during her extraordinary, tragic and short life. I have used the tools of creative writing combined with historical research to present the remarkable story of Kate's life from her viewpoint.

Kate Kelly was a reluctant celebrity. She had the Kelly X-factor, a charisma and an allure that people could not get enough of. It was unheard of for a young woman who was a semi-educated, first-generation Australian from a poor, criminal family to be relentlessly sought after by the public, or to have a notable media presence. Even if her reputation was mostly negative, the press was talking about her and people were flocking to see her, long after the death of her outlaw brothers.

I first heard of Kate Kelly while growing up in Forbes, a small town in the central west of New South Wales, the place where Kate spent the last fourteen years of her life. When I was a teenager, my uncle told me stories about Kate that had been passed on to him by relatives who had lived near her. These stories suggested a kind woman who wanted to help anyone out if she could.

In 2007, some of my social commentary paintings focused on Australian icons such as Sir Sidney Nolan's Ned Kelly, but I did not give Kate Kelly another thought until a conversation I had with someone in 2010 who told me amazing stories about her that I'd never heard before. It was never my intention to wade into the controversies of the Kelly legend, but from that moment it was like a rip current pulled me out to sea where I have been swimming for much longer than I imagined.

I started to research Kate the day after that conversation. I soon discovered that it was my relatives who hired Kate when she came to Cadow Station, thirty-five miles outside Forbes, under the alias Ada Hennessey in 1885 to work as a domestic servant. That knowledge made me feel even more connected to Kate and cemented my drive to really understand her and to shine a light on her intriguing story.

Throughout the last ten years I have researched, written and painted Kate's life. I have exhibited my paintings and discussed my research across New South Wales, Victoria and in London where I also presented a talk about Kate Kelly at London's Central Library in 2018.

I have gathered facts and folklore about Kate from far and wide, trying to piece it together and understand what it all means. A major challenge has been the many gaps in information and the huge amount of conflicting information. Many sections of Kate's life are undocumented, some records have been destroyed and there are differing accounts of key events—including from Kelly family members themselves.

It has been a treasure hunt that has led me to all kinds of records, newspaper articles, letters, certificates and more. I have visited museums, family history groups and locations of key events in Kate's life. I have accessed archival interviews and talked to other researchers as well as medical and police experts. I have read suicide reports, missing persons information, material on peri-natal depression and anxiety (PNDA) and post-traumatic stress disorder (PTSD) and much more, all in an effort to get to know the real Kate, to understand her circumstances and her suffering, and to try to interpret her choices and actions. Through that process I have uncovered new information about Kate and some of the key figures in her life. It has been a pleasure and an obsession to try to catch the essence of Kate Kelly and incorporate everything I have learned about her into this book.

Part 1

THE DISAPPEARANCE OF KATE KELLY

Of course she helped her brothers in their trouble. Yes, she fooled the police time after time. They drove the girlishness out of her. And instead of the girl, they found that they had to do with a woman and not an ordinary woman, but one who knew the bush and knew no fear and who loved her brothers with as great a love as a woman's bosom could hold. Poor little Kate!

Jim Kelly, Kate's brother
Cookson interview for *The Sun*, 1911

1

Finding Kate

An unusual object floated in the water. At first glance, someone might have thought the jumble of black and white was a pelican. The pale white flesh of a woman's lower back revealed itself to the sky. Her black dress had worked its way up and jellyfished over her head.

Her arms were drifting out by her sides, her legs in dark stockings were gently bobbing underneath. If she had been going for an innocent paddle, she would have taken those stockings off. A pair of tired old boots, her only shoes, sat on the bank. Next to them, two empty beer bottles rested.

Almost as if time had stopped, Kate Kelly floated alone. The locals knew this little sister to the bushranger Ned Kelly as Mrs Ada Foster. Below the water, Kate's decay was delayed, but along her exposed back the heat of the day hurried it. Her body drifted in the lagoon for eight long days, waiting for someone to care.

Soft gargles from currawongs gently split the air. Fish and turtles burst the surface of the water, but silence embraced the body. In the surrounding bushland, clumps of enormous river gums and eucalypts, hundreds of years old, stretched themselves up and out of the ground in a twisting motion as if to guard her.

Ancient behemoths, diprotodons, roamed here millions of years before, leaving their pristinely preserved bones suctioned into the clay. This secluded lagoon, located on the outskirts of Forbes in the central west of New South Wales, was eerie and quietly held many secrets, like a wise old woman. Anything could happen at the lagoon and no one would know.

If you were unlucky enough to be passing through the isolated area in times gone by, bushrangers might have relieved you of your money or your arms. Unhappy men had been known to go there to shoot themselves. Drowning or poisoning was more what a woman might do.

So, what was Mr Thomas Sullivan, known to the police as 'Tommy', doing at the lagoon on Friday, 14 October 1898, when he stumbled across Kate Kelly's body? Did he really only discover her body or was there more to it?

From the still location of the corpse, birds scattered and shrieked, their privacy interrupted, as Sullivan walked away from the body and pointed himself towards town. The last place he wanted to go was the police station, but there was no way out. Many eyes had spotted him on the way to the lagoon, and they weren't going to tell any lies to cover him.

Sullivan dragged his feet in an easterly direction, slowly weaving his way through a web of timber huts and stained canvas tents. He passed rough shanties where dirty-clothed fossickers exchanged their fly-shit specks of gold for rocket fuel to forget their troubles. He thought about getting a shot of it for himself, but the drinkers glared at him from their log seats.

Peering eyes disappeared behind fast-closing tent flaps, and tough-looking women in petticoat skirts with revealing bodices swept dust in his direction, signalling him to keep moving away from them, unless he had money for services they could render.

He pushed past Asian hawkers wearing hats like small umbrellas as they shuffled along with bamboo poles stretched across their shoulders. Sullivan couldn't help but snigger an exaggerated *'Neee how'* as he watched the little men balancing baskets on either side of themselves. He kept his head down to avoid any further trouble, increasing his pace just for a moment.

The stench of too many poor people living in close quarters made the hairs in his nose twitch. The smell of himself didn't do him any favours either. Sullivan's residence was a tent on the outskirts of town, near Bartley's Creek. He was just one in a row of vagabond neighbours, allowed to stay there by the grace of the landowner.

His palms were sweaty and his mouth was dry when his soles hit the dry clay of Lachlan Street. To buy himself a little more time he walked to Victoria Park, a leafy, tree-filled refuge in the heart of the town square. The park was surrounded by proud and extravagant Victorian buildings: the town hall, the courthouse and a couple of churches. Next to the courthouse and facing onto the park was the police station.

Nearby, the clock of the post office made itself known through twelve loud gongs while Sullivan was catching his breath and splashing his face at the elaborate water fountain in the middle of the park. Two cyclists wheeled passed him with their trouser legs rolled up and jackets flapping behind them in the wind. Sullivan smirked, jealous of the riders as they exchanged greetings with young women who were strolling together, seeking respite beneath shady canopies. Women like that never stopped for him; he had nothing they wanted.

Opposite the park, the wide verandah and red brick of the lock-up keeper's residence drew his attention. No one was there.

He wondered who was around at the courthouse next door and scanned through the pike rails bedded in sandstone blocks. Sullivan shuddered a little at the huge coat of arms that dominated the entrance, while he remembered stories about the foul stench of stale urine at the overcrowded lock-up next to it. His pulse raced thinking of what he would say to the police, and by the time he finally plucked up the guts to get his dodgy arse through the police station door, he declared, 'It wasn't me! I didn't lay a hand on her!'

Senior Constable J.J. Garstang watched the panicked mess of a man stumble through the door. 'What have you done this time, Tommy?' was all Garstang could muster in response to Sullivan's urgent plea. The policeman leaned on a high wooden counter, bored with the day and hesitant to place any confidence in whatever this familiar figure was about to reveal.

Garstang knew Sullivan, and the dishevelled man carried a hot smell of guilt with him today. Indeed, Sullivan would be branded a 'bad character' by the police in the near future for stealing and maliciously killing a horse in a fit of rage. He would soon spend three years in Bathurst Gaol for his wild actions against the innocent animal and his violent threats designed to warn trial witnesses from testifying against him.

Just like Kate's family, the Sullivans stuck together, and they would find themselves in legal hot water in the next few years. Sullivan's sister Mary would take a successful shot at an ex-boyfriend with a pistol and be charged for 'wounding with intent to kill', while his brother John would wear charges as an accessory before the fact, supporting his sister's violent revenge as if it was a normal thing to do.

But on this day, Garstang's ivory skin turned sticky with perspiration as Sullivan revealed that he'd found Mrs Foster's body at the lagoon. The policeman ran his finger under his tight collar, failing to find any relief. Of all the people to find the woman they'd known was missing, it had to be this man? What did it say about Garstang's police work that a smelly homeless man found Mrs Foster before he did? How did Sullivan even know who it was?

Regardless of how much Garstang's pride was stung, he knew that he had to get to the body. Sullivan, on the other hand, had a desperate need to get the hell away from the police. Garstang wanted Sullivan to take them to the body, but Sullivan said he would meet them at the lagoon and then shot through.

THE BODY

Senior Constable Garstang and his offsider, Constable Kennedy, made haste in their wagonette to the lagoon on the Bedgerabong Road behind the new racecourse and showground. Trudging their way through the surrounding scrub, watching out for snakes as they squashed stringy clumps of rushes underfoot, Garstang looked around from the highest bank he could find and spotted Kate's body. There was no sign of Sullivan. He yelled out to Kennedy to keep watch as he sidled down the bank, swatting flies and mosquitoes in the heat while he approached the corpse.

Brown sticky mud rimmed the waterhole, the water shrinking hour by hour in the drought. The chocolate mud sucked Garstang's boots downwards, and each step released a putrid stench and swarms of insects into the air.

He waded into the water. Nervous that he might become stuck there, he stretched to his limit to dislodge Kate's body, which had become snared on a tree stump about twelve feet from the bank. The snare would one day become known to locals as 'Kate's stump', and even when it rotted and disappeared, its memory would be recounted to further generations.

Garstang pulled Kate's body through the water back to the bank and signalled Kennedy to fetch the stretcher from the wagon. The two policemen counted the days since Mrs Susan Hurley, Kate's neighbour, had reported as missing the woman she knew as Ada Foster.

The distressed Mrs Hurley's young legs had swiftly carried her the two hundred yards or so from her home on the corner of Browne and Sherriff streets to the police station at 10 p.m. on Thursday, 6 October.

Susan's home was on the opposite corner to Kate's, and the loyal neighbour had finally concluded that she had better let the police know that Kate had been gone since Wednesday afternoon. Kate's absence had left her infant and three children with no one to care for them, and Susan found herself filling that role. 'Where could she be?' Susan had asked the police as she made her report, disturbed about Kate's welfare.

In the midday heat at the lagoon's edge, Garstang and Kennedy rolled Kate's body onto the stretcher, attempting to do no further damage to it. They trampled across the undulations of empty waterholes, kicking up clouds of bulldust, until they reached the wagonette and escorted the corpse to Mrs Ryan's Carlton Hotel in Rankin Street.

Mrs Ryan was known for having a clay pipe permanently fixed to her face, like a smoke-breathing dragon. No one was willing to mess with her or her stern shadow. Many hotels came and went in the district but hers had stood the test, lasting nine years already. She directed the corpse-carrying men through the back door to the cellar as she blew smoke out her nose and stepped out of the way.

Garstang barked orders while he wiped his sweaty brow, wishing he could have a beer or something stronger. 'Kennedy, go find Doctor McDonnell.' He needed the government medical officer to examine the body and establish a cause of death. Meanwhile, Garstang went to find Mrs Hurley so she could identify Kate and confirm his suspicions. He hated to admit it, but Sullivan was probably right.

Once he located Mrs Hurley, she would, of course, want to know why Kate's husband had not been pulled in to perform the horrid and gut-wrenching task instead of her.

Where *was* Mr Foster?

2

The Absent Husband

Kate's noticeably absent husband, William Foster, aka Bill, aka Bricky, was a horse tailer and labourer working on a sheep and cattle station known as Burrawang, about thirty-four miles from Forbes. He had been staying out there for five months, ever since an abusive tirade he'd directed towards his pregnant wife.

Charges had been laid against Bricky, and he'd paid a reasonably hefty fine of over five pounds on 20 May that year for 'use of abusive language towards his wife within his own house, within the hearing of the public'. The incident and continuing tensions between husband and wife had been the impetus for Bricky to start working away from home.

In the 1890s, calling someone 'Bricky' meant they were tough. Kate's husband lived up to his name with a reputation as a wild man who liked a drink and could hold his own if it came to knuckles. A tall figure with a wide face and generous features, the crown of his hat was always pushed right up as if he were a Canadian Mountie, a style unique to Bricky. Beneath the felt of his hat, a side-parted, slicked-back crop of straight brown hair could be found.

Burrawang Station stretched across a staggering five hundred thousand acres over Wiradyuri lands, nestled on the banks of the Kalari River, named the Lachlan by the English. Hundreds of hard-working shearers would offer their sweat for money at Burrawang as the wool clip mounted to five thousand bales in its peak seasons off the backs of over two hundred and seventy thousand sheep.

Positioned on flat flood plains, Burrawang had many magnifi-cent tall eucalypts. The colour of their bark, ranging from yellows to reds to whites, matched the clays found at every bend in the river. Ubiquitous kurrajong trees displayed dainty white flowers that popped against bunches of black seed pods, while thick tufts of native grasses and rushes in hues of yellow and beige raced each other across the uneven ground from the river's edge.

Mustering sheep was exhausting work across such vast country-side. Men in loose shirts, wide-brimmed hats, worn trousers and old boots would scour the bush for the sheep. Their hips would rock from side to side in rhythm with the horse beneath them, and much cursing and cussing could be heard from the men above the disgruntled noises of the sheep as the crafty ewes scattered just when the riders didn't want them to.

Tailers like Bricky would set up camp, keep the station's horses in working order and hobble them in the quiet of the night for grazing, resting or saddling up. Horses were something Bricky understood. He knew how to look after them, break them and train them. The bush was where he belonged, in his swag and under the stars. Just like all the other men who shared the campfire and whiskey with him.

↶

While Bricky was under the stars, his wife Kate was under the roof of their small basic home in Browne Street. Dirt lay beneath her family in every room.

On 7 September, with her three young children at home, she gave birth to the couple's sixth child.

Bricky had come home to meet the new baby on Tuesday, 4 October, nearly one month after its arrival. The next morning was, supposedly, the last time he saw Kate alive, before leaving between 8 a.m. and 9 a.m. to get back to work.

Bricky and Kate had been arguing again before he left. He couldn't tolerate her drinking and demanded that she change her ways. With her hipflask under her pillow and the baby asleep next to her, she had simply rolled over and exposed her back to him before he swore at her and departed. Kate had breathed a sigh of relief knowing he was gone. She could hardly lift her troubled head from her pillow.

After Mrs Hurley had reported Kate missing, the police had duly notified Bricky of the news the following morning, Friday 7 October, while he was out at Burrawang. That his three young children, all under the age of ten, and his baby girl were unattended, let alone that his wife could not be found, did not seem to concern Bricky a great deal. He did not return from Burrawang to search for Kate until the next day.

Comfortably stationed in his saddle, Bricky meandered along the edge of the Forbes lake under a dry spring sky, looking for his wife. He suffered a momentary shock when a pink and grey crackle of galahs landed in a stand of river gums, bickering among themselves and watching him.

He cut across South Circle, passing his deserted home. He moseyed up to the station and told the police that he had no idea where Kate was and that he simply could not find her. He made the point of telling Garstang that he didn't think Kate would 'destroy herself'.

'And, wob, wob, what's more, if she don't, wob, wob, wanna be found, she won't, you know.' Bricky had his own way of speaking, and for some it was a job to understand him in between his mumbling and stuttering.

He slept alone in the empty house that night, slightly disturbed by the absence of his family. He rose with the sun and left the way he had arrived, repeating the familiar trek to Burrawang. Bricky did not return again to look further for Kate or to visit his children. Not even once. They remained with Susan Hurley across the road.

A week later, when Susan Hurley had completed the overwhelming job of identifying Kate at the Carlton Hotel, she had quietly wept by Kate's side. Susan had never seen the dead body of an adult before, and she regretted that events had conspired to bring about this terrible moment in time. She wondered what on earth had happened to bring such a conclusion to her neighbour's short life. Kate was only thirty-five. Susan nodded to Garstang to confirm the body was Kate's, but when she went to speak her tears choked the words away from her.

Senior Constable Garstang was sure now; it was definitely the missing Mrs Foster. The police contacted Bricky around 4 p.m. to inform him that his wife had been found dead in the lagoon. A couple of hours later, Bricky was back in Forbes and he took himself directly to Garstang as instructed. The senior constable escorted him to the hotel, and Bricky concurred that it was indeed his wife.

Garstang knew it had been at least six days since Bricky had made any effort to find Kate. He watched Bricky intently, studying his movements, trying to ascertain what level of guilt he was carrying.

Bricky's hat was in his hand as he held it against his chest as a mark of respect, but Garstang was suspicious, he had to be. Years of seeing the worst of human behaviour had taught him that much.

Outside the Carlton, the pair walked away from prying ears and eyes. Bricky looked straight at Garstang, shaking his head and blurted out, 'Wob, wob, wob. She was always on the bloody grog. Wob, wob. She talked about suicide all the time.'

Garstang took a step back. This was not what Bricky had told him just last week.

Concerned, the policeman privately considered Susan Hurley's answers to his questions earlier in the day. She was adamant that Mrs Foster never spoke of suicide to her; in fact, she had never mentioned it at all. And as for being under the influence, Mrs Hurley thought that she had only seen Ada drinking since the baby was born.

Garstang had a lot to think about.

Before he started making accusations, or indeed laying any charges, the senior constable needed to talk to McDonnell and establish what the doctor could tell him about Kate's demise.

Mrs Hurley returned to her home and to Kate's children, devastated. What must she say to them? Surely, she did not have to carry this burden, too? She decided to say nothing of their mother, at least until after the inquest, unless Bricky came to see them before, which she suspected would not happen.

Susan was realising how little she really knew about Ada Foster. She wondered about her neighbour's childhood family, surely they would need to know what had happened to her. Ada Foster must be someone's daughter, perhaps even someone's sister.

In days to come, Garstang would share with Susan what he had been told about Kate's Kelly family in Victoria, and everything would start to make sense. The rumours Susan had heard about her friend in recent times were true after all.

3

A Glimpse of Kate's Childhood

Ellen Kelly would mostly be remembered as such, even though her last name had been changed to King after her marriage to George many years before. She was standing at the old wooden gate of the farmhouse she shared with her grown son Jim when she was interviewed for *The Sun* newspaper in 1911. As Ellen shared precious memories of her deceased daughter, the Kelly clan's devoted mother told reporter B.W. Cookson, 'Dear little Kate! I can see her now, bustling about the place, keeping things tidy, helping outside whenever she got a chance; always bright and cheerful, just like a sunbeam about the house. And the police dragged her poor mother away from her and lied, and sent me to prison. After that, nothing but misery and it has been nothing but misery ever since.'

Despite Ellen's fond memories of her beautiful daughter and the genuine love shared among the Kelly family, she remembered the bitter reality of Kate's childhood. Catherine Ada Kelly, born in Beveridge, Victoria, on 12 July 1863, had an upbringing that was far from bliss.

In 1865, on a brisk August morning, Kate was proudly sitting on the bed next to her mother in their Avenel home. A swaddled bundle was passed to her for a brief moment, which made her feel important. It was her baby sister Grace. With her mother helping her to hold on to Grace, the two-year-old kissed the soft forehead of the latest Kelly family member, and then Ellen took the baby back into her arms.

At the end of 1866, sadness enveloped the small household when Kate's father, Red, died. He'd not been long back home after a six-month stint for cattle stealing. Three-year-old Kate had no idea what it all meant, but she was sad her pa was gone. Her young eyes watched her adored big brother Ned standing like a man, even though he was only twelve, by their mother's side as she sobbed. Kate hadn't seen her mother crying before that, and she had no understanding of what it meant for someone to be 'dead'. But she knew by the tears that the whole household had changed and it was not a good thing.

Red had died of dropsy. Early in his marriage, Red had tried his luck successfully on the Bendigo goldfields. He had then enjoyed the physical labour involved in building a life together with Ellen at the homestead they had purchased. But he had supposedly shrunk away from his true self since then. Clouded by the darkness of depression, he needed to be soothed by the bottle until it took him completely.

When Kate was older, Ellen told her stories of how depressed Red had become. 'It were why he started drinking; looking for answers in the bottle,' Ellen would lament. 'He drifted from his fit and active days. There were nothing could be done. He was lost to me.' It was rare for Ellen to speak about it. She had often wondered if her husband's depression was due to the harsh days he'd spent as a convict in Tasmania.

Ellen became a single mother with seven children: Anne (fourteen), Ned (twelve), Maggie (nine), Jim (seven), Dan (five), Kate (three) and Grace (one). They were a family who relied on each other and stuck together.

The family moved from Avenel to Greta in 1867. They lived with Ellen's sisters and their children, and they all helped each other start over again despite many setbacks, including a house fire lit by Red's brother.

A year or so later, the Kellys moved to Ellen's new 'selection', a homestead in Eleven Mile Creek, about four miles from the township of Greta. As a selector, Ellen could pay for half the land value up front, pay rent on the other half and, after a period of time, could pay the remaining value on the land for complete ownership. She had to fulfil certain requirements, like fencing and other land improvements. The homestead was a basic, two-roomed wooden slab hut, which was divided only by hessian, hanging blankets and rags. Unbeknown to the family, their home would later feature in much of Australia's dramatic bushranging history.

Police observations and opinions indicated that Kate's family had very little. Some records suggested that they lived in poverty and squalor, but at least the homestead was theirs and Ellen managed to hang on to it despite the odds against her. They did almost lose it in 1881 when the government illegally voided the Kellys' ownership of it, a matter that Kate and Maggie went to Melbourne to successfully rectify.

During her early childhood, Kate, her siblings, cousins and friends would tease each other with typical games and irritations on their daily walk through the bush-lined dusty streets of Greta to a small wooden structure, the Catholic school known as Greta Common. This time together firmed up their bonds and rivalries for years to come.

In 1870, when Kate was only seven, she burst into tears as her mother exploded with fury, telling Kate and her sisters that the police had taken Ned and put him in gaol. Maggie stood on the other side of the kitchen table and watched as Ellen pulled Kate onto her lap to soothe her, putting her arm around young Grace as she leaned in to her mother and Kate for comfort, too.

Ned had been charged with violent assault and was given a twelve-month sentence. He had acted as a father figure to Kate for over half of her brief life, but she wouldn't see her oldest brother again until she was about eleven. Not long after finishing his assault sentence, he was nabbed again, falsely accused of horse stealing, when Wild Wright lent him a horse that Ned didn't know was nicked. By that time, Ellen had started a sly grog shanty to create an income and was housing travellers and lodgers.

Kate's big sister Anne had left home and married her sweetheart Alex Gunn, who also ended up in gaol. During 1872, penniless, Anne was forced to move back to Ellen's home after losing hers in her husband's absence. She was also pregnant to a policeman, Constable Flood.

Flood was running a horse-stealing racket and had rewarded Anne with gifts and money in return for creating false evidence for him so he could maintain his racket. Ellen believed her daughter when Anne told her Flood had raped her. The corrupt policeman wanted no part of the scandalous pregnancy and made every effort to keep the information from his wife and children.

Kate, who was still only nine, thought her big sister was the most beautiful belle in the region and was devastated that Anne had been tricked and used by the policeman. She wanted to help her sister during the pregnancy and was excited to be an aunty, despite the terrible circumstances.

But the discomfort and anger the family may have felt about

Flood's treatment of Anne turned into deep rage and mourning when they lost her.

During the birth, Ellen couldn't stop Anne's bleeding. Kate knew it was serious when she saw her mother throw herself onto her knees beside Anne, who had become so weak she could hardly even groan with the pain of it all. Ellen was saying urgent prayers, desperate for some ethereal assistance, which failed to present itself. After the hours of effort Anne had exerted in bringing her little girl into the world, the new mother bled to death. Later, the child passed away, too.

The dark earth of their yard was dug into and Anne's body, wrapped in brilliant red, blood-soaked sheets, was placed within it, later followed by the child. Kate felt cold and numb. Ellen's screaming and cursing rattled through Kate's bird-like frame, and the knot in her stomach remained tight for days. Such a harsh and shocking reality pushed Kate back into herself as their little home was engulfed in grief and loss once again.

If Ned had not been behind bars, he'd have quite possibly murdered Flood to avenge his sister's torment and demise.

Kate's family was shrinking around her. In 1873, her brother Jim was sentenced to two and a half years for cattle theft. In 1875–76, Dan was in and out of trouble but in 1877 he did a stint in gaol for wilful damage. Kate's heart was broken with each brother the law removed until finally she had none left who were old enough for them to take.

The thread of injustices Kate perceived against her family only made her more loyal to them, but the fragile tapestry of her existence was constantly shifting, creating a persistent feeling of uncertainty and vulnerability.

Kate's other idol, sister Maggie, also moved out, having married William Skillion, who would later do time as well.

Ellen's ramshackle shanty was at times a wild place filled with ugly men in filthy clothes whom her mother wrangled with perfection. Police were paid off when they visited as a necessary business transaction, and the rough venture kept the Kellys afloat. Kate became used to the presence of drifters, visitors and drunks.

Over the years, Kate watched her mother take up with various lovers, including much younger men, who were often lodgers staying with them. One of the men, Frost, fathered a child with Ellen. He shot through and the child died.

Kate didn't mind having the handsome George King around for a while, but he felt more like a brother than a father figure, since he was younger than Ned. He was another of Ellen's lovers, and he fathered Ellen Junior and Jack.

Kate helped her mother by keeping her half-brother and sister in tow. She would let them follow her around, feeding the chickens and cleaning the pen, feeding the dogs, and taking the horses out into the paddock or further afield to find fresh herbage to fill their big guts. But George also abandoned Ellen, leaving her with the children they had together.

There was a third child around this time, Alice King, whose story was more complicated. George King had been absent for a very long time when baby Alice arrived. Alice was always portrayed as Ellen's daughter and Kate's sister, but she was the result of a love affair between Kate and a policeman, Constable Fitzpatrick.

The romance between Kate and Fitzpatrick had started with a day at the local races. Kate was chaperoned by her oldest brother, Ned, who was out of gaol at this time and friendly with Fitzpatrick.

'C'mon, Ma, let me go,' Kate had begged her mother. 'Neddy will be there. There'll be no harm in it, Ma. Please!'

Ellen had agreed, thinking nothing would come of it, but when it became apparent that her daughter was seeing more of Fitzpatrick, she protested vehemently, suspicious of his motives.

Fourteen-year-old Kate challenged her mother, sitting defiantly in the saddle and telling her she would do exactly as she pleased, before riding to a secret rendezvous with Fitzpatrick. The 21-year-old policeman was keenly grooming and manipulating her. 'I look after your family, Kate, and I protect your brothers from harm, more than you could ever know,' Fitzpatrick would say to Kate, toying with her constant worry about her brothers' wellbeing.

Ellen became irate, forbidding Kate from seeing Fitzpatrick but it was no use. The affair may well have continued, but on an infamous April day in 1878, Fitzpatrick arrived on the Kelly doorstep drunk and proclaiming he would arrest Dan. From this point, everything in the Kelly's world would become a sensation that would unravel over the next two years; there was so much more to come for the unsuspecting Kate Kelly.

The only time none of the torment in Kate's childhood mattered was when she was on her horse. It was the greatest legacy Ellen passed on to all her children. Understanding horses was in their blood. The freedom, the speed and the agility offered up by the animals were exhilarating.

Throughout her childhood, Kate, along with her cousins, sisters and brothers, when they weren't in gaol, would ride for as long as their backsides could stay in the saddle and their horses could take it.

The rhythmic thumping of horse hooves would drum together as the Kellys and their friends raced each other to the river or chased each other keenly around a paddock of obstacles, an extra log here or there to make it interesting, delicately directing their horses' footwork around the chicken coop, galloping along a fenceline and launching over the sliprail to the finish mark. The courses they set out were deliberately designed to set their hearts on fire and create a space in which they could enjoy each other's company.

When she was older, Kate would take off on her horse at a moment's notice, flying into the surrounding dense green bushland, dodging wide trees, racing through the low-lying scrub, dispersing kangaroos and wallabies.

Escaping into the wild mountains, riding up hillsides and investigating caves, travelling across creeks and plunging into clear-water rivers to cool her horse were a constant joy. She would climb to granite lookouts through precarious ranges and admire the landscape below her. Breathing in the fresh air, she worked with her horse as one to navigate and traverse the land.

From the Warby to the Wombat and Strathbogie Ranges, the Kellys knew the countryside like the back of their hands. From 1878 to 1880, when Kate's brothers and their friends became wanted men, these rugged landscapes would hold them safely, despite them being hunted for months on end. Their teenaged sister helped to protect them, and their ability to evade capture was credited partly to her efforts. Stories of her riding as a decoy and delivering news to the gang in the bush were just the start of Kate's fame.

Ned Kelly and his gang's exploits and misfortunes would scoop Kate up like a relentless wave throughout her entire adolescence. She would find herself spat out at the end of it all with two brothers and their comrades dead by the time she was just seventeen, and would remain the subject of inescapable public curiosity. By the time Kate turned twenty-two, she would be worn out and wishing she could escape her life.

KATE KELLY

Is about 21 years of age. She is about 5 ft. 2 in. in height, and slightly built. Her general expression is of extreme melancholy. She can scarcely be called handsome, although when pleased her countenance assumes an exceedingly prepossessing aspect, and her smile is dangerously fascinating. No one, to meet her casually, would imagine that the girl was imbued with the reckless courage that made Ned Nelly so infamous. She is only slightly educated, but is endowed with great natural intelligence, which to a great extent compensates for her lack of tuition. Kate is a dashing horsewoman, and on numerous occasions has defeated the efforts of large numbers of police to follow her into the Strathbogie Ranges. It is more than hinted that the immunity enjoyed by the outlaws so long, was largely due to the dauntless energy and activity of Miss Kelly, who seemed to be ubiquitious. She was repeatedly seen by the police in all parts of the northeastern district, but none of the police could trace her.

'Dangerously fascinating.' Kate Kelly was actually only 17 at the time of this article, 10 July 1880, and the detailed description of her activities demonstrates the infatuation the press had with Ned Kelly's little sister.

If it weren't for a friend of Kate's who had moved to New South Wales, she may never have found a way out of the public eye.

4

An Invitation to New South Wales

On 15 January 1881, *The Ovens and Murray Advertiser*, a Beechworth newspaper, publicly slammed Kate's prospects:

> No respectable person, unless a very courageous one, would give Kate domestic employment, even if she were fitted for such. What, then, is to become of her? Her mother will be shortly out of gaol and no one will say that a fresh companionship with such a woman will be to the advantage of a young girl, already so hard pressed.

Hugh McDougall was a little older than both Ned and Jim Kelly. He had been fond of Kate, as he was of all the Kellys throughout his youth, and, living in Benalla, he held no illusions as to the way the family was viewed, the illegal activities many of them had been party to and the consequences of that for Kate. He understood the limitations of poverty and the Kellys' damaging record with the law, but he also understood that Kate was a good person brought up in regrettable circumstances.

North-eastern Victoria had been an unsettled place since the late 1870s. The tensions created by the roaming, lawless Kelly Gang, known originally as part of the Greta Mob and then as the Mansfield Murderers, deeply affected and divided the people of the region.

The gang both suffered and caused tragedy and torment. The family members of the police who had been murdered, terrified locals and regional Kelly sympathisers had to find a way to live alongside one another in their small communities. There was talk of a revengeful uprising after Ned Kelly was hanged at the end of 1880, but it never took place. Hugh thought it was a good time to leave the area and make his own way in the world.

Hugh arrived in the north-west of New South Wales with his mate 'Burrowa', aka John Wright, to work as a shearer at Gnalta Station, near Wilcannia, in 1881. The unwelcoming local shearers made life on the station unpleasant, so Hugh and Burrowa tied their swags to their horses early one morning and no one saw their heels for dust as the young men rode off in search of other opportunities. Hugh could see no reason to stay in the dry, godforsaken place to plug their way through 30,000 sheep with men they had no time for.

After they left, Hugh and his mate were blamed for the theft of two cheques, worth nineteen pounds, but Hugh was none the wiser. It was reported in the police gazette, but no warrant was issued. It was assumed that the two young shearers were heading to Queensland since they were so close to the border, but after a day's travel they each went in different directions.

The accusations of theft were a reflection only of the men they had left behind, and this singular shadow of doubt over Hugh dissolved into history. Unlike his friend Kate Kelly, Hugh was able to keep his good reputation.

Later, Hugh became the first stock master at Lake Cowal Station. Not far from Forbes, it was an extraordinary patch of dirt expanding across one hundred thousand acres, which included the extravagant Lake Cowal covering about twenty thousand of those acres. Fed by local creeks and intermittent flooding from the Kalari River, it managed to hold the bulk of its water, even through the droughts.

The lake sustained an abundance of birdlife and fish species. Dark purple Macquarie perch, colourful freshwater catfish and a host of cod and other fish were a source of delight for fishermen. Black-feathered ducks could regularly be seen floating along the surface with their sapphire-like, blue bills and, on the shores, long pink legs carried black-necked storks through the shallows while they stabbed their hard beaks into the water and mud.

Samuel Wilson, another Victorian, was taking a gamble on this new area and on Hugh McDougall. Mr Wilson was a well-heeled Scotch College graduate and a Mansfield local. Hugh knew the importance of connections and, on this occasion, it had paid off for him. Wilson's son later took over the management of the station, and Hugh found employment as the property manager at Warroo Station, further up the river, even closer to Forbes.

Warroo's nearest neighbour was Cadow Station, only seven miles away, and Burrawang Station was across the river from Cadow. The water frontage enjoyed by each property was essential for the survival and longevity of its people, animals and crops.

Warroo had its own church, a police base and telegraph station with a general population of seventy-two that would rise during shearing.

Hugh's boss, C.S. MacPhillamy, was known as 'The Squire of Warroo'. The entrepreneurial and dedicated owner was best known for his superior horse stock, having bred and raced many prize winners. Alongside his horses, he was proud of the excellent quality of the sheep and cattle they raised and bred, running more than fifty thousand sheep across Warroo in the good seasons.

Hugh worked every step of the way alongside the visionary MacPhillamy, who acquired the station from his father in 1883. The Squire planted extravagant gardens and created fertile orchards, building up his property, raising a family and devoting his life to his beloved horses. In the role of property manager, Hugh was entrusted to keep things humming.

WORKING AT WARROO

Kate had been no stranger to violence in her short life, nor had Hugh. He continued to deal with it in the blokey world of bush shearing sheds and station life.

Shouting, swearing and a lot of thumping and cheering could be heard coming from the shearers' quarters at Warroo one hot night. As Hugh approached the huts, which were still filled with heat from the summer sun of the day, two men rolled out the door, landing at his feet while gripping onto each other. One had hold of the other's shirt, heaving him to his feet, but the other man's large clenched fist landed on the side of his captor's moosh, spraying sweat and blood into the air. Hugh could feel a hint of it as he jumped out of the way before a left hook landed the other shearer on the dirt behind him and the instigator rolled his sleeves up and dove in for more.

The other shearers, yelling and laughing, had spilled through the doorway to see what the result of the argument was going to be. They all pulled up when they realised that Hugh had arrived. The two fighters were wrestling on the ground but both were running out of energy by the time they noticed that everything had gone silent around them. The tired and bloodied men looked up to see all the workers gathered in a heap looking at Hugh. The property manager was staring at the men on the ground and shaking his head.

Hugh was known to wrangle some wild situations in his time, some of which ended up in court, where shearers were charged with indecent language and riotous behaviour. This wasn't one of those occasions. Some kind of wager had gone south between friends, and tempers had flared.

Calmly, Hugh addressed them all. 'Are you lot done?' Silence all round. The smell of rolled tobacco burned in the air. 'Get yourselves cleaned up and back in the huts. That's enough for tonight. You start this again tomorrow and you can pack your swags. The MacPhillamys aren't paying you lot to cause trouble here. I could bring the police in to sort you out but I don't want to have to do that. You don't want me to either, I'd say.'

'All right, McDougall, all right.'

Some of the men who had been watching lingered outside; others followed his instructions. The two brawlers slowly pulled themselves up off the ground and made their way to a barrel of water to wash up, deciding to stay off Hugh's radar for the rest of their run.

Hugh considered such incidents part of his job, and he could cope with the roughness. He thought it should be expected with a workforce of men working long and hard in hot, remote circumstances, and mostly it worked out just fine. The shearers weren't getting paid a hell of a lot, and he knew how hard they worked.

Other issues could crop up, like the theft of thoroughbred stallions and the occasional stolen supplies. All in all, he could handle it or, if he couldn't, the police could. A bag of spuds nicked from the large shed of food stores could see you in the lock-up for seven days.

After about four years working in New South Wales, Hugh got wind of a domestic position coming up at the neighbouring property, Cadow Station. He knew from his connections back in Victoria that his friend Kate Kelly really needed someone to give her a break. He'd been worried for a while about how she could possibly get a job. She was a poor Irish Catholic girl from the bush whose family name was a public shame. Her big brother could possibly be the most infamous bushranger of Australian history, and she was known to have helped him. What chance did she have?

Hugh decided that he would sponsor Kate and bring her to New South Wales. He had a word with the folks at Cadow about a young woman he would vouch for as being a good person for the role, and they agreed to take her on.

Hugh's gesture would provide Kate with the gifts of employment and a new start. But first they would have to find a way to conceal her identity so she'd be given half a chance.

5

Cadow Station

Pierce Collits was a wheeling and dealing convict, assigned to work for his wife Mary when they first arrived in Australia in 1801. Together with their children, they worked their rural property on the banks of the Nepean River, near what would become Penrith. But later they were lured by a new vision, and it was widely rumoured that Mary was the first white woman to cross the Blue Mountains, the pair having made their way over the hills before the official track was mapped by the explorers Blaxland, Wentworth and Lawson, and forged by Cox and his men.

In a parallel existence, Western Sydney always belonged to the Darug people; they shared the Blue Mountains with the Gundungurra to the south-west. Wiradyuri country opens up from the western side. This mountain range was not seen by them as a 'dividing range' but as a meeting place for thousands of years. These Aboriginal neighbours negotiated special agreements for sites where they could meet, trade and pass safely through each other's country until access to their lands was interrupted by the practices of the new settlers.

The Collits family worked their stake on these foreign lands, and when Pierce was pardoned by the governor, they were given permission to build an accommodation house in Hartley Vale. They finished building the Collits Inn around 1823, and the small homestead was ready for business, anchored at the foot of Mount York.

The inn was the only place where weary travellers and their horses could rest, eat and drink after making the epic journey across the mountains. Everyone, from businessmen and politicians to new settlers and their families, would stay there, heading either west or east on their journey between Sydney and Australia's first inland settlement, Bathurst.

Cox's track, built around 1814, was steep and perilous. Horse teams had to travel down it backwards, weighted by heavy logs dragged from uphill to slow their descent. It was nothing to see masses of debris and the wreckage of commuters' carriages, luggage and dead horses piled up at a wide bend where they had been abandoned.

The government needed a new road that was less dangerous, and Pierce Collits's son James put in a bid amid huge objections from the surveyor-general, Thomas Mitchell, who had nothing but contempt for James Collits, calling him an illiterate idiot. Despite work starting on the new track selected by Collits, Mitchell managed to bring that work to a halt. The surveyor-general insisted on the track that he had selected, making sure it went nowhere near the Collits Inn, consequently ruining their business.

Despite this, James's submission to the government in 1829 was rewarded with a grant of a large chunk of land near what would become Canowindra, making James among the first of the European settlers in the area. He named the property 'Canoundra', which he had supposedly derived from the Wiradyuri term for 'home' or 'camping ground'.

James Collits pushed out even further west than Canowindra. On 26 March 1836, Mitchell and Collits had a chance meeting when both were exploring that region, and Collits suggested to Mitchell that there was no decent land, an obvious ploy. Mitchell noted in his diaries how James had mentioned that without the help of the local Aboriginal men whom he was travelling with, he would not have been able to find adequate drinking water. The white settlers referred to the river at that time as being in a stage of 'emptying itself'.

James Collits was one of the first squatters along the Kalari River in the region that would later become known as Forbes, and Cadow Station was one of his first properties in that location.

In later years, James Collits' niece Elizabeth Scott managed Cadow Station after her first husband John Strickland died. With her second husband Edward Jones, they built the station up as a hugely successful farming business. Located along a popular stock route, Cadow Station had many visitors as people made their way from or to Victoria.

White settlers like Elizabeth and Edward had set to work removing trees so that grazing stock and the business of commercial agriculture could pave a new existence for them and their future families. Squeals could be heard as koalas' homes were toppled while they were still in the canopies. If the animals were lucky, they hit the ground running, nursing their injuries and babies as they fled. Extraordinary numbers of koala were killed. Their lives intentionally taken and their sought-after skins harvested and sold.

Elizabeth and one of her sons contracted typhoid and, despite the efforts of those who loved her, which included her neighbour, Mrs O'Nions, who kept a relentless bedside vigil, Elizabeth soon died. There were only a handful of pioneering women in the region at the time, and the loss of Elizabeth was intensely felt by the small network of new settlers.

Edward had adopted Elizabeth's four sons to Strickland, and together they had seven additional children. With his next wife, Georgina Breathour, Edward had another nine children. It was Edward and Georgina who agreed to hire Kate.

ADA'S ARRIVAL

Ada Hennessey cut across a flat grassy paddock filled with roaming cattle that parted in front of her, sending out a few deep echoes from their lungs in protest at the disturbance. Dogs barked wildly at the visitor and her horse. Ada slowed from a canter to a trot as she approached, her dark wavy locks reaching down her back and bouncing in step with the horse's rhythm. Her neatly shaped jacket highlighted her curves, and the exquisitely sewn detail of her skirt was on display as it flourished across the back of the mare she was steering. It was her finest riding outfit with tailored boots that helped her cut such a fine figure, designed to impress anyone who laid eyes on her.

In the next paddock, fine horses with shiny coats trotted around jerking their heads. They could be heard whinnying and snorting as workers reached up to bridle their heads and bring them in for training. Groups of men were scattered around the stables and sheds, busy at work but not too busy to notice the attractive visitor from a distance. Hugh admired the shape of the petite woman as she sat upright and elegant in the saddle. As she neared the station house paddock, he walked towards her, so glad to see her face.

'Welcome, Ada!' He lifted his palm in a wave, and she pulled the reins back, slowing the horse's pace to a walk. When Hugh reached them, he took hold of the animal, pulling the horse to a halt. Kate excitedly slid down the side of her ride, relieved to see her friend who had thrown her a lifeline.

'Hugh!' Kate let out a sigh with a smile in her gentle Irish lilt. She was a first-generation Australian, and the influence of her parents' accents could still be heard. 'You're a true champion! Bless yer! I'm thrilled to see yer!'

The pair embraced and examined each other's faces. Hugh could see the tracks of torment and grief in her eyes, but she was still young, only twenty-two. She had so much life in front of her, and she was as beautiful as he remembered. It had been a journey for her to get there, nearly a full week of riding. 'I'm so tired but no way could I rest,' she said. 'I'm delighted to be here! Delighted!'

Kate had been known by many names in recent years: Ada Hennessey, Kate Hennessey and Kate Ambrose were a few of them. For her new start at Cadow Station, everyone except Hugh would know her as Ada. Hugh had agreed to meet her at Warroo first so they could catch up and get their stories straight before they rode over to Cadow for introductions.

There was an air of hopefulness, in the same way that New Year's Eve is filled with resolutions and new beginnings. Kate felt that maybe her life could turn around. She imagined that she could become someone new and escape her painful past.

Visitors to Cadow entered the property along an avenue of pine trees designed to create a grand entrance to an impressive property. At the heart of Cadow, the main building had two L-shaped wings with a verandah all the way around. Towards the back was the kitchen, which boasted ceilings twelve feet high and dimpled glass above the kitchen doors, which allowed light to fill the room. A breezeway led to the right wing, which had rooms at least twenty feet square and a ballroom. Not far from the rear shed, a walk through the first of two orchards would bring you to the servants' quarters, only a stone's throw from the banks of the river. Logwood sheds and stables were scattered across the property, and fences were being added every year to create the paddocks and stockyards needed to cater for the range of stock being bred and raised. Tireless work was dedicated to creating a pleasant house yard with gardens to sustain the household and its staff. The attractive orchards grew alongside productive vegetable gardens. Winding dirt paths surrounded small plots of lush, green plantings, which provided pleasant settings to take tea with guests. It required many hands and hard work to create and maintain.

For two years from 1885, Kate worked dutifully for the Jones family in Cadow's comfortable environment. The Joneses may have been family-oriented people, but there was no mistake to be made about her role with them. Hard work was expected in return for her keep, and it was to be remembered that she was the maid. The wealth and status her employers enjoyed held Kate and anyone like her in her place.

Dirty plates were to be cleared immediately from the dinner table, and the 'help' were never invited to join their employers for meals. Even the children knew they were above her. Kate cleaned dishes, made beds, belted rugs free of dust, polished silver and washed clothes down at the river's edge amid the yelling, taunting, tears and laughter of the many children and teenagers of the combined Jones families.

Screams of delight could be heard as children swung from a rope over the river, making splashing noises as they plonked heavily into the brown water, which slowly carried them downriver while they hurriedly dog paddled themselves back to the bank. Scrambling up it and covering themselves in muddy clay, they would walk back to the swing to start all over again. Older kids would yell at the young ones to get out of their way, and tears would be shed over hurt feelings. Amends would be quickly made when a call-out for lunch was heard, and they would all race each other back to the homestead to fill their hungry bellies.

At the end of a long day, Kate could ride through the trees across country to raise her heartbeat and forget everything or to simply be alone and remember her family far away. When she needed a friend, she could talk quietly with Hugh, sitting on a rock somewhere private where she shared stories of her recent life.

During Kate's time at Cadow, there were also some inclusive get-togethers where all the nearby property owners and their workers socialised. They had picnics and set up steeplechase courses in the paddocks, just like the old days for Kate. Burrawang visitors would often stay at Cadow late into the night, and Warroo friends would ride across to join in the races and activities through the day. Kate would impress them all with her graceful elegance but competitive edge, galloping bravely ahead of the others, unafraid of ramping up the pace as she cleared logs, sticking her heels into the horse's guts to kick her into another gear and edge eagerly ahead of the other riders, her heart racing and the horse keen to do well for her.

The extensive property at Cadow was in the process of being divided up for the future of three particular sons: Philip, Sidney and Rudolph. Edward Jones intended to retire with Georgina to a comfortable abode on the shores of Neutral Bay in Sydney. When Edward had first arrived in Australia, he'd walked empty-handed from Parramatta, over two hundred miles, to the region he now called home. He had worked hard for everything he had achieved, but the land he had loved and toiled upon would soon become the concern of a few sons.

Manna, Ina and a portion of the original Cadow were the final divisions; three properties that would be left in the care of the men. The effervescent Sidney or 'Sy', who was only nineteen while Kate was at Cadow, would one day breed fine thoroughbred stallions, be reputed for his precise marksmanship at the clay pigeons and, most detrimentally, be known for his voracious gambling appetite. He loved horses as much as Kate did. They shared many conversations about quality horses and riding, and sometimes she would be asked to help them break in new horse stock. Kate was only a few years older than Sy and he would watch her moves. Keen to learn and compete, he was always trying to outdo this Ada Hennessey.

Sy was generous and friendly. He was a person well thought of throughout the district as he grew into an adult, but his well-heeled position created a sense of expectation that others, like Kate, could never indulge in. It would have been impossible to predict the terrible end that awaited him.

Many years after Kate had been and gone from Cadow, a housemaid named Jessie Cattanach would be the focus of a scandal that terrorised the Jones family.

The Scottish-born Cattanach was given a .32 calibre pistol by her employers, similar to one that Kate was given during her time at Cadow. It was a small pocket gun they had deemed suitable for young women to use to protect themselves if needed. A gun was considered a necessity out in the sticks as everyone was armed. The men all owned shotguns for times when animals needed relief from their suffering, birds had to be kept off food supplies by shots fired into the sky, snakes were shot and rabbits were hunted to eat and, if it came to it, humans with bad intentions could be deterred.

On a dry summer night, Jessie had cleared the table, as usual, after the evening meal and hadn't been seen again for a long while. Sy and his brother Dolph had been playing cribbage with their neighbour Chas from Burrawang and Sy's nephew Stanley. Dolph eventually gave up on the cards and dozed on the settee. The sound of noisy crickets magnified through the warm air, and the haunting calls from a lone boobook echoed from a distance.

The other men were sat at the card table ribbing each other about who owed money to whom and who was bluffing who until their tired eyes were getting the better of them. Sy left the table to change into his pyjamas, and Chas and Stanley leaned back in their wooden chairs, talking about Jessie.

A while ago, Jessie had confided in Sidney's sister-in-law that she needed a husband, and it was considered a given by the meddling women that if she started to work at Cadow, Sy would fall madly for her and there would be a fairytale ending. But Sy didn't love her. He had made it plain to the maid over the eighteen months she had been working at Cadow. In the last three months she had threatened to shoot him on many occasions. He had to get away from Cadow for a while, until they figured out what to do with her. 'It's gone on so long now,' Chas said. 'She's mad.'

Stanley added, 'That's twice now I've had to hide my shotgun from her just in the last two weeks. The conniving wench stole Dolph's yesterday. I snatched it off her and hid that, too. She promised me it was the end of it.'

Stanley was very worried. 'She knows that he's leaving tomorrow morning just to get the hell away from her.'

It seemed unfathomable to Chas that it was Sy who had to leave, not the disturbed servant. Jessie's friendship with Sy's sister-in-law was keeping her there.

Just then, as if she had appeared out of nowhere, Jessie called out to Sy from her room on the verandah, where she had been staying while the servants' hut needed repairs. 'Can you bring me a match, Sy? I can't see a thing.'

'I'm busy, Jessie, find your own match,' Sy called back from the lounge room where he had returned to the others for one more game. He rolled his eyes at the other men.

'Sy, I can't see a thing, won't you help me, please?'

Jessie waited in the darkness, and Sy walked softly in his pyjamas from the lounge towards her room. As he rounded the corner and lit the lantern, Jessie fired at him with a double-barrelled shotgun. In the dim light of the kerosene lamp, Sy was thrown backwards with the impact. Blasted by both barrels, the material from his pyjamas was blown to shreds, and his guts spilled out of his body as he landed on the floor. Blood raced across the wooden floorboards, and Sy was left quivering, unable to make a sound.

His fellow card players jumped up at the loud boom from the gun. Dolph sprang from the lounge and ran through the dining room, thinking the worst as he ran. He heard another shot just as he got to the verandah. Jessie had shot herself in the thigh and still had the gun in her hand. She raised the long weapon and was poised to release another shot as Dolph landed on her and pushed her arm downwards, the spray of lead sending splintering shards from the floorboards flying but somehow missing their feet.

'Let me have another shot!' Jessie screamed, and she struggled as Dolph pushed her onto the floor and held her there.

'You're mad as a cut snake! What have you done to my brother? This is unforgivable, Cattanach. You mad fool!'

Chas and Stanley were only moments behind Dolph. Stanley grabbed the shotgun away from Jessie. 'It's my gun! This is the other one that's been missing!' Stanley was crushed that she had deceived him so easily and attacked his dear uncle with his own weapon. 'You've betrayed me, Jessie, betrayed our family.'

'Watch her, will you?' Dolph rushed to his brother's side. 'Sy! Sy! Can you hear me?'

Sidney was lying on his right side as if he had been trying to drag himself away from his attacker. He made some final gasping sounds but was unable to say a word.

'Get the doctor out here, now! Sidney's not going to make it! Get me some rags or sheets, something!' Dolph had removed his shirt and was pointlessly pressing it onto the huge open wound, unable to contain the force of so much blood but trying to comfort his silent brother.

Jessie lay there, rambling and twitching. She had swallowed spoonfuls of strychnine and honey between the shots, the bottle sitting on her dresser, gleaming under the light of the lantern. Next to it, the small handgun that she referred to as her 'toy thing' was loaded but rested innocently. The strychnine was used to poison rabbits, and Jessie had stolen the small bottle from the poison house only two hundred yards away.

From the floor she yelled out to no one in particular. 'I didn't want anyone but him! I heard you all planning to take him away from me.'

Poor Sy Jones painfully bled to death while Jessie continued to convulse and squirm, moaning from the poison eating her insides and the pain of the gun wound in her leg, dying only moments before the doctor finally arrived at 1 a.m.

Kate's time at Cadow had been somewhat simpler than Jessie's, and her ownership of a similar pocket gun had not ended in such trauma.

Kate's employment at Cadow had allowed her to catch her breath. The obscurity of life on the station had provided her with possibly the most stability that she had ever known, but at the end of her two years of service she was ready to move into town and meet people.

'Ada' could be recommended as a hard-working and reliable maid who was a pleasant soul. Kate could see future possibilities in the small town of Forbes, a place where the inhabitants could not judge her if they didn't know who she was. Missing her brother Jim and mother Ellen, she wrote once or twice to her family in Victoria when she could muster the enthusiasm, but what could she tell them? She was lonely and far away from them and that would probably never change. The only relief was that here no one knew who she was.

Having employment and anonymity had been a blessing, but it didn't banish the night terrors and flashbacks that she silently endured. A little tipple every day seemed to ease the pain. Sometimes more than a tipple was needed.

Hugh continued to sponsor Kate as she moved into the town and then from family to family, never lasting for long periods. Her steady time at Cadow became a memory. Kate found herself cleaning houses and answering to people wealthier than her again and again. The knowledge that this would be her life began to wear her down in the same way that her struggle to run from the past was exhausting her.

Kate wanted to fill the anxious and lonely void created by the absence of her family. She would come to know the handsome Mr Foster, but it was his younger brother Artie who thought that he was the better man for her. His interest in Kate would cause problems between the brothers.

6

Bricky and Kate

After working for the undertakers, Mr Luthje & Son, Kate went to the Gunn family. Her reputation as a hard-working domestic then earned her a position helping Mr Prow who was left with ten children when his wife died in 1884. Mr Prow was the owner of the general store, and Kate would often run errands between the store and the home, during which her good looks and cheerful manner caught the attention of many admirers.

Scrubbing the floor with her tired hands, kneeling in her long smock, Kate could hear Mr Prow's daughters running down the stairs. She hoped that they wouldn't skid into the back room and mess up the linoleum she was so fastidiously soaping. 'Spoiled little so-and-sos,' she whispered under her breath. Kate loved the Prow children, but she was over the hard slog of her life.

It was three years since she had first arrived in the area, and the shine of her new beginning had worn off. In between the torment of her memories, Kate held quiet hopes of the vague possibility that she might meet someone and create a life with him. Returning to Victoria was never going to happen. If she held any hope at all for the future, it was most likely going to play out in this little town by the lake.

Local dances and singalongs had been busy social events that Kate enthusiastically attended in the beginning. Handsome men in their smart pants, floral waistcoats and long coats with their shined-up shoes eagerly gathered in groups among the sweet perfume of the red rose bushes outside the hall. They stood watching with anticipation as pretty girls arrived in homemade dresses with billowing skirts, showing off tiny waists and their mothers' jewellery. In their minds, each of them was making plans about potential dance partners.

Everyone knew each other around town. The people Kate worked for wouldn't welcome her to socialise with them, as she and her friends were of a lower class. But there was no shortage of interest from men in Kate, regardless of their class, which only added to the jealous insults from other women.

'So poor she wears the same dress week after week! Surely no one will dance with her.'

Kate's prospective employers and their families were a small, connected pool in the town, so her responses to catty remarks remained unspoken. Instead, perhaps a drink would accidentally be spilled over a dress or two later in the evening.

The men took covert hits from hipflasks for a bit of Dutch courage. The women pretended not to notice the adoring men staring at them while they whispered among themselves about which of the men looked the finest and who may or may not be granted permission to take them for a twirl on the dance floor. The men would make their advances and request the pleasure of a dance while taking the woman by her hand and pulling her in as close as they were allowed to be in public.

The freeing sounds of the fiddle and the piano rattled loudly through the dancers' chests and up to the ceiling, while the floorboards shook with all the youthful energy that the country lads and lasses exuded. Carrying themselves rhythmically, lifting arms and swinging around while flaring their skirts, they entertained themselves through the night. Smiling and staring into their dance partner's eyes, they were filled with the thrill of kicking up their heels and the excitement of meeting a potential mate or even stealing kisses under the midnight sky on the walk home afterwards.

Kate was excited when she dated a very tall and attractive chap, a great dancer, who seemed very keen, but she landed flat when he ended up leaving to try his luck on the goldfields in Western Australia without her.

Bricky, the tall and strapping manager of the livery stables, had got Kate's attention when she was running errands for the Prow family, but nothing came of it for a while. Kate had no idea at that time that she would end up working with Bricky with horses from the stables, and that they would be some of her happiest times, doing something she loved.

It was Bricky's younger brother Artie, a very religious man, who first asked Kate out. Artie Foster was well pleased with himself, and Kate went along with it even though she knew that she was too old for him. Over time, as she was sitting with the Foster family on their verandah watching the world go by and having a yarn, she would come to know all of the family a lot better, including Bricky.

Bricky could not have been further from Artie in his disposition or his interest in religious talk or rituals. Bricky had a wild element that reminded Kate of the men she had been around all her life; men who were fit and active, raw and unapologetic. There was something daring or maybe even dangerous in Bricky that attracted her to him.

Like Kate, Bricky was also a first-generation Australian. His grandparents had arrived with their children, Bricky's father and siblings, in 1848 on the *Agincourt*. Although his grandfather was a lacemaker, the patriarch found himself on the goldfields with his wife and family in the Pyramul region, between Hill End and Sofala. He became known for his sly grog shanties and licensed inns, before moving to Forbes around 1863.

One night, after Bricky and Kate had been out riding together, they ended up alone by the lake. After a few too many drinks, Bricky made a move on Kate that she didn't resist. Down by the water's edge, their kisses became much more intimate.

A few months later, the two brothers were abusing each other out the front of the Foster home. Artie was calling Bricky a grass cutter. 'You knew she was with me, you mongrel bastard. You selfish queer dog.'

The pair moved in close to one another. Artie pushed Bricky, violently shoving his shoulder and throwing him off balance. It irritated Bricky, who stepped in towards Artie and shoved him with both arms in the chest, sending his younger brother a few feet back with a shocked look on his face.

'You've got no respect,' Artie said. 'You're not my brother anymore.'

'Wob, wob. You don't want to, wob, wob, do this, Arthur, you know I'll belt you, wob, to kingdom come.'

'Don't be so cocksure, Bricky. I'll give you a run for your money, you can be sure about that, you rat-faced, cheating liar.'

The knowledge that Artie's beautiful Kate was pregnant with Bricky's bastard child was too much for him to bear.

'Put 'em up, Bricky!' Artie ordered his older brother. Bricky had no choice, that was a challenge.

'Wob, wob. You're gonna regret this, Artie.'

'We'll see about that, William. We'll see.'

With their fists poised, they circled each other, shuffling their feet like a dance. Artie wanted to take a few really good swings at Bricky, but he knew he had to make them count. His brother was a harder man than he was.

'Wob, wob. She don't want to be with you, Artie, get used to it.'

That was enough to spark Artie into action. He came flying in, belting Bricky with strike after strike. The fury rising from his belly fuelled him to keep going and going, a *thwack* heard with every connection of fist on face. Blood vessels burst in Bricky's eye, making it a red mess. Artie was proudly surprising himself as he watched Bricky reeling from each punch. Bricky was raising his hands to cover his face and tucking his head down while retreating with each blow, trying to regain his balance. Bricky was stunned by Artie's power as his younger brother's anger kept propelling him forward, pounding and pummelling Bricky until suddenly Artie ran out of gusto.

That was when Bricky retaliated. He slammed his brother with two or three hits, and Artie landed on his arse. Bricky strode forward, picked his little brother up by the shirt and whacked him with a final blow that made him see stars. Bricky considered that was enough.

Exhausted, the men sat apart from each other, gathering their breath and assessing their wounds. Neither said a word. Eventually Artie, with his bruised face and bloodied nose, walked dizzily through the front door, seeking a mattress, while Bricky made his way to the Carlton with a bruised and bleeding head, a sore eye that he knew would become a big black shiner later that day and an eyebrow that felt like it needed stitches, too. One thing he knew for sure was that he and his brother would never speak again. His planned wedding to Kate was clearly not going to be a big family affair. Bricky was grateful that Kate hadn't been there to see the fight that caused the final wedge in the relationship with his brother.

✑

On 25 November 1888, at the small, dark-bricked Anglican Church known as St John's, Bricky's sister Evelyn and one of his brothers were witnesses as Minister Dunstan performed the wedding ceremony joining the two legally. That side of things was sorted. The baby would be born in four months, and there was a lot that Bricky, only twenty-two, and Kate, twenty-five, needed to do. Creating a home was at the centre of it.

The fresh start at Cadow had helped transform Kate's life three years earlier, but after she married, Kate had little control over her circumstances once again.

From the time of her marriage she was known, like all women were, by her husband's name. Mrs William Foster had, since their union, adopted the legal status of 'femme covert'. This legal creation of the courts upon marriage rendered a woman and her husband as one person in the eyes of the law. Her very being or independent legal existence was suspended during the marriage or at least consolidated into that of her husband.

No matter how things unfolded in their marriage, she would be stuck in it and dependent upon her new husband to provide for her while she raised children and engaged herself in the demanding, repetitive and often solitary tasks of keeping house and serving her husband. The freedoms Bricky had before he was married didn't really change. He had fought off his rival and won, and life would carry on, while Kate's new duties would tie her to him and their home.

From the time they got together, the couple were often seen breaking in horses together down by the lake. Kate, or rather 'Ada', was known for her superior horse skills, much to the ire of her husband. Kate thought Bricky was just young and immature, but she'd soon realise that Bricky couldn't let it go nor could he live with being second best to his wife. His insecurities were exposed even further when a handsome man called Johnny arrived with his young colt named Whiskey one morning.

7

Breaking in Horses

Horses are hyper vigilant creatures of flight, and so was Kate. Both knew what it was like to be hunted. She understood their fears.

Bricky was quick to lose his temper with the animals, but Kate would always tell him, 'To blame a horse for anything is like blaming the night for being dark, Bricky!' She could not bear cruelty. ''Tis humans who are mistaken, Bricky, in believing that cruelty is a way to gain respect.'

The couple would break horses in, down at the South Circle where a fenced circular pen held Kate in the middle of it. The lake snaked around the paddock behind them, and beyond the tree-lined banks, black swans elegantly glided past with their fluffy cygnets. Large pelicans stretched their wide wings as they took a break from the water and rested on the banks. Fluffing up their black and white feathers, shaking their large pale-pink bills and extending their clown-like webbed feet, they were calm and restful in this peaceful place.

Johnny, the owner from a property out of town, had brought in a dark chocolate-coloured colt, leading it behind him as he arrived on his own horse. He greeted the couple warmly, singing out with a smile, 'Morning, Ada!'

Bricky said hello, but Johnny didn't really seem to care. He led the colt into the ring, holding on firmly. A long line was attached to its headstall and bit, and he handed it over to Kate. Then he exited the ring, calm as the still lake behind them, even though the horse was not.

'What's his name, Johnny?' Kate asked, not losing eye contact with the young horse as it pulled and bucked, cantankerous.

'Whiskey.'

'Aah, Whiskey, you're a fine fellow!' Kate said as the colt jolted and strutted around, snorting and wondering what was going on. His energy was electric.

Johnny leaned on the fence, watching intently. His eyes followed the outline of Kate's lips and her hair. He watched the way her body moved, admiring her in a way that made Bricky bristle.

'He's well bred, Ada, from a good line. I think he's real smart. Maybe a champion in him yet. What do you think?'

Kate had ridden and trained prize winners before. Highlander, a favourite thoroughbred she'd owned in her wild days in Victoria, took out numerous prizes as both a hunter and a high jumper in Western district shows and even at the Melbourne show after she had reluctantly sold him.

'To be sure, Johnny!'

Bricky closed the pen off and shot a threatening look at Johnny, who saw it from the corner of his eye but paid no heed. Bricky positioned himself on the fence where he could stare straight at Johnny, who grinned a little.

Kate looped the long line and held it in her left hand. She reached out gently with her right hand, but the colt pulled his head back, unsure about her. They did a little circle in the middle of the ring.

Whiskey was nervously bucking, and Kate needed all her strength to hold him.

Whiskey sussed out Kate's heart rate and smell; he could sense everything he needed to know about her, while Kate quickly slid her hand under his jaw to do the same. She could tell that his heart was beating fast, maybe 120.

'Aah, Whiskey, of course yer a bit edgy, for sure, for sure! All right, Whiskey, that's all right.'

The colt pulled his head away from her, defiantly rejecting her touch. She walked backwards, maintaining eye contact, tightening the line a little, asking him to walk with her to the edge of the ring. He tentatively followed. He was flighty and flung his head a little from side to side as if he could shake her away from him.

Releasing the long line, she worked her way back to the middle and encouraged Whiskey to follow his instinct in moving around the edge of the ring clockwise. He was wound up but he started slow, not sure of what she was up to. She slapped the rolled-up long line on her thigh, which sparked him; he kicked the dirt behind him and sped up.

'That's it, Whiskey! Burn it off! Go on away now!' Standing in the middle of the ring, she threw the long line so it unravelled in the air and the end of it landed at his hind legs. He shook his head a little and worked up to a canter very quickly, while she brought the long line back to the middle with her and kept watching his body skirt around the ring before she cast it out again. He was happy to build up pace and keep moving away from her. She was letting him burn off his surge of nervous energy and follow his natural instincts.

'Eyes on eyes, shoulders square, see how I'm doin' it, Johnny?' She sang out softly while never losing eye contact with Whiskey. She raised her hand in the air with her fingers spread, and the colt sped up again. 'He's leading with his right, the inside legs. See, Johnny, his right eye be watching me. I'll make 'im turn now, Johnny. Watching?'

Johnny was watching all right, drinking in the image of this competent woman, and it was driving Bricky wild.

Kate moved a little closer to the edge and slapped the long line on her thigh again, this time with a criss-cross motion. She made a slapping noise from the left to her right thigh, and Whiskey changed direction with a shake of the head and a little buck. Now he watched her from his left eye, and she sent him back the other way again.

'Oh, Whiskey, see now, that's better, ain't it?

'See how he's more relaxed now, Johnny? He knows me from the right eye already.

'Yes, Whiskey, we've been here before, ain't we? Yer know me now!'

Kate was speaking gently to Whiskey, but Johnny was hanging on every word. Whiskey slowed down a little. He was calming, but Bricky was quietly seething. Restless and edgy, he moved closer to Johnny.

'Now watch his ears, Johnny,' Kate continued. 'Watching? See that he's put his ear on me, this inside ear. That one's listening to me now, the other is paying attention to outside the ring. See it?'

'I see it for sure, Ada.' Kate's smile thrilled Johnny, and he threw his head back with a chuckle and a smile of his own.

'Now I'm waiting to see him do a bit of a lick and a chew.' The signal Kate had been waiting for would show that the colt's adrenaline was settling. 'Aaah, that's it, Whiskey, good boy!'

Whiskey lowered his head.

'Good fellow, you're a fine fellow, Whiskey. With his head down, he's saying he's gonna let me be the boss. Keep moving, Whiskey.'

Whiskey had a calm rhythm now, and Kate could tell that his heart rate had lowered. She watched his flank to monitor his breathing.

'He'll come in for a smaller circle in a moment. That's what I'm waiting for now, Johnny.' Kate's eyes darted to Johnny, who was staring straight at her. She gasped a little and looked quickly back at Whiskey. 'Aah, Whiskey, me boy.'

Whiskey slowed. He had calmed down and finally moved in, doing a lap just a little closer to Kate. She let him keep going. 'That's it, Whiskey.'

Kate got him back up to a canter by raising her hand up with her fingers extended and, after a lap, she closed her fist and lowered her arm. Whiskey slowed right down in response and eventually walked briskly around the edge. Kate moved towards him and then turned her back on an angle and walked away from Whiskey. She looked a little over her shoulder to see if he had decided to follow her. Yes.

She turned slowly and Whiskey stood still for her. She put one hand to his mouth, letting Whiskey lick and smell her, while she patted him with the other. 'Well done, Whiskey, so well done! Whiskey, you are a fine, fine fellow!' She turned and walked away again, and he followed.

They did this for a while, with pats in between. Kate attached the long line again and looped the excess, holding it in her left hand. They were centred in the middle of the ring again. Snapping Bricky out of his focus on Johnny, Kate called out to him, 'Bricky, get the saddle gear and bring it round this side.'

The process had taken a long time, maybe an hour or more, but patience was what mattered and each horse was different. Kate was patting Whiskey and feeling for his heart rate, maybe sixty or so now, it had slowed right down. They were new friends, and he wanted to do what she wanted.

Kate wanted to try the saddle on him. Both Kate and Whiskey were calmly standing together, the long line attached and held firm for control, when Bricky came in slowly.

Whiskey was a little edgy, suddenly pulling his head back and moving his legs, wondering what was about to happen to him. They waited for a while, Bricky standing next to Whiskey holding the saddle, until Kate gave the word for him to gently place it over Whiskey's back, making sure the stirrups were crossed and resting atop the saddle so as not to dangle and spook the horse. 'Don't throw it rough like. Just place it there, softly. Don't spook him now.'

The horse shook his head a little and ruffled himself, pushing his neck up to let Kate know he was not thrilled. 'Just leave it there, don't strap it yet, just let 'im get a feel for it.'

With the saddle resting on his back, Kate thought Whiskey was doing okay so she got Bricky to fasten the girth strap firmly but not too tight. Whiskey was suspicious and reacted strongly against the unusual feeling underneath him. He tensed, kicking and pigrooting, snorting a little, very unhappy with these latest movements. Kate looked up at Whiskey's face while she pulled the long line in tight, calming him and patting him. She waited for him to relax a little.

She knew she couldn't be nervous or Whiskey would sense it. But would Bricky follow her instructions?

'Now, you have to listen to me, Bricky,' Kate said. 'When I say so, I want you to just lie over the saddle from the side and stay there. Don't go raising your legs over him like yer gonna ride him. Got it?'

Bricky nodded, annoyed that Kate was telling him what to do. He had worked with horses long enough, he knew all this stuff, but he couldn't argue with her in that moment because too much was at stake.

Again they waited for the right time and then Bricky slowly lifted his big body up and rested his upper torso on the saddle, letting his legs flop gently alongside the horse.

'That's it, Whiskey. He's just gonna stay there, until you get the feel of it, Whiskey. It's gonna be all right now. That's good, Bricky, just stay there and we'll keep walkin'.'

Whiskey jolted and pulled, not really sure about this new experience. Bricky wasn't worried because his feet were not that far from the ground, so if things got rough he could abort quickly. Kate led them around.

'Keep low, Bricky. Keep low.' Slowly the horse accepted the idea, and he carried Bricky as a side passenger for a long time. 'Ah, Johnny, you have a gem in Whiskey. He's a gem!'

'Well done, Ada! You worked a treat on him!'

'Bricky, do yer wanna try sitting up?'

'Wob, wob, well I don't wanna just hang here being dragged around the paddock for much, wob, wob, bloody longer for God's sake!'

Kate and Johnny laughed, trying not to unsettle Whiskey, but Bricky was fuming. Whiskey frisked up a bit, feeling Bricky's anger.

'Johnny, can you bring your ride over and lead Whiskey just like yer did coming into town? Come over to the gate here and Bricky will ride him with yer.'

'Try an' sit up, Bricky, give him a go. Come on, Whiskey boy, let Bricky hop up there.'

Bricky swung his big leg up and over the horse, lifting himself very slowly until he was upright in the saddle with his torso low. Whiskey did a little jump and kick but was calmed again by the arrival of Johnny and his horse. Kate opened the gate and passed the long line to Johnny, who was smiling from ear to ear.

Bricky and Whiskey headed out of the pen and did a slow lap of the paddock with Johnny leading them. Johnny said gently from his saddle, 'Ada, you've got talent, woman! Got a gift there, gal. I can't thank you enough, what a great start! He'll be a champion one day, Ada!'

Kate smiled, watching them walking around for a while until Bricky got moody, saying he'd had enough and telling Johnny to walk them both back to Kate.

Bricky dismounted and was put out when Johnny complimented Ada again. 'Wob, wob, that's enough, Johnny! Wob, wob, probably good for you to start heading back home now!'

'Whiskey, me boy, it's been a pleasure.' Kate gave Whiskey a goodbye pat while she shot Bricky a glare before Johnny set off.

'You're a talented woman, Ada!' Johnny snuck in one more compliment, just to annoy Bricky, before he laughed openly and waved to Kate. He didn't bother farewelling Bricky, who'd had a gutful.

Bricky hurled a mouthful of abuse at Kate and stormed off to the pub with his bruised ego.

8

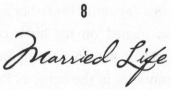

Married Life

Kate knew that her mother, Ellen, had become inconsolable after the death of her first child, Mary Jane, twelve years before Kate was born.

Heartbroken, Ellen had cried endless tears as she and Red placed the little infant into the grave Red had sadly but dutifully dug alongside their home. It was a scene Ellen had never imagined in the joyous months leading up to Mary's arrival. Ellen spent many days in bed afterwards thinking about dying. Her animals remained unfed and the housework untended. She was listless and suffering a serious and intense bereavement.

Perhaps, given her family history, Kate was exposed to the vulnerabilities of depression caused by loss and grief. But what could she do? Infant mortality rates at the time meant that every second child a woman gave birth to was destined to die. Having a baby was the riskiest thing a woman could do. Many women did not survive the gruelling demands of childbirth, mainly due to loss of blood or infection, and medical assistance was rare or rudimentary if provided. Kate had seen the worst of what was possible with her sister Anne. It was an experience that never left her thoughts.

Much of Kate's married life involved birthing and raising children. Only months into being wed, on 15 March 1889, her son Fred was born, just five days after his father's birthday. Registered by Bricky, Fred was named on his birth certificate as Arthur Bertram, but he would be known to everyone in his family, and later in life to his comrades in the army, as Frederick Arthur. The following year, his sister Gertrude arrived on 8 July 1890, four days before her mother's birthday. It was after the difficult birth of Gerty that things shifted in Kate. The first signs of postnatal depression revealed themselves, but Kate had no idea what it was. Her outlook on life dulled, and she never returned to her previous good health. Friends thought she was never the same again.

Another child didn't come along until 1893, but William died when he was only eight and a half months old, after two weeks of acute gastritis that Dr McDonnell was unable to remedy. Kate sobbed as she held her dead son in her arms until she surrendered him over to Bricky. She wished that the hole in the ground made for her son would swallow her.

On 28 February 1895, Ethel Maude, to be known affectionately as Elsie, came along, and Kate was relieved to keep her alive, making it three living children in the Foster clan.

In January 1896, Kate received word that her beloved older sister Maggie had died from 'untreated rheumatoid gout'. This rocked Kate's world. Maggie's body had tried to fight the infection that left her shivering with fever, sweating and confused. Although she had been in extreme pain, and became unable to even move her limbs, she hadn't asked for help. Her stoic, silent suffering allowed the untreated infection to escalate to septic shock, and by the time the family was able to seek medical assistance, her condition had deteriorated morbidly.

Kate wondered why her sister had refused treatment. Had she shared the same horrid nightmares that Kate suffered? Did she not want to live? Now it was too late to know. Maggie had finally abandoned Kate completely. Another loss. Another family member returned to the dust. Kate was reminded of her own loneliness and suffering while grieving her adored Maggie and their lost years. Kate carried on with life, from one sadness to the next.

Kate endured another birth in 1897, when she welcomed baby Ruby into the fold. But one November morning, Kate discovered the still features and lifeless body of her baby, who had given her last breath to the world. Dr Calder described the six-month-old's cause of death as *debilitas*. Ruby was simply too weak to continue. For a second time, Kate lost a young child and was sent into grief over the loss. She had not recovered from the death of her sister and this time the loss felt insurmountable. Kate's sadness could not be contained as she wrapped Ruby in a favourite cloth for the last time.

Fred and Gerty had grieved the loss of their baby brother William with their mother, so they were overjoyed to welcome Elsie as their baby sister after that, but all were saddened again by the loss of baby Ruby. The children were able to understand in their own way what it meant when the babies their mother had cared for weren't around anymore, but once they were gone no one talked about them again.

Like every woman of the time, Kate was more or less unable to control her fertility and found herself pregnant within a few months of losing Ruby. The last addition to the Foster family was Catherine, arriving on 7 September 1898.

No other adults were with Kate for the delivery. No midwife. No support from an older woman or family member. Fred was almost ten, Gerty eight and Elsie nearly four. It was customary in some households for children to be sent to stay with relatives during births, but that was a luxury Kate didn't have and so she had to keep the children close by her. Kate would endure the delivery unaccompanied and enlist the help of Gerty when needed. Kate had grown up experiencing the same circumstances; she and Maggie had assisted Ellen with the birth of Jack and Ellen Junior.

The doors and windows of the Foster household were open wide, funnelling the freshness of September through the house while the squeals and murmurs of children playing echoed along the hallway. Barefoot and wearing a loose nightshirt, Kate was slowly following Elsie as she ran into the yard. Kate could feel some familiar muscle spasms around her back and then her abdomen. Her waters had broken half an hour before, so she knew things were getting closer. Kate's plan was to keep moving around for as long as she could.

'Gerty!' Kate sang out to her daughter to come and join her and Elsie in the yard. 'Fred! Come out here now, boy!'

The fire out the back nursed a huge pot containing water, rags and towelling. Kate had been poking and prodding at it with a large stick in preparation for the imminent event. Her bed was as clean and neat as she could prepare it, and it would remain as hygienic as one could hope considering the simple mattress of calico stuffed with feathers, straw, wool and rags was positioned on the dirt floor.

Standing by the metal vessel, she gave instructions to Gerty about placing towelling and hot water into a bowl without hurting herself. A stern warning came with it that these would need to be brought in to her mother when she asked. Fred had to keep feeding the kindling and small wood into the flames and make sure the water was kept on the boil.

Once the youngsters had repeated their mother's instructions, to show her they understood, Kate went inside to locate the opium she had purchased from Quong Lee's store down the street. Her hope was that, as the approaching pain became too intense to bear, the opioid would take the edge off.

She mixed up her poppy-based concoction in a teapot and placed it beside her bed, noticing her contractions as they became more painful, sharp and frequent. Using the opioid was immoral to most. The pain of childbirth was considered to be 'God's wish', as if women were meant to suffer and ask for God's help. Pain relief was considered intoxication, and it was suggested that, by using it, a woman would remove her 'maternal instinct'. Kate didn't care about those kinds of beliefs.

Facing hours of labour on her own, she paced around her room, gently bending and leaning over in an attempt to find comfort, squatting and kneeling, sighing and panting through her contractions.

She asked Gertrude to bring in the soapy water and cloth like she had shown her. Gerty ran quickly to the boiler and did what she was told, asking what else she might do as she wrung out a hot towel, leaving it for her mother to place behind her lower back. Kate relaxed into its soothing warmth momentarily. 'Go on now, Gerty. Keep an eye on Elsie. Yer a good lass. I'll need you later. Good girl.'

Gerty followed her mother's instructions and got her sister ready for bed. She had promised to look after Elsie, and now they were cuddling each other in the room next to their mother, trying to fall asleep. Fred kept to himself, knowing this wasn't his business, but he listened astutely to the noises his mother was making in case he needed to go get help. He'd been through this many times before.

Kate worked up a sweat, resisting the urge to push for as long as she could take it. She used the soapy water to wash herself down and try to sterilise her vaginal area in preparation. Propped up with bedding, so her back was supported, she brought her knees up and reached through, gently applying pressure to her perineum in anticipation of slowing the arrival of the baby's head. The distressing sounds of Kate's labour emanated through the house while the children kept quiet, doing what their mother had told them, mainly to stay out of the way.

It was late into the night and Gerty was half asleep when Kate called to her again. Rubbing her eyes, running down the hall, she stood beside her mother's bed while Kate gave directions in between groans and rapid breathing. 'It's gonna be here soon, Gerty. I need yer to get the towelling out of the hot water like we talked about.' She was breathing heavily and concentrating on her body and the final stages of the birth. 'I'll need to wipe the baby down soon. Yer know what to do.' Kate panted and groaned with the movement of the child as it began to crown.

Excitedly, Gerty ran outside to the pot of hot water again. The moment she'd been waiting for was nearly here. She had been an assistant to her mother before and she knew she was a good helper, but the mess of blood she knew was coming always made her queasy. It was a sight that made her grow up and be prepared for her own future.

Outside, the fire had gone out long ago. Fred had been sleeping on and off and listening to his mother so intently that he had forgotten about the fire. Enough heat remained in the pot, and Gerty delivered a large bowl of warm water and soaking towelling to Kate, staying to witness the arrival of her newest sibling.

With her mother panting and pushing her into the world, little Catherine's head revealed itself and Kate pushed it down a little to prepare for the next stage. Panting, she paused, catching her breath as she awkwardly reached down with both hands ready to grab the pink-skinned and bloodied creature as she started to push again. Kate groaned and guided the child as its little shoulders squeezed through. Gerty was a little shocked, thrilled and nervous all at the same time.

The remainder of the perfectly formed body smoothly followed, and Kate brought it up to her chest. She was feeling exhausted in a way that felt as if she had just finished a long cross-country ride at great pace. Gerty gave a little squeal of excitement as she wrung the towelling out and handed it to her mother.

Dazed and tired, Kate began wiping her baby clean, clearing the child's nostrils and mouth with her fingers. She rubbed the baby's little sides and back vigorously up and down, almost begging it to breathe. There was a moment when she was unsure about whether it would happen until finally the new arrival cried loudly. Kate released a deep outward sigh of relief. 'Meet yer new sister, Gerty.'

Gerty was filled with delight and Kate leaned back, feeling relieved and tired. 'Good girl, Gerty. Give me a moment now and a little later yer can bring the others in.'

Gerty left reluctantly and went back to the bed where Elsie had fallen asleep. She climbed in next to her but she was too excited and woke Elsie to tell her the news.

The new bundle of flesh continued to exercise her lungs relentlessly. Kate focused on the strong contractions delivering the placenta. She was hoping it would all exit her body as she pushed it along. Leaving the placenta connected, she closed her eyes and leaned herself back, looking for a moment of rest. Opening her eyes a few moments later, she wrapped the soft tiny baby in a flannelette.

Then she tried to put her on the breast, but the baby wouldn't take to it. Crying loudly, the baby and Kate were becoming distressed.

The opium had done its job for a while, but it was the hipflask she was sipping from now to take the edge off it all. Kate began to realise that the baby was not of great interest to her. She stared at it blankly. After a while she put the child to her breast again, but the infant continued to squeal and turn its head from side to side, refusing to latch. There was palpable tension already between the two. Wiped out from the athletic and life-threatening challenge she had endured over the last ten hours, Kate drifted away, affected by fatigue, opioids and alcohol.

In the small hours of the new day, Kate was rudely awoken by the screams of her newest daughter. The shock sent her mind reeling for a few very long seconds until she finally remembered the new human she had brought into the world now lying by her side.

The first sign of the sun gently shone on the eastern-facing walls, and there was a stillness and quiet, it was a sacred time. Shaped in the spaces around the quiet were the shrieks of the new baby suffering pangs of hunger that its mother could not satiate.

As the morning progressed, Kate pegged the placenta cord in two places and cut it with a knife, wrapping it with muslin to absorb the blood. She left one peg attached. She wondered why the child wouldn't take her milk and was both irritated and defeated by it.

Kate could hear the other children talking to each other beyond her bedroom door and called out to them to welcome their new sister. Each of the scruffy-headed kids flocked in sheepishly, looking exhausted and a little shocked themselves, after all the screams and noises they'd heard through the night. Elsie had been so alarmed by the stressful sounds that she had needed a lot of cuddles from Gerty, but now she was happy to hold her new little sister.

With all of them in the bed with Kate and Catherine, there was a brief moment of togetherness as the children stared with awe at the baby. They were too young to notice how exhausted their mother was. Kate turned them out with things to do to help her around the house, telling Fred to light the fire again so she could have a wash. She needed to clean herself up and freshen her bedding, all the while wishing she could run a million miles away, but feeling so guilty for it. Another drink would surely help.

Over the coming hours baby Catherine still wouldn't settle, refusing to take Kate's milk. 'Yer little imp! What's wrong with yer?' Kate rustled up some coins and sent the kids to Quong Lee. 'Tell him I need something to put in a bottle for yer new sister. Off yer go now, take Elsie for a walk.'

Kate felt herself slipping into a dark place. The post-birth hormones were wearing off and lowering her mood. She was hot and bothered, sore, moody and tired. So very tired. Catherine's screams were becoming weaker from a lack of sustenance but, for Kate, it was a relief not to have to listen to her anymore.

She lay herself down while the children were out and closed her eyes and ears to the sounds of the baby. Waking up again sometime later, the crying child's vocal demands had increased again and Kate decided to boil some more water. Sprinkling a handful of oats into a cup, Kate poured hot water over them and waited. Separating the liquid and the mushy oat mixture, the new mother dipped a rag in the milky substance and poked it into the baby's crying mouth until it finally started to suck the fabric. It was better than nothing.

The first few weeks after the birth, Kate grappled with her depression and the difficulty in feeding the baby. It was a tug of war, with the depression increasing the more the child wouldn't feed. The intense pain in her breasts was developing into mastitis.

She hadn't had a baby that wouldn't take her milk before. Kate had no choice but to put the infant on the bottle or she wouldn't survive. The lack of attachment between the mother and child was causing deep anxiety and distress in both of them. Bricky had not met his new daughter yet, but he would be back from Burrawang in the next few days. Kate wasn't sure how she felt about his pending arrival. It had the potential to be another stressful feature in her already dim world.

Desperate for a distraction and despite her precarious mental state, a few weeks after the birth of Catherine, on Saturday, 1 October 1898, Kate decided to get out of the house and see this new travelling show she had heard about. Susan would keep an eye on the kids for the night and relieve Kate of the agitation caused by her infant. Kate's enthusiasm for a few moments of freedom quickly evaporated not long after her arrival at the marquee, and nothing could have prepared Kate for the shock that was to come.

9

The Bohemian's Travelling Show

The Bohemian Lecturer's travelling entertainment, which had been drawing in the crowds, publicised its latest productions and performances in *The Western Champion*, a newspaper published in Parkes, on 30 September 1898.

> On Friday last [the 23rd of September] the Bohemian Medical Company gave another very interesting entertainment. The programme consisted of many fine views ... of the world ... On Saturday night [the 1st of October] they intend giving an account of the origin and destruction of the Bushrangers of Australia. All of these entertainments have been well patronised by the public.

A four-sided hessian tent with no roof was set up behind the Foster family home, where Bricky's mother and father lived, near the goldfield flats.

The travelling show consisted of a group of performers and a side business of 'wellness' tonics and pills. The troupe's leading showman, the Bohemian Lecturer, claimed that his bottled wares could cure many things, and there was a huge buzz all over town about their novel entertainments.

Kate sat in the audience alone, her once-smart black dress looking worn and old; her hair was messed up, making her look a little wild. She squinted as she peered around the crowd, trying to see who else was there that she knew, but she could only see two of the hideous women from the singalong group she used to go to. She quickly looked the other way, but the women had already seen her and sat smirking at each other.

The crowd was growing as people found their seats, chatting excitedly among themselves and waving to others in the audience. A man dressed as if he were someone important presented himself to the crowd. *So this is him? The Bohemian Doctor or whatever they call him*, Kate thought to herself, unimpressed and suspicious. In his top hat, long black coat and twirly moustache, Mr Cole (for that was the Bohemian Lecturer's real name) launched into an announcement, speaking of himself in the third person as the onlookers reduced their noisy conversations to an eager quiet.

'This show is brought to you by the Bohemian Lecturer's wellness tonics. All our reputable products are safe for children and adults alike.' He raised his bottles of oils and potions as he spoke and waved them from left to right like a snake's head hypnotising the audience.

'Our tonics and pills cure the common cold, stomach ailments, headaches and nervous tension. Ladies and gentlemen, be sure to see our assistants during the intermission to make sure you get your supplies before they are sold out. No home should be without our modern medicine! Beware of imitators!'

Mr Cole continued with his sales pitch, looking at the locals who were dressed in their finest outfits, some of whom had travelled for miles in their horse and carts to be there for a night of entertainment and relief from their mundane and unremarkable lives. He reminded them all that he was also a dentist, a thought that made Kate shudder.

'For the rich and the poor, note that I am here with practical experience. Why, I have extracted over one million teeth! Without artificial aid! In fact, one fine, delicate lady left my surgery pleased and happy within fifteen minutes. Extractions are performed daily while we are in your town, and I provide medicine and advice on all diseases!

'Indeed, I am the only travelling member of the Bohemian Medical Company, and these are positively our last few days here! Our wellness tonics and pills are imitated but unequalled!'

The crowd was impressed and applauded loudly.

Kate knew about these kinds of travelling showmen; she'd worked with them, and she didn't like this Mr Cole. 'Self-praise ain't no recommendation,' Kate blurted out loudly. It made people about her shift in their seats, uncomfortable. They looked down their noses at her and wished she would shut up.

Mr Cole then announced the commencement of what he called the Cycloramic Exhibition. The crowd rallied loudly with anticipation. Everyone was thrilled to witness something so new and exciting. There was a high canvas, twenty feet or more, that functioned as a screen. On it appeared a series of lifelike pictures of places from around the world. Giant images of New Zealand, Honolulu, San Francisco and the amazing World Fair in Chicago were magnified onto the canvas wall. Majestic rivers and mountain ranges transported the audience's imagination as they were dazzled by the enormous images that were enabled by a new contraption and lit by a gas lantern.

Forbes.

(FROM OUR OWN CORRESPONDENT.)

At the Police Court on Monday, Thomas Molloy was charged with riotous behavior at Warron, and indecent language. The case was postponed for a week, bail being allowed. This aggressor was again arrested on Tuesday, with others, for the same charge.

The Half-holiday Sports, under the auspices of the Forbes B.C. and the Half-holiday Association take place to-day (Wednesday.) A good number of entries for both bicycle and foot races have been received. Last night a lantern procession of Cyclists took place; being, however, poorly attended.

On Friday last the Bohemian Medical Company gave another very interesting entertainment. The programme consisted of many fine views of the greater part of the world. A drama, entitled "Queen's Pardon," was played, the proceedings terminating with the singing of comic songs, etc. On Saturday night they intend giving an account of the origin and destruction of the Bushrangers of Australia. All of these entertainments have been well patronised by the public.

Mr. H. P. Smith, chemist, late of Sydney, has opened a pharmacy in this town. This gentleman is well-known here, having been a resident of Forbes some time ago.

A paragraph was published in

This article dated 30 September 1898 (above) and advertisement from 21 October 1898 (right) confirm oral history about the Bohemian Medical Company visiting Forbes and presenting its performance of 'The Life and Adventures of the Kelly Gang'.

'It is a breathtakin' view,' Kate whispered. Descriptive songs were performed by the acting troupe to accompany the images. Comical outfits and slapstick acts with humorous banter about events of the day were also carried out in between the giant slide-show of pictures. Kate relaxed a little; it seemed that this was the escape she needed from the misery of her life after all.

After the last of the images was shown, a brief intermission was announced. A rush of people pushed their way outside and purchased tonics and pills, oils and remedies, which promised relief from human suffering of every kind. The Bohemian and his staff looked down on the excited consumers from an elevated platform on their wooden caravan and took money hand over fist, relishing their own success.

Kate remained seated. She scanned the audience again and spotted an old friend, Clara Rae. Her long blonde locks were neatly twisted and tucked, and she was dressed elegantly in a dark corset, long black skirt and gloves. She was sitting next to her husband, who looked equally sharp. They were quite a distance away, but they gave a little wave to her.

Clara gazed a while at Kate, wondering what she was doing there unaccompanied. It was unusual for a woman to attend an evening like this alone. Kate couldn't care less. Everything about her right now was unusual and unhinged. She had a wild edge, a tension that was accentuated by alcohol and illness. Her reality was altered.

Bells started to ring, encouraging the return of the punters, newly armed with their fresh supply of mysterious antidotes tucked into pockets and bags. Minutes later, a gleeful Mr Cole reappeared, having happily counted his money. Now he intended to guide his viewers to the next chapter of their entertaining evening.

'Ladies and gentlemen! Ladies and gentlemen! A show like this you'll never see again! The only true representation of the thrilling episodes enacted in the 'Life and Adventures of the Kelly Gang'. Yes, the "Origin and Destruction of Australian Bushrangers!" A new, original and novel entertainment!

The crowd cheered and clapped excitedly, keen for the action to start.

Kate was horrified and frozen in her seat. Everything she had tried to escape had followed her here to this moment. *Entertainment? This ain't no entertainment. Dear God!* The word 'entertainment' was like a stab in her heart, and her throat felt like it was closing in on her.

Seemingly out of nowhere, the cast was in sight, gathering in the wings and dressed up almost like cowboys. Kate sneered at the costumes. *What would they know? This is too much. How do I get out of here?* Looking around from her seat, she couldn't see the exit. Panic grew within her. Then the Bohemian enticed the crowd with a new announcement. It took a few moments to sink in.

'Ladies and gentlemen, I have a special announcement, indeed a special announcement!' The crowd found its silence. 'Do you want to know this special news? I have been informed, ladies and gentlemen, that in fact, we even have a member of the infamous Kelly family in the tent with us tonight!'

There was a collective gasp from the crowd, and people started to look around, chattering like excited monkeys.

'Yes! A member of the infamous Kelly family . . . here . . . in the tent!'

Kate remained dead still; everything around her was moving in slow motion. She cast her eyes downward and covered her face with her hands. *How could this be happening? Bastard, feckin' mongrel!* She felt raw with humiliation.

Clara Rae knew exactly who Kate was; they used to go to dances together in their single days and Kate had told her much about her early life. But she would never have given her away. Now, Clara looked over at her desperate friend awkwardly, not knowing what she could do to help her.

She stared at Kate, hoping she would not do anything to make it worse for herself. She noticed how sick Kate was looking. She'd heard that Kate had had another baby and assumed that's why she was so pale and gaunt. Fragile-looking.

There was confusion and movement among the audience. Some thought it was a joke, just part of the act. Embarrassed and humiliated as she was, Kate refused to buckle and she glared at the Bohemian, thinking about what she'd like to do to him to get even. The travelling charlatan had purposely and publicly tormented Kate so she would reveal herself, but she was not playing along.

Kate's cover in town was blown, though, and the privacy she had clung to for so long had been betrayed. *It were them whores from the singalong, I know it.* Kate was livid and looked around for them. *It must've been them. Those whores, those boot-licking, God-loving whores! They must have told him. What dogs!*

Kate's anonymity had been compromised at a social outing just a month or so before baby Catherine came. Her friends had been absent and instead other women had surrounded her, looking for information. Kate's large belly protruded boldly, and two of the women had cast a harsh look from the bulge to each other. How could she be out in public in her condition?

Sweetly, they had asked her about her pregnancy, then more brutally, about the absence of her husband. The ambush had made Kate feel smothered and trapped. She'd wanted to get away but then they'd started stirring her up about her brothers being the infamous Kellys. 'Your brothers, we know about your brothers!' they'd said to her. 'Murderous bushrangers, devil's spawn. What a shameful family. Shameful.'

Kate had pushed her heavy self up off the chair and spat every cuss and curse she had ever heard her brothers use at the women until she got herself away from them. She had been in a disturbed state after the encounter. Who else knew? Who else would they tell? Kate had scurried back to her home and faced night after night alone with her children, dwelling on it. *But how did they know in the first place?* She'd racked her brain about whose big mouth had dumped her in it. Which friend had betrayed her?

From her seat at the travelling show, Kate glared at those treacherous women she'd seen earlier. She could feel her life unravelling along with her anonymity. In this small town, where not much happened, Kate's past offered up salacious controversy that would not be ignored by keen gossipers. The pretentious singalong women had gobbled it up, and tonight was an ideal opportunity to humiliate Kate and put her in her place. But Kate was not going down without a fight. She was doing her best not to reveal herself or respond to Cole's manipulative efforts.

With the audience now gazing at Mr Cole, somewhat disappointed with the lack of climax, he fidgeted on stage for a moment. He didn't know what Kate looked like, and he realised that his sensational plan was a flop. He had no choice but to keep the show moving and introduce the act.

Kate was agitated and emotional as she tried to regain her composure, waiting for everyone to settle into the play so that she could make her exit when an actress came on to the small stage. Kate gasped at the sight of a fake Kate Kelly, dressed like a cowgirl, twirling in front of the patrons in the front row. The crowd began laughing at the actress who was delivering a parody of Kate's supposedly misguided loyalty to her outlaw brothers.

Kate's lifetime of tragedy, all the social judgement and misrepresentation were wrapped up in the form of this public entertainment. Her pain and trauma reduced to a devastating public amusement. They were ridiculing her.

Still seated, her shabby dress was visibly moving as Kate's shaking became overwhelming. Unable to contain her hysteria, she shouted profanities and abuse at the stage, her rage wild.

'Why did you bring this here? You don't know nothin'. Nothin' at all! This is an outrage! Yer a rotten mongrel! You rat-faced coward, Cole.'

She jumped to her feet and screamed at the pretty actress. 'And you whore, what the hell do you know about Kate Kelly? Yer not Kate Kelly, you'll never be Kate Kelly!'

Trapped in a nightmare, Kate continued her tirade at the stage. The crowd grew excited by it. From the front of the stage, Mr Cole pointed his fat fingers at Kate. 'Someone help this lady out, please, the excitement is too much for her! Too much for her, I declare! Such is the power of our remarkable entertainment.'

He signalled an assistant to escort her out. Amid the thrilled audience, captivated by the action both on stage and among them, Kate wrestled with the assistant, hurling abuse as he yanked her out of the tent.

Outside, she was dizzy and confused. Someone pushed her onto a chair, opened a bottle of their tonic and passed it to her. 'This will help you, Madam.'

Kate gulped it down then hurled more abuse at the man. 'What in damnation were you playin' at in there? You wretched thing!'

He muttered defensively at Kate.

Her face was red, she was sweating profusely and her throat was raw from yelling. Her heart was pounding, and she was mortified by both the exposure of her identity and the shock of how the evening had panned out.

The face of the man transformed before her eyes. He looked like a wild bush rat. 'What have yer done to me now?' she asked suspiciously, hardly able to get the words out. Kate stood up in a hurry only to fold back down as her legs disappointed her.

'Madam, please stay seated until you feel better, the tonic will work directly, just wait a moment.'

'Unhand me!' she shrilled as she pulled away from him. 'You know nothin' about me! Get away from me! What a scandal, what an outrage! You mongrel.' She took a swing at him and he ducked to avoid her closed fist, but she let another one fly on his way back up, connecting firmly under his eye and sending his head backwards. He groaned. Her knuckle print remained red on his face as she made her getaway.

Dizzy and confused, Kate stumbled away from him, striking the air and protecting her face from the large eagle she could see above her. Its wings opened wide, and it hovered, fanning wind on her face. She had seen this eagle before, terrorising a roo across a paddock at Cadow. The eagle's heavy legs bludgeoned the roo's head, knocking it over each time it got up, until it sank its large talons like knives into the animal's shoulders and rattled the exhausted creature to death.

Kate had been worn down like the kangaroo, bashed every time she got back up. She wished that her hallucination would swoop down on her. 'Take me away from all this,' she whispered with her eyes closed. When she looked up again, the bird was gone.

Kate rushed down a back lane and retreated to her house.

Four days later, Kate could not clearly remember her return but she had remained in bed since. Bricky had arrived the previous night and was about to make his exit again now that it was early morning.

'You smell like whiskey,' he said to her.

Kate couldn't look at him as he stood beside her bed, making demands and reprimanding her. 'You need to straighten up, woman. What do you have to say for yourself?'

'All right, Bricky. Leave it alone. I'll straighten up.'

'When?'

'Today.'

'The children are unclean. When did you wash their clothes last? When did they bathe?'

Silence. The baby next to her was weak and quiet. Bricky threw six shillings on the bedside table. 'That child ain't right either. Why can't you feed it? What's wrong with you? Get out of bed and be a mother, for God's sake. You're an embarrassment.'

10

Visiting Kate

Later that afternoon Kate's neighbour, Susan, opened the front door of the small white weatherboard house and called out to Kate. She could faintly hear the baby, but all other sounds were absent. Susan trod the hallway. As she turned into the living room, she found Kate sitting in her only armchair amid the darkness of the enclosed space, which offered no window. A dirty white woollen blanket with a soft blue stripe rested on the floor underneath the four-week-old Catherine as she lay on her back, crying.

'Ada?' Susan said her friend's name like it was a question. 'It's just me. Susan.' She spoke softly from the doorway. With her weight on one leg, she leant on the doorframe, waiting to see if Kate was going to greet her. If not, she would just leave.

'Mmmm.' Kate was dozing. With her head leaning on a bulge of protruding stuffing at the side of the chair, a donation from old Mr Prow, it took a moment for her to realise that Susan's voice was not in her mind.

Susan tapped Kate on her shoulder as she moved beyond the

chair, saying hello and scooping up the infant, rocking her gently while she bobbed up and down to soothe her. Kate's hair was messy, and she looked weak and tired. Susan gave her a moment to wake up properly.

'All right, Ada?'

'I don't like her.'

'You what?'

'She's still on the bottle, Susan, she won't take me milk.'

From this side of Kate, Susan could smell the liquor on her breath and she sensed Kate's desperation.

'Me breasts are paining me. Can you take her?'

'What d'yer mean, Ada?'

'Can yer take her? Bricky's got money. He'll pay yer.'

'No, Ada.'

'Ah, go on now, Susan! I need to straighten up.'

'Where is Bricky?'

'Gone again.'

'Burrawang?'

'Mmm. He hates me. Says I'm embarrassing, that I should be ashamed.'

'Oh now, Ada, it's just a tiff. Just some strong words.'

'Take her, Susan. Just for a couple of days. Let me get away.'

'Ada, I don't want to do that. You need to stay put. Anyway, what would I tell Ted?'

'Bricky can give yer money to look after her.'

'Where are the children, Ada?'

'Gerty and Fred took Elsie wiv them to the lake. I told them to get out and don't come back 'til sundown.'

Susan felt anxious about the children and grimaced slightly at what Kate said. Catherine squirmed.

'Take her, Susan, will yer?'

Susan was silent for a while. 'When did Bricky leave?'

'This morning. Glad he's gone. I need to get away just to straighten up. Let me do that, Susan, will yer?'

'What about the other children?'

'They'll be fine here until I get back.' Kate looked at Susan desperately. 'Susan, help me out. Yer know she's on the bottle, something's wrong.'

At home, across the street, was Susan's three-month-old baby, Ethel Alma, born on 5 July. Susan was breastfeeding her daughter without any issue, but she wasn't expecting to be a wet nurse for anyone. Is that what Kate wanted? She rocked and rocked the unsettled baby in her arms, feeling the pressure of what Kate wanted her to do.

Susan had suffered child loss of her own. Her daughter Rose had died five years ago, when Susan was only twenty, and yet another child had died just two years ago. Ted and Susan had been able to keep their young son, William, now four years old, alive and well, and he was at home with his new baby sister under Ted's watchful eye. Susan and Ted only got hitched in January. The Hurleys didn't have much money, but Ted was a good man, only twenty-two years old, and he worked as a coachman and in the fire brigade. Life was hard enough for Susan's own little family without any further complications.

Susan understood Kate's dilemma, though, and had real concerns for the baby's health after watching her friend struggle over the last month. She thought that Kate's request was an act of complete despair. She could not imagine how it must feel to have to ask someone else to feed your own child or to be in such pain because your baby wouldn't take your milk. Wet nursing was a common practice for the time, but Susan had not planned to take on another baby, especially under these circumstances, even if it was just for a couple of days. And she wondered how she could make the baby feed if Kate couldn't. Yet she was persuaded by her neighbour's plea.

'All right, but just tonight. You have to be back tomorrow. I'm just helping you this one time. I don't know what Ted is going to say, for goodness sake.'

'Write me a note will yer?'

'You can write yer own note, Ada.'

'Susan, write a note for me. Write it down that you'll look after her and that Bricky will pay yer.'

Unwell, exhausted and slightly drunk, Kate then simply walked out the door. Susan called out a farewell but received no reply. She watched Kate, who was squinting with the shock of the daylight, as she headed off alone.

Susan looked at the scribbled note Kate had asked her to write and wondered if there was any point to it. A feeling of nervousness overcame Susan as she walked back to her own place, nursing little Catherine.

Where was Ada going?

11

Going to the Lagoon

On that Wednesday afternoon, 5 October, Kate walked away from her young family, desperate to be alone. Lost in her own suffering, her mind was elsewhere as she made her way down Browne Street towards the lagoon. The tragic image of her little ones coming home to find her gone made her ache. It didn't feel right, but she couldn't make herself turn around.

She was painfully reminded of the travelling show as she rushed past the tent. A flood of anger pulsed through her body but quickly receded as she gave in to the humiliation she had suffered at the hand of the Bohemian, Mr Cole.

Kate passed the miner's claim that had been worked by Artie Foster and his father not far from their family home. The illusory pursuit of gold was familiar to Kate, her father had been lucky with it on the Bendigo goldfields. She also had memories of handling gold on her brothers' behalf years before. One of the many rumours that followed Kate around when her brothers died was the suggestion that she had access to a secret stash of gold from their exploits, hidden in caves. If only it had been true, she wouldn't be in this place anymore.

Ted Foster, Bricky's youngest brother who adored Kate, spotted her and sang out, but she was oblivious to him in her trance-like state. He was standing with his friend Violet Dargon, out the front of her house, and they stared at Kate as she disappeared from sight.

All of those features she was known for—beauty, charm and humour—seemed absent on this day. Kate's long, wavy, dark locks were pulled back tight but random curls dangled, unthreading themselves as she walked and walked until her legs felt like stone.

Kate's trauma was vibrantly tormenting her. 'I can hear the voices of m' loved ones, vanished and gone. When the stars are out or in the daylight hours, it don't matter when. Their faces float before me. It torments me. Give me rest!' she exhaled. 'Ghosts. Hauntin' me with memories of bastards and betrayers. Blast yer into damnation. Yer no good mongrels. Devils, against me. Born a Kelly, what damned fate is it? Wish I'd never been born at all.'

She made her way to a shanty. Desperation was all around her and within. Without even speaking, she handed over some coins and took whatever they gave her; she didn't care. The old lady knew Kate and wondered what the hell had gotten into her, but she handed over two heavy brown bottles. Only slightly intrigued, she watched Kate walk away, slumped and defeated, slugging the beer straight from one of the bottles, ignoring the collection of day drinkers nearby.

Kate stopped once she was past Foo's crossing. It was full of old stones, and the water was only ever low enough to use it during drought. Alone and far away from anyone, Kate could feel a faint, hot breeze. She thought that she could hear some male voices carrying in the wind from the nearby brickyards, but she vacantly stared through the surrounding bush, unable to detect any movement.

Across the still, brown water of the lagoon and through the colourful, thick stands of trees, Kate could see the white paling fence of the new racecourse. On a nearby bank, kangaroos halted their movements and stood upright as they watched her.

Kate recognised the swirls of jade and viridian greens that she figured must be the back of the Chinaman's garden filled with spring vegetables. Within it, there were patches of lilac. She knew the colour belonged to Ah Toy's poppies.

Kate stood still. She ran her fingers over the brooch pinned to her dress, as if caressing it would bring her mother closer to her in that moment.

Plonking herself at the base of a tree near the largest waterhole, Kate unlaced her tattered boots, revealing her delicate feet covered in stockings. She put one bottle of beer in the water to keep it cool and returned to her spot under the tree, lowering her narrow back into its bark and tilting her head to consume the remainder of the contents from the first bottle.

She was distressed by her dilemma. Her secrets were out, and she had been publicly humiliated. She had worked so hard to reinvent herself, to conceal her past, but the game was up. The complicated mixture of intrigue, fascination and disgust, coupled with a desire to punish the Kellys, had stuck to Kate like shit to a blanket for what seemed like her entire life, and it had finally worn her down.

There were different rules and expectations for women when it came to crime. Kate knew it. She had seen for herself how the female of the species could receive an overly harsh sentence; just look at her mother.

Through the alcohol, she could still feel the pain of her breasts, and she was burning up with a fever. Her new child was one of the sources of her pain. She continued to ply herself with alcohol, despite telling Susan and Bricky that she planned to get straight.

She was too depressed to figure anything out. *That damned baby ain't no good.* There was a pounding force in Kate's head. *I'm so shameful. They are better off without me.* Many thoughts were clashing in her brain at once, and she couldn't stand it anymore. She was in such a sorry place that she couldn't see how she could possibly navigate her way out of it.

Her passions and adventures had been replaced by domestication, a mostly absent husband, hungry mouths to feed and one mouth that would not. 'Me breasts are useless, can't even feed me own child.' The space she filled in the world had become confusing and dark.

Her inebriated vision made her dizzy. Kate stretched herself out, sinking into the dirt and immersing herself in the spinning world of blue above her.

12

The Investigation

Senior Constable J.J. Garstang was English born, and although he was proud of it, his 'stiff upper lip' attitude and innate sense that he was better than everyone else annoyed a lot of people.

If you asked Garstang, he was an outstanding policeman. It was a goal of his to make sergeant as soon as possible, and it seemed that landing in Forbes had been a good move for his career. After moving around from post to post, he had promising prospects in the small town, and he didn't want anything to ruin them. Investigating the death of Kate Kelly had become a sore point, but he wasn't letting on. How she had remained at large in such a small place baffled him, but mostly he was annoyed that he had not been the one to find her body. He was no stranger to wild criminals or dead bodies, but Kate had managed to simply vanish.

How hard had Garstang and his men searched for Kate? A missing person's case needed to be investigated immediately. The first port of call should be the missing person's house to establish what belongings they may have taken or if they had a means of transport. The police might even perform door knocks or check hospitals.

Kate had travelled solely by foot, so how far could she have gone? How difficult could it be to locate her in the small town? Ted Foster recollected her passing by, and Kate bought two bottles of beer from the nearest shanty, but Garstang didn't visit either of them.

Garstang's angular face bore a painful scar, which ran from eyebrow to lip, and was acquired in Lithgow, his first posting as a policeman outside of Sydney. A cranky worker had bashed Garstang with blue slag, the by-product of a smelting process. It was Garstang's first taste of the kind of resentment held by some towards men of his profession, and he'd pursued and charged the perpetrator who then spent three years in gaol for the assault.

Serving at Sofala in the 1880s, Garstang spent a lot of time along the Turon River amid the cultural tensions of multiple races, mostly miners, working their claims and contending with river floods. Some of the largest populations of Chinese miners were found in this area, and their diligent and industrious approach to gold extraction enabled teams of Chinese to yield results even after a claim was considered done and dusted by European miners. This enraged many non-Asian miners, making community tensions and anxieties palpable, and placed a target on any Asian miner's back.

Garstang was not in Sofala during the Turon Rebellion of 1851–53, when miners rose up in retaliation against exorbitant miner's right fees, but thirty years later, Garstang's daily task was still to collect mining fees from the diggers along the river. The fees were still unpopular enough to have 'Rummy the Chinaman', an infamous Royal Hotel local armed with a double-barrelled shotgun, ready to wipe Garstang out on one occasion. It was only thanks to an Irish woman who gave Garstang a tipoff that his life was spared.

Located in Forbes since 1891 after a posting in Cowra, Garstang had a run-in with a gun-bearing criminal and was, once again, very surprised to still be alive. It was in his early days at Forbes, and the senior constable had chased down and pounced on a brazen thief. As they rolled around on the ground in broad daylight, fighting over the weapon, the criminal forced the gun behind Garstang's ear and pulled the trigger. It was only the fabric of the policeman's collar, caught between the revolver hammer and the cartridges, that had prevented the gun from going off. Garstang's stories of close shaves and hot pursuits were like badges of honour to him, and he didn't like the idea of his investigation into Kate's death interrupting his good record.

Garstang had failed to get a lead of any kind about Kate's whereabouts within the first twenty-four hours, which meant that as the hours had ticked forward, the chances of finding her alive had ticked backward. He was accountable to no one.

After the window of forty-eight to seventy-two hours had passed by, memories would have faded, diminishing any chance of reliable testimony if he had bothered to ask around. Garstang had nothing other than what Susan Hurley had told him. His contact with Bricky had been fruitless.

After a week, it was usual for the investigation to switch from the focus of finding a living person to locating a body, but it would seem that Garstang wasn't focused on finding Kate at that time, dead or alive.

The final stage in the sad trail of a missing person was when a body had been discovered, but Garstang had not even done that, Sullivan had, and even then, it was eight days after Kate had been reported missing. From a police perspective, it was necessary to determine if the investigation was then about a homicide, suicide or accidental death. Garstang told everyone that he had searched tirelessly for Kate, but had he? Once again, Kate Kelly had given the law the slip.

On Saturday, 15 October 1898, the day after Kate's body was found, the inquest into the death of Mrs William Foster was held at the Forbes Courthouse. The district coroner C.P. Sowter presided, and Government Medical Officer, Doctor Edward Patrick McDonnell provided testimony as to what had happened to Kate.

C.P. Sowter Esquire was a solicitor, appointed as coroner in 1890. C.P. stood for Charles Pearson. A British subject, he had arrived in Australia in 1887 on the *Bengal* and was described as a gentleman. He married in Forbes and, over eight years as coroner, saw all of the unusual, sudden or suspicious deaths, homicides or suicides and destruction by fire that the district had to offer.

Doctor McDonnell was appointed as the GMO in the same year as Sowter's appointment. He'd arrived from Ireland on the *Mirzapore* in 1883, and he held the official titles of GMO as well as Surgeon and Dispenser at the Forbes Gaol.

Both of these men enjoyed a wealthy background, with high levels of education and the trappings of a much higher social standing than the woman whose death they were investigating. It would be easy for Kate not to matter to them. She was just another dead poor person.

Garstang, in his fully starched and pressed uniform, walked through the arched front entrance of the courthouse precinct that led to a small courtyard. He was keenly followed by his subordinate, Constable Kennedy.

Looking around for Sullivan, Garstang was suspicious as to whether the man who'd found Kate's body would turn up. He hadn't shown up at the lagoon when the police went to retrieve Kate's body, even though he'd said he would. He was unreliable. Garstang spotted Bricky and then Mrs Hurley, each sitting at opposite ends of the verandah that ran along the outside of the courtroom.

Nodding his head at Bricky, Garstang told Kennedy to go into the courtroom and see if the coroner was ready. Garstang then approached Mrs Hurley, whose eyes nursed dark circles on her kind face.

'Morning, Mrs Hurley,' Garstang offered up gently, but he received no reply. He took the hint and walked towards Bricky.

The horseman was trying to look respectable in his worn-out old work pants and clean shirt. He still donned his chewed-up work hat; it was the only one he had. Sheepishly avoiding the woman who was looking after his children, Bricky had chosen the dented wooden pew furthest away from her. He was dreading the moment he would have to give his testimony. Words were not Bricky's strong point.

The coroner looked down his long nose through his tiny round spectacles at Kennedy and confirmed that he would like to commence. By the time Kennedy, a much younger man than Garstang, had come back out to the verandah to pass on the coroner's instructions, his jacket was off due to the uncomfortable heat. With his coat under one arm, he greeted the newly arrived and handsome Doctor McDonnell, while Garstang gave Kennedy a dirty look for having removed part of his uniform. Kennedy ignored the look and told Garstang that the coroner was ready and went back inside.

Garstang signalled to McDonnell and asked if he could have a word. Standing to the side, the policeman opened the large wooden door to the officious and intimidating courtroom and instructed Bricky and Mrs Hurley to enter first, saying that he would follow directly. One entered well ahead of the other, and Garstang closed the door behind them, turning to McDonnell.

'McDonnell, you said something yesterday I'm not clear on.'

'Yes?'

'You spoke of milk fever and delirium.'

'Yes, Garstang.'

'You said you can't tell how Mrs Foster died, but you talked about those things. What might cause them?'

'Infection caused at the time of the birth is my guess. Fever symptoms are common. Delirium can set in with severe chronic illness. Medical experts would notice emotional disruption and mental confusion in a patient. Commonly a lack of awareness of the environment around them occurs. It does sound as though she was melancholic in my opinion. But, Garstang, none of that contributes to my assessment of her death. The body was simply too decomposed to draw accurate conclusions.'

'I understand.' Garstang opened the door for the doctor and ushered him through.

After closing the door behind McDonnell, the senior constable walked back through the entrance to take one more look up and down the street for Sullivan. As Garstang turned sharply on his heel, he noticed Sullivan arriving in the distance. 'Sullivan!' the policeman sang out. 'You're late!'

Sullivan, with his pushed-down hair and suspicious eyes, kept walking towards Garstang with his hands deep in his pockets, looking nervous and saying nothing. He knew that he was better off to provide no excuses and just go along with him. 'Pommy bastard,' he mumbled under his breath.

Garstang accompanied Sullivan to the courtroom door, but Sullivan said he needed to have a smoke first, lifting a small pipe from his pocket and waving it at the policeman. Garstang was irritated no end by Sullivan, but he didn't think it really mattered, at least Sullivan was there. 'Hurry up then!' Garstang grunted. Sullivan was already lighting his old pipe and taking a seat on the verandah as Garstang disappeared behind the door.

As evidence was deposed about the sad events of the day prior, Garstang poked his head up to the window to see what Sullivan was up to and saw him pacing up and down. Sullivan was done with his pipe but was now wringing his hands and muttering to himself. Garstang crankily tapped on the window, signalling him to get inside. Moments later, Garstang marched out, intending to give a sharp serving to the man, only to discover that Sullivan had vanished.

Part 2

KATE'S TUMULTUOUS LIFE IN VICTORIA

The daring Kate Kelly, how noble her mien
As she sat on her horse, like an Amazon queen.
She rode through the forest, revolver at hand
Regardless of danger—who dare bid her stand?

May the angels protect this young heroine bold
And her name be recorded in letters of gold.
Though her brothers were outlaws she loved them most dear
And hastened to tell them when danger was near.

Anon, 'Ye Sons of Australia', folk song lyrics (extract)
Circa late 1800s

13

Kate and the Kelly Gang, 1878

FITZPATRICK'S VISIT, APRIL 1878

Stonkingly drunk, still on duty from the races and trying to big-note himself once again, Constable Fitzpatrick put himself in the wrong place at the wrong time. And, once again, it was everyone around him who paid the price.

'You weasel-faced little scoundrel! You wait 'til I get a hold of yer!' Kate's mother Ellen shouted at the constable, who was running away from her around the kitchen table, gun in hand, as he dodged a heavy skillet aimed at his head and tried to make his way to the door of the Kelly hut at Eleven Mile Creek in Greta.

'What d'yer mean you don't have any responsibility to Kitty?'

Kate sat nursing the three-day-old Alice King in her arms, watching the shenanigans happening around her and shooing her younger siblings back into the sleeping area behind some hanging blankets and the hessian divide.

'Ma! Ma! Stop!' Kate yelled, worried that Ellen would kill Fitzpatrick with the iron pan. He took a tumble, scratching his wrist on the way down. He then clumsily scrambled to his feet and exited in a hurry but not before Dan had wrangled the Webley revolver from his hand.

'What was you planning to do with that pop gun of yours, sonny?' Ellen scolded Fitzpatrick as he ran for his life. 'Yer not getting my Danny boy either, not without no warrant.'

'I told him already I woulda gone with him after me meal, Ma. He must be daft.' Dan winked at his sister, who sighed as she cuddled baby Alice. Perhaps Dan's promise to Fitzpatrick had just been a way to delay the policeman until he figured something out but that was no longer his concern.

'Good riddance,' Ellen spat out as she put the skillet down and reached for the kettle. 'I'll make tea. Dan, get the whiskey for yer old mother, will yer?'

All the police had been warned by their seniors not to attend the Kelly homestead alone. Fitzpatrick had arrived an hour earlier under the pretence of arresting Dan, but he had not brought the warrant. It was a ruse to see Kate.

Kate, a few months out from turning fifteen, and Fitzpatrick, twenty-one, had been having an affair, and she was holding the product of their time together. A plan had been hatched to cover up Kate's pregnancy, and Ellen was raising Alice as her own, a story as old as the wind. Women in traditional societies who had breastfed for many years would often relactate for their daughters' babies when they shared the same house, which made it possible for Ellen to help Kate conceal the truth.

Fitzpatrick had worked hard to infiltrate the Kelly family. He had befriended Ned and then wooed his sister. He had told her all kinds of lies about how he was protecting her brothers and that he was on her side; he even said that he was Irish. Ellen never trusted him. Never. She was now regretting the fact that Kate had been so defiant and insistent on seeing the irresponsible and troublesome constable. Kate was regretting it, too.

From the Kelly homestead, the wayward constable made his drunken journey back to Benalla via yet another public house and then he located a doctor. He told the medic it was a bullet wound in his wrist from the infamous Ned Kelly, but the doctor doubted the story and noted how strongly the officer smelled of brandy.

Fitzpatrick declared that the Kelly family had tried to murder him. His confabulating grew the sensational story bigger and bigger, implicating ever more people, including Ned, family friend William Williamson and Maggie's husband William Skillion.

Fitzpatrick's claim that Ned had shot at him caused a sensation that would mark itself in the Australian history books forever and leave a stain on Fitzpatrick's name along with it. His altercation in the Kelly family home that evening would become known as the 'Fitzpatrick Incident'.

Within a few days, Kate's life was turned upside down. Right before Kate's very eyes, her mother Ellen was accused of interfering with the arrest of Dan and attempting to murder Fitzpatrick, then dragged away to Beechworth Gaol. Kate watched her mother argue with the policemen who arrived like a pack of wild dogs to devour her. They also took baby Alice, who was held with Ellen for three months at Beechworth Gaol. The lies of Kate's treacherous lover, Fitzpatrick, the father of her child, had stitched her up. If those police had pushed Kate to the ground and kicked her black and blue, it would not begin to match the pain and distress of being rendered motherless, childless and suddenly alone with three younger siblings to care for: Grace, Ellen Junior and Jack, who were also shattered by the events. Dan had gone again, to try his luck at gold in the local ranges, and Ned was stealing horses, so it would be a while before they even knew what had happened.

After three months waiting for her court case, Ellen was bailed out by a family friend in June. In October, Ellen returned to Beechworth for her court case, where she was found guilty of 'wounding with intent to prevent lawful apprehension'. After two weeks in a cell in Beechworth Gaol, she was taken to Melbourne Gaol, where she would stay for almost three years. Alice was returned to the care of Kate and Maggie, who were taking turns looking after all the children between the two homesteads. Williamson and Skillion were also gaoled, but for six long years, despite the fact that they were way out in the paddock chopping wood when Fitzpatrick had visited.

Ned and Dan were accused of attempted murder and, with their two friends, Joe Byrne and Steve Hart, they would remain at large for the next two years as everything escalated. Ned proposed many different scenarios about what had happened that night when asked, including one story that he was out stealing horses, adding that he would never fire a weapon in his home or surrounded by his family. In fact, each of the Kellys put forward different and unverifiable accounts of events, creating a permanent sense of confusion for outsiders.

By July that same year, the rampant Fitzpatrick had been coerced into marrying a young woman, Anna Savage, who was also pregnant to him. The Kellys would find out about other girls he had impregnated and tried to abandon. Anna's solicitor father suggested that he would make life very difficult for Fitzpatrick if he did not honour his responsibility to make Anna an honest woman. Indeed, her father had written to the police insisting that Fitzpatrick be forced to do so by his superiors as a matter of morality.

Until that point, Fitzpatrick had made a concerted effort to shirk any obligation to Anna. Kate and young Anna, also about fifteen years of age, were clearly not the first victims of Fitzpatrick's reckless and selfish behaviour. A woman in Meredith had been left with a daughter to him when he'd skipped town. Unable to support her child, she gave her up for adoption, and soon it was reported that the little girl had died. Kate and the others had all become trapped in Fitzpatrick's terrible web.

THE HIDEOUT, SEPTEMBER 1878

After the fateful night of Fitzpatrick's troublemaking visit to the Kelly homestead, the Kelly Gang continued business as usual. Their main trade was stealing horses, and Ned considered himself one of the best at it.

Kate and the Kelly family referred to the gang as 'the boys', and the tag even caught on in the press as their notoriety grew. They were all young men in their twenties roughing it at the gang's hideout near Bullock Creek in the Wombat Ranges in between horse jobs. The basic bush camp was a well-concealed wooden shelter in the middle of nowhere, and it was a hive of much plotting. How would they get Ned and Dan's mother and innocent friends out of gaol? How could they get the government to listen to them about the injustices being committed against them?

Kate was keen to do her part and excitedly delivered news and supplies to the boys, which became harder and harder to do because the police followed Kate and Maggie everywhere they went. The police were even making home visits to harass Kate in the small hours of the night to ruffle the Kelly feathers and lure Ned and the boys out of hiding.

'I played a wee game with those pigeon-livered traps!' Kate told her brothers. 'They forced their way in again last night. I pointed to the corner of the hut, behind the blanket curtain, and whispered, real soft like, that you was in there havin' a rest, Ned! I made out like, "Oh no, be kind to him, don't hurt m'dear brother!"'

'Kitty, you are too much!'

'Ah, Neddy. They fell over themselves, the cowards. When they pushed the curtain back, proddin' it with their rifles, they was relieved it weren't you. I told them to get out of our home, which they did but not before smashing all our eggs and tipping the flour on the floor. Ellen Junior and Jack was crying their eyes out with all the commotion.'

Although Kate had watched the troopers in amusement as she taunted them, it was hard not to be afraid. The police arrived unannounced at any hour, unashamedly abusing their powers. Without warning, they would grab her and her siblings and use them as human shields so that if Ned or the gang had really been in the house and taken a shot at the police, they would shoot their family member first. The unwelcome visitors made a point of leaving the impoverished family with the mess of their ruined meagre supplies and nothing to eat.

Many a night Kate and her siblings could hear the footsteps and conspiring whispers of police moving around outside their hut. Prying eyeballs could even be seen staring at her through cracks in the bark slab walls. She was being observed at all times. The police had even stolen her horse on more than one occasion to prevent her from visiting her brothers. She would wake up to find that Oliver Twist had disappeared, and the horse would somehow materialise again in the following days. It only strengthened her resolve to help her brothers.

On her trips to the hut at Bullock Creek, Kate made sure that she ducked and weaved a course through the trees and scrub that no trooper could follow. She would sit hidden on a rock ledge in the bush, watching the lost souls below. Only when she was convinced that the troopers were out of earshot and committed to the wrong track would she ride towards the hideout. It was a relief to see that the boys were okay and bring them what news and supplies she could.

Ned was also masterminding something new. In the days prior to one of Kate's hideout visits, Ned and his team of men had travelled through Daysdale under the cover of night. Ned had woken the blacksmith at gunpoint to shoe the best of the horses they'd stolen. The rest would be traded, and the men would be cashed up from the sales. He also instructed the blacksmith to shoe Kate's horse, Oliver Twist, back to front.

On the way back to the hideout, Ned let Oliver loose, smacked him on the behind and told him to go home, which he was happy to do. Kate greeted her horse in the early hours of the morning in a far corner of a paddock, thrilled to have him home.

Oliver was not happy about the new arrangement hindering his footing, and Kate had to soothe him on her way to the camp. 'Hang in there for a few days more, boy! It's good to have yer back. I've missed yer!'

Ned asked what she thought about the back-to-front shoes, and she concurred that they were useful in confusing the police. She had witnessed for herself that the tracks sent them the wrong way but she wouldn't like to be in a situation where she had to get away in a hurry, nor would it be good for more than a few days at a time as Oliver didn't like them.

At other times, her adventures through the bush presented different requirements. Sometimes she could just trot along and lead the police astray, encouraging them to follow her on a mystery tour to nowhere, a distraction while Maggie or the boys were taking care of other business. Other times she would have to be crafty and lose the traps cross-country style. In those instances, she needed Oliver to gallop as fast as he could, zigging and zagging while being chased.

Without Kate's complete balance and control in the saddle, beast and rider could easily find themselves crashing into trees or becoming unsure of their footing, or even worse falling over. It took enormous skill and an intimate knowledge of the land as well as the stamina and athleticism of both rider and horse.

Ned knew Kate was much braver and probably smarter than most of the troopers harassing her, and the police didn't stand a chance trying to follow his sister across the ranges.

Even people who didn't really know the gang members very well were being watched or hauled in by the police and held in custody, in the hope of extracting information or recruiting informers. The Kelly Gang used money from their robberies to bail their friends out and pay for people's legal representation to compensate for the harassment that Kelly loyalty attracted. Ned and the men felt that everyone in their life had been victimised by a corrupt and unfair system of law.

Some locals were won over as spies or double agents and relayed accurate information to the police, betraying the gang. But by the time the police were onto it, the Kelly Gang was long gone. Ned and his gang were always many steps ahead of the traps, thanks to their networks, instincts and the news and supplies delivered by their sister Kate.

Kate sometimes found Ned and Dan at Bullock Creek operating a sluice they had built themselves, trying to find enough gold to pay for lawyers to help free Ellen and fund their future endeavours. At one point the men had even offered to hand themselves in, if the government would agree to release their innocent mother and anyone else who was held unnecessarily and unjustly. But the government wasn't interested in cutting any deals with the Kelly Gang. They were furious that a group of poor, ex-convict youth had the audacity to see themselves as equals or even above the law. Not only had these troublemaking youths avoided capture, but they were also achieving fame and notoriety. The press was obsessed with the drama and adventure of it all, and Kate became a focus of the media's obsession.

The gang also considered kidnapping Fitzpatrick or the other person driving them crazy, Detective Ward. Ward seemed to be everywhere, which annoyed Ned; he was a bad smell that wouldn't go away. The detective had a lot to do with their close friend and ex-gaolbird, Aaron Sherritt. It made the Kellys suspicious. They had every right to be—Sherritt was playing both sides.

The gang had a notion that if they took someone like a police officer or an even higher-ranked official as a hostage, they could somehow do a deal with the government and trade them for Ellen and be allowed to tell their side of the story.

Under Ned's instructions, Aaron Sherritt had approached both Fitzpatrick and Ward, proposing to lead either of them to the gang. Ward was informed by Sherritt about Ned's plan to capture and trade him off, so of course he declined the offer. Fitzpatrick, on the other hand, was terrified that the gang wanted to lure him in and kill him. He knew that his false testimony had caused all sorts of trouble. He wasn't going to fall into any trap. Sherritt's visit only made the guilty Fitzpatrick very, very nervous, so Ned's plan gained no traction at that time.

THE LOCAL RACES 1878–1880

Ned and the gang continued their rebellious plotting and planning, keeping in touch with and relying on family and friends, and like wild horses, making sure to avert their own capture. But no amount of police pressure would deter the gang whenever they desired a great day out watching their family and friends compete at the races.

A day at the races was a great community event bringing in people from all around the region, and there were competitions for women and men alike. The hack races were a chance to display their skills and win a prize, but the recognition and reputation among the people of the region meant so much more than any prize.

The races drew in plenty of friends, family and supporters of the Kellys. Many people were too afraid to take sides against the Kellys, who had extraordinary networks helping to protect them. As a consequence, the wanted men and their sisters went with confidence where they pleased, despite the huge fortune that would eventually be offered to betray them, and they were seen from Wangaratta to Benalla and Wagga Wagga to Moyhu.

On one occasion together at the Moyhu races, Maggie and their Lloyd cousins were competing while Kate was stationed as a lookout for her brother Dan, who had joined them for the day. Kate remained on duty near a heavily timbered part of the field where she could watch the riders but also prevent anyone from continuing past a certain point while Dan watched the events from the cover of trees. Kate wasn't letting anyone come near him unless it was planned. They wanted no surprise approaches from the police or others who might want to betray them.

Sitting on a smart-looking bay thoroughbred, Dan proudly watched his family competing in the races. The girls' rides were all impressive: elegant in appearance and displaying the excellent self-carriage only quality thoroughbreds who are well trained and looked after could present. Ned's horse-stealing racket had served them all very well, and they knew how to look after their equine stars. If you needed a horse to get away fast or last a good distance, you wanted a quality vehicle, a thoroughbred not a hack.

In the corner of Kate's eye, a flash of movement attracted her attention, pulling her stare away from her sister's performance on the field. An unfamiliar face riding a grey mare was approaching and moving in Dan's direction. Holding herself up out of her saddle, Kate trotted through the stand of trees shadowing the male rider, trying to see who it was. Unable to place the man, she dug her heels into Oliver's sides and they sped towards the rider. The man was unaware of Kate's presence until she and Oliver were almost on top of him, blocking his path.

'There's nothing along here for you to see, friend.'

The man pulled his horse up, startled by the arrival of this woman from nowhere. He tried to walk his mare to the left of Kate, but she shimmied with Oliver to block him, skilfully using only the slightest hip and leg movement. 'Friend, you need to go another way.'

'Like hell I do! There is a man I am trying to meet with up ahead. He looks familiar to me. Move your horse, woman, and let me through.'

Dan noticed his sister moving from left to right, elegantly blocking whoever was trying to pass. He sank back into the bush and, ghost-like, he was gone from sight in a moment.

Kate insisted that the man return to where he had come from and then turned to see if Dan had relocated himself yet. 'Friend, there is no one there for you to see.'

The man looked over again and realised he'd been had. 'Well, there's no reason for you to block my path any further, is there?'

'I'd be guessin' there ain't no reason for yer to continue in that direction any further, friend.'

He knew for sure now that he was dealing with the Kellys and figured it was in his interests to let it go. He turned away, irritated, smouldering while looking over his shoulder at the teenage girl as he sauntered away.

The prize position results that day were each dominated by the girls, a Lloyd cousin on either side of Maggie's second place. People had no choice but to admire the striking girls in their smart outfits and riding boots. Kate was itching to be out there, too, but she would contest the honours on the turf another time. She'd rather know her brother was safe.

There were many other occasions when Kate took out prizes for her skilled horsewomanship, and from Benalla to Wagga she was respected for her admirable skills, humour and warmth by people of her class.

For a short period of time, the family's odd existence split between hiding out and mixing in the community started to feel somehow normal to Kate. When they could all enjoy moments of family and community life, it was almost as if nothing was ever wrong. Kate's need for a constant state of alertness would never go away but, temporarily, she could ignore the huge absence of her mother and brothers from home and the true pressure of their circumstances.

These moments, feeling like a family, emphasised that there was a deep desire in Kate for a normal life. She daydreamed that, someday, the Kellys might have a peaceful existence together like other families. But yearning for that kind of simplicity only high-lighted the opposing truth: it was impossible.

There was a tangible feeling of heaviness for Kate, and living with nervousness and worry for such a long time took its toll. Regardless of the support around the Kellys, everyday life for Kate and her family had become an unusual existence.

More Kelly Rumours.

It is rumoured that the Kellys and their mates are still in close proximity to Mansfield, says the Melbourne HERALD of June 21. Mrs. Skillian and Lloyd were in Benalla yesterday, and took away a drayload of provisions with them in the evening. Wild Wright is here to-day, having come from Mansfield. He tells his friends that he is going up to the Murray. He spent money freely at the hotels. The police and black trackers express an opinion to the effect that the outlaws will not attempt to travel until the dry season sets in, as it would be a very easy matter to follow their trail in the present heavy state of the mountains. The relations and sympathisers have been daily in and out of Benalla. They do not confine their purchases to a single store, but pay each a visit. In conversation with one of the publicans he remarked that the township would have been in a state of insolvency long since had it not been for the Kelly outrage. Only two hotels are visited by the friends, and at both these every night a kind of free-and-easy concert is carried on, in which some of the most prominent friends may be seen. They generally leave the township late at night, and return between noon and 4 o'clock in the afternoon. A Melbourne photographer here offered a good sum if he could get an interview with Kate Kelly, Mrs. Skillian, Wright and Lloyd, for the purpose of inducing them to sit for their portraits. They consented through a friend to do so, and the sitting was to take place to-day. When the party returned from Melbourne, they proceeded to one of the publichouses mentioned, and were shortly afterwards called upon by Superintendent Sadlier and a party of police to produce their luggage, which they readily consented to do. The only articles found to have been brought from Melbourne consisted of some female wearing apparel, and a small quantity of good tobacco. These things, of course, could not in any way be interfered with. Several questions were asked by the officers, but the friends were not at all communicative; and upon the officers leaving, they were asked to have a drink, which was refused. Immediately afterwards the concert was started, and kept up till very late in the morning. The person whom the detectives lost sight of in Melbourne arrived in Benalla late on Thursday night, but did not come by train. He was met at the house by a number of friends, and congratulated very warmly for the manner in which he had hoodwinked the police. A communication was received from Kate Kelly, stating her intention of again visiting Melbourne shortly, and she averred that the authorities should not have the opportunity of seeing her at all.

The movements and activities of Kate, the Kelly family and their sympathisers were observed by the press, as seen in this article from 25 June 1879, as well as the police for years, increasing the need for Kate and the others to work at protecting the gang.

THE SYMPATHISERS 1878–1880

Some Kelly sympathisers wore their chinstrap resting under their nose as a symbol of their allegiance. The only other indication was a particular flash style of dress. In the good old days when the gang was still a part of the Greta Mob, they all used to attend dances and the races in fine clothing and show off their horse skills. To help the Kelly Gang, the sympathisers offered food and important information about police movements when times were tough.

Up and down the train lines, the Kellys and their friends created distractions and decoys to confuse the police. They often travelled in packs to Melbourne, and on their return two supporters would get out at Euroa, Maggie and another would alight at Benalla, and Kate and cousin Tom would grace Wangaratta with their presence. Each pair would be met by supporters at every station, and the police wouldn't know who to follow.

On other days, Kate, Maggie or Tom would go to Benalla or neighbouring townships on horseback or with a wagon in the afternoons and make extensive purchases of supplies right under the noses of the police. They made a point of visiting many stores, finding out the latest observations and news from the locals, and making plans to assist their brothers. After their errands were done, Kate and the others would head to a sympathetic inn to share in Irish ballads sung to remember their heritage and forget their troubles, while important messages were conveyed between drinks. Kate or the others would then leave late at night to make their way home, with the police following each of them like lost puppies.

By 1879, Kate and Maggie were accused in the press of using the proceeds of Ned's crimes to ride on extravagant, twenty-guinea saddles and pay off locals every week for information on police movements, but they didn't care what was being said. By that time, it was also crystal clear to the police that there was a code of silence, which local supporters were proud of, and being on the outside left the police facing a virtually impenetrable wall. Because of that, senior police were getting more and more uptight. And as the police presence grew along the north-eastern train line and across the region, Kelly sympathisers made their feelings known.

Embarrassed police tried to hide their red faces as they were humiliated by loud bursts, sung with gusto from inside the train carriages and along station platforms.

'Three cheers for the Kellys!' Defiance filled the air as the trains rolled in.

'Hoorah!', 'hoorah!', 'hoorah!'

Keen for a breakthrough, the police rounded up familiar Kelly and Hart friends and relatives, and dragged them into court: Thomas Hart, James Quinn, Francis Harty, Richard Strickland, John Lloyd, John Quinn, Daniel Clancey, James Clancey and, of course, Wild Wright.

The solicitors Mr Zincke (who had represented the Kelly family many times) and Mr Bowman defended the men and protested their detention vehemently, but they were all, one by one, remanded in custody. Wild was seen muttering to himself, refusing to wait for permission as he hurried out of the dock in a deliberately contemptuous gesture. Mr Zincke was outraged at the clear misuse of the legal system by the prosecution and at the magistrate, for holding the men without due cause. But Zincke only managed to get Thomas Hart released before a second bout in Beechworth Gaol. The others were forced to remain and would face up to another thirteen remands without any charges being laid.

Victorian correspondents for the *Brisbane Courier* in 1879 wrote anti-sympathiser commentaries: 'Villainous-looking scoundrels lounge about Benalla, dressed in offensively green neckties. They openly defy the police to catch the Kellys.' And after the Kelly friends were remanded, reporters went even further, saying, 'During the incarceration of the eight sympathisers, the outer doors were iron sheeted and all preparations were made for an assault. Unfortunately, the settlement of the district is bad.'

Events were about to get even more serious, but neither the Kellys nor their sympathisers could have anticipated what was about to happen at Stringybark Creek.

STRINGYBARK CREEK, SATURDAY, 26 OCTOBER 1878

Constable McIntyre and three police colleagues were camped in an isolated bush location near Stringybark Creek, in the Wombat Ranges, disguised as prospectors but on the hunt for the Kelly Gang.

The search party had set up camp, and two of the four policemen were out in the bush on their horses, patrolling the area and searching for tracks, when Constable McIntyre foolishly drew attention to their location by shooting parrots. The shots fired from his rifle rang out like an alarm through the bush air, notifying the Kelly Gang of their presence.

Ned and his gang of men set out in the general direction of the noise to investigate. Without making a single suspicious noise, the men surrounded the makeshift camp like dingoes and watched their prey innocently fumbling around. McIntyre fiddled with a canister trying to extract tea-leaves, while another policeman, Lonigan, gathered wood for the fire. He sang out to McIntyre to give him a hand, and it took them twenty minutes to get the fire going.

The gang lay in wait, camouflaged by the grasses and trees, watching. Who were these men, and what were they up to? The gang's weapons were poised, tracking these strangers as they moved in a relaxed fashion around the camp, focused on their tasks, unaware of the surveillance being conducted on them.

With the late afternoon change of light around 4 p.m., the policemen were worried that their two absent colleagues had lost their way, so they started to build the fire as large as they could, adding swathes of thick branches and leaves in quick succession, making the flames jump higher and higher. It was to be a beacon for their mates as night fell.

McIntyre fetched the billy for his tea-making. As he carried it back to the fire and Lonigan watched the tall flames, the words 'Bail up! Hold up your hands!' came from nowhere. McIntyre turned around to find four armed men with weapons pointed at his chest. The billy slipped from his fingers as he lifted his hands in surrender.

The menthol smell of burning eucalyptus leaves was strong in Lonigan's nostrils as he leaped away from the fire and made a dash for cover. As he ran, bullets flew at him, and he landed behind a large log, reaching for his revolver. He grabbed it from his holster, took a deep breath and sat up on his knees to take a shot. Bullets bombarded Lonigan from the moment he raised his head. From the lead shower raining on him, one shot hit its mark. Lonigan fell to the ground with a thud.

Ned told McIntyre to keep his hands up as he patted him down. He demanded to know where any weapons were stashed, and McIntyre trembled as he told Ned they were all in his tent.

'Mind yer don't try to go away or I will shoot yer,' Ned warned him. The other men lowered their guns but kept them pointed in McIntyre's direction while Ned crawled into the tent and discovered a boon of arms.

Ned knew that the standard issue of arms for policemen was a single revolver, usually a Webley, and each officer was only allowed to have six cartridges in that weapon. So, Ned was shocked when he found breech-loading Spencer rifles, fowling-piece shotguns, over thirty rounds of revolver cartridges, three dozen cartridges for the shotguns and over twenty Spencer rifle cartridges. He suspected that these men were incognito policemen and that they intended not just to shoot Ned and the gang but to riddle them with bullets. Ned grabbed one of the shotguns and took it with him back to McIntyre.

Ned waved his new shotgun around with one hand and pushed McIntyre onto a log near the fire with the barrel of his other rifle as he sat himself next to his prisoner. 'Who are yer and who else is here with yer?'

'McIntyre. Constable McIntyre. Are you going to shoot me?'

'You were smart enough to surrender. Why would I shoot you?'

'Because . . . Holy Mary . . . You sshhot Lonigan.'

'That man was not Lonigan, I know Lonigan.'

'It was Lonigan, I'm telling you. It was him.'

Dan piped up with a dry chuckle, 'Well, he'll lock no more of us up then!'

'Who else is with you?' Ned asked.

'Scanlon and Sergeant Kennedy are out on horses, but I think they might be lost.'

Ned looked McIntyre over from his shoes to his moleskins to his light overcoat and wondered about the man's background. Ned noticed that McIntyre's hands looked soft and clean. Not a working man, that's for sure. Ned looked back down to the fowling piece he had a hold of and held it up to inspect it before he stared again at McIntyre. 'This is a curious gun for men to be going into the country with. You have so many arms and so much ammunition. It looks like you are going to war. Why did you come here?'

'To shoot kangaroo.'

'You came to shoot us.'

'We . . . we came to apprehend you.' McIntyre's leg trembled.

'I cannot suffer you lot blowing me to pieces in my own native land. I won't have it.'

With the distant sounds of crunching bark under hooves, Ned was alerted to the other policemen returning to camp, and he pushed McIntyre onto his feet. 'You stand in front of me, McIntyre, over here.' He pointed towards the fire. 'Lads, take your positions.'

Dan, Steve and Joe scurried across the ground and concealed themselves so well in spear grass at the edge of the camp that even Ned couldn't see them. Ned planted himself behind the fire with two guns ready, and McIntyre stood where he was told like a sacrificial lamb.

'When the other two return, yer need to be telling them to surrender or yer a dead man, too. We'll let the rest of yer go, but I'll be takin' yer horses, weapons and yer supplies.'

Ned gave McIntyre his final warning. 'I have you all covered. If you give them a signal I will shoot yer, be sure of that.'

Sick in his guts with fear, McIntyre waited for the other policemen to enter the camp. As they came closer, he spoke up, terrified that he'd be shot if he didn't get it right. 'You had better dismount and throw your weapons down. Ned Kelly has you covered.'

Kennedy looked around as if it were a joke, smiling a little at his friend's dark humour.

Ned stood up and yelled orders. 'Put yer hands up or yer dead.'

The gang members, with their rifles cocked, moved from their hiding places towards the pair. Scanlon threw himself from his horse and ran for a tree, a move that invited a flurry of bullets and brought him down, dead in what seemed like seconds.

Kennedy took his chances, too, and jumped from his horse. He darted between trees and found himself in a shootout with the gang.

McIntyre made a getaway, grabbing the horse Kennedy had

abandoned. Escaping the scene, he galloped through the bush until the horse fell over with exhaustion.

Meanwhile, Kennedy held his own and blasted away at the gang until he had no more bullets in his revolver. His arm was drenched in blood and a large clot was forming at his hand, which he went to raise but the gang closed in on him and ended it all.

They covered his body with someone's cloak and scooped up all of the supplies they could stuff into or strap to their saddlebags: sardine tins, tea, sugar and a small fortune's worth of weapons and ammunition. They gathered the three remaining horses and set fire to the tent before heading back to their own camp. It was supposed to have been the police who ambushed the gang, but it turned out the other way around.

McIntyre scrambled through the scrub as the dark closed in on him, and he took refuge on his elbows and belly, hiding in a wombat hole overnight, praying that the owner of the burrow would not return while he was there and crush him to death. The next morning, McIntyre found his way to Mansfield to tell the story and accuse the Kelly Gang of a possible triple murder.

At the gang's hideout, Ned reflected on the wild events. He couldn't figure out why the other three hadn't just surrendered like McIntyre did. 'Why did the scoundrels not surrender when we told 'em to put their weapons down? They fired at us instead!' He couldn't understand it. 'They were huntin' us like wild dogs. Damn them. If they had found us first, they would have annihilated us, no question. Lonigan weren't going to bring us in. He wanted us dead, for sure! They had enough weaponry for a small army. They were just going to hammer us with bullets until we be dead, to be sure. What right do they have to try to murder us?'

As soon as the word got out about McIntyre's narrow escape, every store and business in Mansfield shut for nearly a week. The locals weren't mucking around. The Kelly Gang had wiped out three policemen and that terrified people. Clearly, the gang was willing to shoot anyone. No one wanted to be the next victim.

The Kelly Gang's efforts to remain at large after the Fitzpatrick Incident would be known as the 'Kelly Outbreak'. And for a while the gang would be referred to as the Mansfield Murderers, which led to them being outlawed. From that point in time, the gang would need even more help from their sympathisers, and Maggie and Kate.

OUTLAWED, 1878

Patrick Quinn was a Mansfield local and possibly a distant cousin of Ellen Kelly. The press had touted Quinn as a betrayer of Ned and his men because he had offered to help police inquiries and guide the police to the gang's location, but it was always a ruse. In truth, Patrick Quinn was as loyal to Ned and the gang as any man could be, and his skills in deceiving the police were vital. For a short time, the police trusted Quinn, believing they had him in their pockets, so they had spoken openly with him about their intentions to shoot Ned Kelly first and ask questions later. After Stringybark Creek, Patrick met with Kate to pass on information and confirm other plans.

'Paddy, they're all callin' the boys murderers,' Kate said. 'Saying it were a massacre. Oh the shame of it.'

'Listen 'ere, lassie, if those mongrel traps had gotta hold of our boys first, it weren't gonna be known as no massacre. Girl, it woulda been celebrated by the traps with no shame. Don't doubt it.'

'They're saying now there's a price on their heads, a small fortune to betray them, four thousand pounds!' Kate couldn't even imagine what that amount of money would look like.

'They won't get our boys, Miss Kate. Even if them bastards in New South Wales double it like they're threatenin'. Pay no regard, Kate. There be a right lot of men marching behind our boys. Never you mind.'

Up until then, the gang had still been moving quite freely around the colonies of Victoria and New South Wales, gathering support and masterminding ambitious robberies. It was estimated that at least two thousand Kelly sympathisers existed among the small population in the north-east of Victoria. Was the bounty on their heads about to change all that?

Paddy lifted Kate's chin to get her attention. 'It weren't no good though, that Ned told Lonigan he were gonna kill him all those years ago. Fitzpatrick were the start of all that, puttin' something in yer brother's drink so they could arrest him for bein' drunk 'n' disorderly. What a set-up! Lonigan grabbed Ned by the balls and belted the living daylights out of him while the others held him down. Ned talked about shootin' him. He said it in front of people. It might catch up to him.'

'That ain't fair, Paddy.'

'Nothin' is ever fair, Kate. Forget about fair.'

Patrick was slamming one fist into the other. He was a violent man, and just talking about the injustice against Ned got him riled up. 'Everyone can see Stringybark were a big set-up, Kitty. First of all, Dan has an outstanding warrant for horse theft, but that ain't no reason for them traps to hunt him down in the bush and try to kill him, for God's sake. That ain't right. We all know the bulldust Fitzpatrick is pedalling about Ned tryin' to kill him that night at the homestead, but even being wanted for attempted murder don't mean them traps had any right to try an' murder our boys. Innocent until proven guilty, right?' Paddy kept slamming his fists, making Kate nervous.

'All right now, Paddy.'

It wasn't just Paddy who was baffled by the events. It left the gang wondering what was afoot. How was it legal for the traps to hide out in disguise and hunt them down? It only cemented the gang's perception of the injustices against them.

The response to the Mansfield murders by the politicians of the day was a swift adaptation of laws from 1865, previously used in New South Wales to capture bushranger Ben Hall. The Victorian Parliament wasted no time in passing the 'Outlaw Act', officially known as the *Felons Apprehension Act* on 31 October 1878, and it appeared as a supplement in the *Victoria Government Gazette* on the following day, 1 November 1878. The Act removed all human rights from the Kelly men and gang members Hart and Byrne. A date was assigned for the gang to hand themselves in by, and when that had passed, they were cast as outlaws.

Being outside the law meant that anyone could kill Ned, Dan, Steve or Joe, and no punishment would be applied. Anyone believed to be assisting the wanted men would be committing an offence that could land them in the lock-up, and that included Kate.

'It ain't lookin' good for the boys,' Patrick continued. 'You need to be real sharp, Kitty, or you'll come undone, too. They be wanted outlaws now, make sure 'n' tell them there's a price on their heads. This makes everything even more serious. Make sure you're letting Ned know that the scoundrel Constable Strachan were bragging about how Lonigan said he were gonna shoot first and ask questions later. Lassie, you make sure and tell him that, right. And let him know that Lonigan's plan were to lay a gun down beside Ned's dead body and say Ned tried ta shoot him. They had no intention of bringing him in alive. Strachan told me that himself. Bloody Lonigan even told Strachan that Ned deserved to die! For God's sake!'

Kate gasped at the revelation, and she felt red-hot anger rising. 'How did they get away with that kind of talk? Mongrels! Yer can be sure I'll be telling Ned.'

The attempted police ambush at Stringybark Creek was just the latest example of disregard for Ned and the gang members' right to fair legal process, as far as they were concerned, and it was like a burning fuse to a stick of dynamite. Born into the wrong class, they felt pushed into a corner at every turn.

What did they have left to lose? The Kelly Gang was ready to take things to another level, and being outlawed was their invitation. The authorities assumed that because anyone could kill the wanted men with no consequence, only a financial reward, that the bodies of the gang members would soon be handed in. But the authorities had always underestimated the skill, knowledge and cunning of the Kellys, their helpers and supporters.

14

Kate and the Kelly Gang, 1878~79

EUROA, TUESDAY, 10 DECEMBER 1878

Only two months after Stringybark, Patrick Quinn promised to lead the police to the Kelly Gang but instead led them on a wild-goose chase. He had deliberately distracted a large number of troopers by taking them in the opposite direction from Ned and the gang, while the bushrangers conducted the robbery at Euroa in December 1878.

Quinn had ridden with the police cross-country over a great distance and at great speed, wearing out the men and their horses so that they were too exhausted to do anything but rest by the end of it.

It was too risky for the gang to target banks any closer to home, so they made a plan to use Younghusband's Station at Faithfulls Creek, not far from Euroa, as a base. There they held station workers and residents, plus some unlucky travellers, as hostages while they commandeered a wagon and a cart to take into Euroa and hit the Colonial Bank.

While Ned, Dan and Steve went into town to rob the bank, Joe Byrne guarded the hostages and worked away at a letter that he and Ned had been drafting. The letter was signed by Ned Kelly, and in it he outlined all the perceived injustices against himself, his family and others in the community. Ned was hugely critical of the police, stressed that he believed himself to be a 'police-made criminal' because of the way he had been treated and complained about the corruption and injustice inherent in the legal and political establishments.

Ned also made sure that all the hostages knew the content of the letter, and he told them all how McIntyre had done a runner at Stringybark Creek. Ned thought McIntyre a coward for abandoning his comrades, and word spread like wildfire, humiliating the sole surviving policeman from that event.

Posted from Glenrowan, the letter was sent to Victorian politician Donald Cameron, who had been outspoken about the failure of police to catch the Kelly Gang. Another copy went to the officer in charge of the police in the north-east district, Superintendent John Sadleir. The letter would become known as the 'Cameron Letter'.

The Kelly Gang's robbery of the bank at Euroa gained them a bounty of at least two thousand pounds in cash, over thirty-one ounces of gold ingot, a stash of silver and several pistols. Their audacious efforts also brought a welcome level of notoriety unknown to them before.

JERILDERIE, MONDAY, 10 FEBRUARY 1879

The gang's plans continued to build and grow, and two months after Euroa, in February 1879, they pulled off the robbery of the Bank of New South Wales at Jerilderie. It caused a deep irritation to the New South Wales Government, and its leader, Premier

Henry Parkes, wrote a letter to the Victorian premier on 14 February 1879 suggesting a united action between New South Wales and Victoria in catching the gang. Parkes then co-signed a proclamation to increase the reward on the gang's heads to a staggering eight thousand pounds.

During the Jerilderie robbery, the brazen capture of the Jerilderie police, Senior Constable Devine and another constable, who were bailed up and locked in their own cell, was just the start of the action. The gang dressed up in police uniforms and patrolled around town, pretending that they were newly stationed police while checking out the bank and surrounds. The boys advised the curious residents that they had been sent to capture the Kelly Gang.

The absurdity and humour of it all was not lost on Ned and the gang as they made their way around town being very social and discussing the Kelly antics, which were hot on everyone's lips. They even helped to decorate the local courthouse for a Sunday morning church service and attended it with all the locals, a task usually performed by Mrs Devine, who had been instructed by the gang to stay in her house and keep quiet.

Early Monday morning, before they went into the bank at Jerilderie to rob it, the gang paid a quick trip to the local blacksmith to have all their horses freshly shod, chalking the bill up to the New South Wales police force account.

The Jerilderie job raised about six hundred pounds in cash and over fourteen hundred in bank notes, plus a lot of documents recording debts to the bank from small landowners, which Ned destroyed later at a nearby pub where locals had been held up under Joe's watchful eye.

For Ned, the most important part of their mission was the publication and distribution of another letter. Written to the Victorian

Legislative Assembly, the Jerilderie document was longer than the first, over fifty pages, and in it Ned laid out all of his accusations and complaints against the police and the government in even greater detail, but this time he included his threats of what was to come if his requests for the liberation of his mother and other men serving unwarranted sentences went ignored.

My brother and sisters and my mother had to put up with the brutal and cowardly conduct of a parcel of big, ugly, fat necked, wombat headed, big bellied, magpie legged, narrow hipped, splay footed sons of Irish bailiffs and English Landlords. Give those people who are suffering in innocence, justice and liberty. If not, I will be compelled to show some colonial stratagem which will not only open the eyes of the Victorian police and inhabitants but also the whole British army. Fitzpatrick will be the cause of greater slaughter to the Union Jack than Saint Patrick was to the snakes and toads of Ireland.

I am a widow's son, outlawed and my orders must be obeyed.

It was Ned's desire to have it printed in *The Jerilderie Gazette*, but the editor, Samuel Gill, had run off when he learned that the gang had captured bank staff and were looking for him. Ned tried to give the letter to Gill's wife, but she wouldn't take it.

Ned handed his letter to the accountant from the bank in place of Gill. Instead of passing it on to Gill for widespread publication like he promised, the accountant showed the document to the police, who concealed it from the public, scared by its contents and the risk of public support for the Kellys.

In addition to the newspaper coverage he wanted but never received, Ned's intention was to have copies of the letter distributed throughout the region, but his hopes were dashed.

Before the gang left town, they visited the telegraph office where Joe cut the telegraph wires while Ned smashed the insulators with his revolver. No word of their unlawful activities was going to leave town that way.

Ned had planned to use the media to his advantage but was disappointed. He knew he needed a wide audience and forum to make a personal plea and to control his message, image and reputation. If only he was able to deliver his message from the small town in the bush to the rest of the world, he figured, people might understand his plight and become his followers, attaching themselves to his revolutionary cause.

KIDNAP THE GOVERNOR 1878–1880

This was my first intention, to capture the leaders of the police and take them into the bush and allow the superintendent to write to the head department and inform them if they sent any more police after me or try to rescue him I would shoot him and that I intended to keep them prisoners until the release of my mother, Skillion and Williamson.

Ned Kelly, 'Letter to the Governor of Victoria,' 1880

Since Ellen's imprisonment in 1878, Ned had been proposing ideas about kidnapping prominent people, like the governor and senior police, to force the government to hear his truth. He wanted to reject and overturn the legal structures oppressing so many poor people.

Seated around the campfire at their hideout, Ned spoke of drastic measures with enthusiasm to his gang members. 'If we kidnapped the governor, he would surely see the truth in what has happened over the years. He could not ignore the facts and betrayals of the law against us. He would surely see that we 'ave all been driven to damn madness by police corruption and abuses of power. Then we trade him for Ma. We go for the meat, not the maggots!'

'I'll raise a glass to that, Ned!' Dan and the young men cheered at the ideas of rebellion.

Ned was fuelled by the gang's support and his own desperation.

'The only way to create a true revolution is to make bold plans. What business has an honest man in joining the police? It takes a rogue to catch a rogue as they say, and them traps are rogues in their heart but too cowardly to follow it up without having the police force to disguise it. I'll never desert the shamrock, the emblem of true wit and beauty. Lads, we must lead the way forward bravely and do credit to Paddy's land. We cannot remain oppressed by the English yoke because we are all paying for it with our lives. We must act.'

What other choice did they have? The line had been crossed some time ago. The lawmakers wanted them dead. Each member of the gang was fully committed to their cause, as unplanned as it may have originally been, and their many sympathisers were equally supportive. The gang felt forced into an untenable situation. They weren't going back to prison again. Their next ambition was an uprising at Glenrowan. It would involve no half measures, but there were things to organise before it could happen.

VISIT TO SANDRIDGE, JUNE 1879

Loaded up with cash and gold, Maggie and Kate headed to Melbourne with their cousin Tom Lloyd. While travelling on the north-eastern train line, the Kellys were identified by a businessman, who notified the police immediately on arrival. By the time Kate and the others arrived at the Carlton Hotel, the press and the detectives were following their every move.

Grateful for a restful sleep on the Friday night after the train ride, Kate and the others rose early on Saturday to make their way to Sandridge. An industrial area, Sandridge was home to the first mills, distilleries and sugar refineries of Victoria's capital city. The rough Port of Melbourne suburb was also the focus of the city's criminal underworld. The same wildness found in border towns existed on the city's docks, and there was a thick tension of possibilities in the air.

The constantly moving ships were pawns in a chess game of many players competing to devise the most lucrative and clever deals for the biggest piece of the black-market pie. The toughest thugs helped maintain the status quo for the main players while alcohol, arms, sex and money were traded.

Walking against the salty air blowing in from the sea of Port Phillip Bay, the Kellys were acquiring weapons and ammunition. A man joined their group as they moved along the dock. Walking close to Kate but looking straight ahead, he slid a bag from Kate's shoulder and walked briskly ahead of her, disappearing away from the group. No one watching would have been able to tell that a transaction had taken place. Stage one of the deal was complete.

After their short visit to Sandridge, Kate and the others returned to their hotel in Carlton early Saturday afternoon. In a quiet corner of the pub, Maggie, Tom and Kate confirmed their plans. Tom and Maggie intended to head over to Rosier's Gun Shop to purchase ammunition. Many of the weapons accumulated by the gang needed particular bullets that couldn't be bought in Beechworth or Benalla. Rosier supplied the police force with their revolvers and some shotguns, so he was clearly on the opposing side to the Kellys but he had what the Kellys needed. A good deal of cunning would be required to make their purchase. With the media hot on their tails, Kate needed to distract them while Maggie and Tom snuck out the back of the hotel.

Kate was up to the same game, but this time in the big smoke instead of a bush setting. Scurrying out the front of the hotel,

Kate created the impression that she was in a hurry. Looking over her shoulder as if to check that she was not being followed, she was actually checking to see who had taken the bait. Heading in the opposite direction to many of the pedestrians strolling past the shopfronts, she ducked and weaved in between passers-by who made sounds to indicate their shock at her lack of etiquette as she bumped into shoulders and kept moving, unapologetic. She peered over her shoulder to make sure the journalists and police were following her.

Police in plain clothes were just a few steps behind her and obvious about it, anxious not to lose sight of her. A scrawny cadet and fat older journalist led a pack of press agents, all waddling like penguins in a row behind them. Kate concentrated on her path, determined to stretch out the detour for as long as possible. Crossing the dusty street in between horses and carriages, she was mindful of avoiding sewage in the street as she landed herself on the other side of the wide thoroughfare. She stopped for a moment to stare into a large plate-glass window.

Looking at her own reflection, pretending to adjust her hat, she counted the trail of followers crashing into one another behind her, all of them surprised by the sudden stop. The followers loitered around, trying to figure out what she was going to do next.

Kate caught her breath, relieved that she had lured the police and media well away from the hotel, and Maggie and Tom. Strolling, she led them on a very long, wide loop back to the hotel where the pointless chase had begun.

Meanwhile in Elizabeth Street, Maggie and Tom made a very large purchase from the old gentleman in suspenders and heavily starched shirt behind the counter at Rosier's Gun Shop. They paid him in cash. His suspicions had already been aroused by the quantity of ammunition they had just acquired, but when they placed another order of the same size again and left a deposit, he was convinced they were up to no good. And even though he didn't know who they were, he had his suspicions. He calmly agreed to supply the assorted ammunition and was more than satisfied when they told him they would return on the Monday to collect the order and settle the account. Secretly, he knew that would be enough time to get the police involved and be ready to catch them.

On Monday morning, many police staked out the shop. Detectives were excited to be a part of such a great sting. As the day drew on, however, the men grew weary as they realised the suspicious customers would not be returning.

Meanwhile, Kate, Maggie and Tom had made their way to Sandridge on the Monday, just as they had planned. The usual pack of reporters and a separate group of police and detectives were following the Kellys. It was all somewhat comical to Kate. The reporters were ruining the police surveillance, and it was driving the police mad.

On Tuesday morning, the Kelly party returned to their Melbourne accommodation, having spent the night at Sandridge, and one member of the group was noticeably absent. Kate had vanished. The detectives couldn't believe it, and the press reported it in their broadsheets for all to read. The Kellys were making public fools of the police once again. The young Kate Kelly had simply disappeared beneath their noses. It should have been impossible. The authorities called on the plain-clothed section for back-up, and senior detectives called Captain Standish back to Melbourne from Benalla to review the situation.

While Kate was absent and the police were in a quandary, Maggie and Tom visited a leading Melbourne bank. The detectives and reporters were desperately following them and were devastated that they had no power to establish the nature of the Kellys' business at the bank.

Shortly afterwards, Maggie and Tom rode the train back to Benalla. Seated together, they were only a short distance out of Melbourne when Maggie felt a tap on her shoulder. She lifted her head from Tom's shoulder, only to discover that they were surrounded by a number of uniformed police and some detectives who had embarked at the last stop.

Tom smirked at Maggie and sarcastically asked, 'Well, what do we have here, Maggie? Looks like we have a visit from half the police in Victoria.'

'What do you want?' Maggie was severe in her tone.

'You're coming undone, Mrs Skillion. You and your lousy brothers.'

'Is that so?'

'Empty your bags.'

'What?'

'Empty your bags.'

Tom was indignant. 'You have no right. What's your case with us?'

'We know about your visit to the gunsmith. Unpack your bags.'

Maggie shoved a small trunk and a canvas bag fiercely at their stomachs, slightly winding the police. The men were furious when they scrambled through Maggie's belongings and found nothing other than women's apparel.

The police tipped the belongings out onto the floor while other travellers in the carriage looked on in silence. Maggie was outraged and told them so.

'So what was that about coming undone? Leave us alone.'

'Mark our words, Mrs Skillion, it is just a matter of time. We'll get you lot.'

Tom ordered them away from Maggie. 'It seems you have misguided intelligence. You clearly have no case to harass us any further, so leave us alone.' Tom stood up, nose to nose with the ringleader of the police party, and it seemed enough to make them back off. The frustrated police retreated to each end of the carriage, watching the couple until the next stop, when the uniformed men reluctantly alighted. The detectives remained on the train to follow them all the way home.

Kate had disappeared with the ammunition on Monday night and was already making her way to her brothers' hideout. This teenage girl had easily outwitted the surveillance team once again.

Despite the slapstick episodes of surveillance and the sense of satisfaction in putting the slip on the traps, the sobering reality was that Kate and Maggie's efforts were essential to keep their brothers alive.

POLICE SURVEILLANCE 1878–1880

Tensions were mounting. Kate and Maggie knew that police were hiding in the bush around their homesteads every day and night. Late in the evenings, the teenaged Kate had a routine of releasing her beloved cattle dogs and walking around the hut with them for a distance of several hundred yards and out across their property boundary. Deliberately muzzled, so that they would not take the poisoned baits distributed around the grounds by the police in an attempt to kill them, her faithful companions would patrol confidently with her. The faint smell of rotten meat from the baits lingered in the night air, spoiling the fresh smell of the soil rising up from the ground as the heat of the day dissipated.

'Who's that?' Kate would whisper to her loyal pack as she let them off into the dark. They would eagerly respond, loving this game. 'Where are they? Good girls! That's it. Find them, off yer go now!' The trusty canines set off at an eager pace with excited whimpers, trying to outdo each other by finding the scent first, dragging their noses along the ground or sniffing the air. It would only take a few moments and then the hunt was on.

Running together and barking like their lives depended on it, the dogs would find the sources of the smells. Gathering together at the edge of the bush with tails and hackles up, growling and snarling at the police, they would successfully reveal the location of the spying eyes hidden in the dark. It was designed to intimidate and unnerve the troopers and push them back a little into the bush or make them choose another location.

One morning, Maggie had business to take care of, and Kate was to be the decoy. Having conducted the canine routine in the late hours of the evening, Kate concealed a parcel inside the hut, hiding it in a cavity beneath the floor for Maggie to collect.

At four o'clock in the morning, Kate came out to the paddock to catch Pathfinder, a thoroughbred Ned had 'acquired' for her, and she saddled up. Tying a small yet conspicuous bundle to her saddle, she pulled herself up onto the horse. Doing a slow and noisy round of the hut to attract attention, she headed off slowly in the direction of Maggie's homestead.

The troops stationed around Kate's place pursued her without hesitation. Imagining that Kate would lead them straight to the gang, they fantasised that they would each be heralded as heroes. Kate made sure that she kept just in sight but with enough distance to make them work to keep up with her. The expedition took the followers past Maggie's place, and the policemen watching the family at that location joined the party eagerly following Kate. Once they were out of sight, Maggie rode to Kate's to retrieve the stashed parcel and head to her brothers.

Meanwhile, Kate pushed up into a steep gap in the Warby Ranges. The policemen had followed her, across country on their horses, but were struggling to make it up the relentless slope through the scrub. The steep trail soon proved to be too difficult for them, so they had to dismount and trudge it on foot.

Kate selected a pleasant spot to rest her horse, placed herself on a rock and waited. The first of the exhausted men arrived, without their horses, and were greeted by Kate, who was thrilled with the torment she had created.

'Fancy seeing yer here, Constable! What a lovely mornin' for a ride! It's a long way for a walk up that hill, though, don't yer think?'

Fuming at the humiliation of the trek the young girl had taken them on, the cranky constable demanded to see what was in the bundle.

'Very smart, Miss Kelly. Playing games with us like that. What's in the bundle?'

'Ah now, that's none of yer business as far as I know!'

'You may have achieved a humorous lark at our expense, Miss Kelly, but we are still the law. Undo the bundle. Now!'

'Ah, all right then, if I must.'

Undoing the bundle with great suspense and theatrical effect, Kate shook a simple tablecloth out in front of her as if removing crumbs after a meal. The constable groaned in annoyance while she laughed at how she had fooled them. She began folding the cloth back up again and secured it to her saddle for the trip home, which she was now very much looking forward to.

'I hope you have a pleasant walk back down the hill, Constable. You and all yer friends! I'm sure to be seeing yer again soon, no doubt.'

'It's just a matter of time, Miss Kelly, before we catch your brother and his gang, and then you won't be so smart, young lady. You can be sure you will see us all again very, very soon.'

As a trickle of officers was arriving up the hill, Kate was gently descending on horseback. She was soon out of sight, leaving the men to contemplate the joke they had just been made the butt of, all the way back to their hideouts in the surroundings of the Kelly homesteads.

But pressure was mounting on the Kellys, and Kate was feeling it. She was only sixteen years old and in the second year of being pursued by the police. Under constant surveillance, she was being followed everywhere by the media, and she and Maggie had to help her brothers survive and carry out their plans, while maintaining the homestead and caring for her siblings and Alice.

One evening on her return to the homestead, the police took things to a new level. They had received intelligence that Ned was coming back to the homestead that night and, hoping to knock him off his horse, they had replaced a slip rail that Kate had deliberately removed.

Kate noticed the rail at the last moment and threw her weight up out of the saddle in unison with Oliver Twist. Together they worked urgently to clear the extra height. Horse and rider cleared the fence despite the wicked trap, but a flighty policeman took aim at Kate and a bullet caught her in the hip.

Kate wondered if those wombat-brained police thought she was one of the boys as she rode astride, or if they had tried to harm her so that she could not continue working for her brothers. Either way, she was painfully wounded and livid about it.

In pain and shock, she rode to her sister's place. 'It were so quiet, Maggie. As I approached, I had to think quick smart. We only just cleared the rail. I had to use all me strength to get Oliver as high as I could but then I heard the cap go off. It were only a slight sound over the noise of Oliver and meself panting. Then damn it, Maggie, it were like a red hot poker in me hip! Damn them traps!'

Kate was lying on one side on Maggie's kitchen table, hoping her sister could help her. 'Can yer get it out, Maggie?'

'Let me see. Hold still. Stop squirming around!'

Kate flinched and flexed as Maggie splashed alcohol on the wound. 'Ah . . . that is killin' me, Maggie.'

'I've got to clean it, Kitty, it surely will sting but there's no choice. Hold still, damn yer!'

Kate was gritting her teeth and moaning.

'Looks like the mongrel bullet has really sunk in there, sister. Can yer move your leg all right, Kitty?'

She swung her leg and grimaced a little. 'It's more like the flesh aches. I can move all right, I suppose.'

Maggie poked around in the wound with a knife but couldn't reach the bullet.

Kate screamed. 'Stop it now! Just stop it!'

'I can't get it out if yer squirming around like that.'

'Yer killing me, Maggie!'

'Here, bite down on this.' Maggie handed her a scrunched-up rag before having another go. 'Stay still! Jesus and Mary, I can't get it, Kitty! I'll wrap it up in rags, you'll just have to keep it clean.'

'What those bastards did makes me wild! I looked behind me when I was singin' out abuse at the weasels, I thought I saw that hog-faced constable from Benalla, I think it were him. But it were so dark, it were just the outline of him so I can't be sure.'

Maggie wrapped Kate's hip and sent her home, but the bullet remained in Kate's hip for the rest of her life.

As the Kelly girls continued to support their brothers and friends, the fascination with Ned and the outlaws grew. The Kellys sold newspapers. Their activities were labelled and publicised:

'The Fitzpatrick Incident', 'The Kelly Outbreak', 'The Stringybark Creek Massacre'. It was like a play or adventure story. The whole saga was a public feast.

Another trip to Melbourne was about to show Kate just how much the public was obsessed with the Kelly story.

15

Kate and the Kelly Gang, 1880

KREITMAYER'S WAXWORKS, APRIL 1880

The unfolding Kelly events were making headlines and history, defining a new concept of celebrity and fame, and captivating generations of spectators globally. Indeed, the extraordinary public attention paid to the law-breaking Kellys was like nothing the colony had seen before. Adding to the extreme fascination were the stories of how the gang was supported by the defiant Kate and other sympathisers.

Next door to the Apollo Theatre on Bourke Street East in Melbourne, the entertaining and innovative Mr Kreitmayer's Waxworks drew crowds of everyday people looking to be thrilled and amazed. Mr Kreitmayer was a clever businessman, and his wax replicas were as close as the masses would ever get to the people who were creating the narratives, fashions and sensations of the day.

The public's attraction to the macabre, the gory and the criminal was demonstrated by the ongoing, outstanding attendance and interest in Kreitmayer's changing displays. Kreitmayer had created a special Chamber of Horrors for his truly gruesome effigies, and there was always a huge window display to get the public in. The waxworks was open into the late evening, which added to the ambience of mystery, fear and drama.

From 1870, he had exhibited a variety of wax figures starting with Mary Queen of Scots, before and after her beheading! He had also displayed effigies of the criminals Mrs Kinder and Mr Bertrand. Mrs Kinder, a New South Wales woman, had been accused of poisoning her husband. Mr Bertrand was her lover, and he was sentenced to death for shooting Mr Kinder in 1866, when the poison that Mrs Kinder administered had failed to kill her husband. A drunken sailor had paid the one shilling entrance fee late on a Saturday evening and was found with his arms around the wax Mrs Kinder, begging her to answer his questions and to give him a kiss. He was ejected in tears after getting no response from the silent, wax woman.

Kreitmayer didn't need to make judgements about taste, he just had to give the colonial public what they wanted and sell tickets. Previous exhibitions of Kreitmayer's had toured widely. In 1872, an exhibition of artefacts from the South Sea Islands and Australia was shown in conjunction with the waxworks and then taken to England. The collection contained two busts based on the Tasmanian Aboriginal leaders Truganini and her husband Wourrady, of the Palawa tribe. *The Argus* distastefully described them as notorious traitors and their son as the last Aboriginal man in Tasmania. It was a supremely white attempt to continue the absolute myth that colonial power had triumphed in extinguishing the last of the Tasmanian people. Additionally, a cruelly preserved corpse of an Indigenous man from Queensland was on show. He had been shot while hiding in a tree during a massacre and was heartlessly reduced to nothing more than novelty value for paying customers, apparently devoid of any ethical code.

By 1876, Madame Tussaud, founder of the famous wax museum in London, had teamed up with Kreitmayer to create a grand waxworks collection, and it toured parts of Victoria. Two years later, in 1878, Kreitmayer sent a number of wax figures to feature in the Paris Exhibition. His figures depicted colonial life and included a replica of a generic, hairy-bearded digger from the goldfields. Upon the wax figures' return to Victoria, Kreitmayer noticed that the digger's head had been repaired in France after some damage. As he unpacked the delicate figure, he found that the unfortunate digger had been fitted out with a humorous, freshly twirled French moustache, displaying the latest Parisian trend!

The public taste for criminals was growing stronger, and well-publicised local murderers appeared next to a dying soldier who displayed a breathing chest 'of a wonderfully natural manner', which contained an apparatus that moved up and down to create the effect of the poor man's last breaths on the battlefield.

There was also the infamous Mrs Smith, who had been charged with the murder of her young son. However, Kreitmayer had overlooked the small detail of her innocence, and she took him to court to demand that her wax double be removed.

Occasionally, Kreitmayer's plans were rejected, such as when he requested permission to take a cast of various criminals who had just been executed. Mr Howard, guilty of the Frankston Murders, was one corpse that got away. The family simply refused the outrageous request, and Kreitmayer was most disappointed that he couldn't capitalise on the attraction that the local story would have brought.

With the approaching Easter Fair of 1880, Kreitmayer planned to present a collection of no less than fifty waxwork figures, with Captain Moonlite among the famous faces, all celebrated alongside a beer and wine competition.

It should have been no surprise to anyone in Melbourne when Kreitmayer announced that the key attraction would be wax models of Ned Kelly and his gang, set in a scene replicating the Stringybark Creek massacre. The figures of Lonigan, Kennedy and Scanlon would also feature, regardless of how their relatives may have felt. A play about the Kelly Gang had also been proposed, but the government put an urgent stop to it.

After one of her trips to Melbourne, Kate had rushed to tell the boys about what she had seen on display and how everyone was talking about it. The musty smell of the rooms had given her a sickly feeling as she stood beside other spectators at the Easter Fair in a state of disbelief at the scene before her eyes. The other spectators were clearly impressed by the display, but they were also whispering about how the famous Kate Kelly was in the audience with them. Here was Kate's life reflected back in the art and popular culture of the day, and it blew her mind. She may just have lost her mind completely if she had known in that moment that in just two years she herself would appear as a wax figure. In March 1882, a new waxworks exhibition included the daring Kate Kelly, and she was a hugely popular feature, visited by thousands and promoted in the press.

'Everyone were lined up, Neddy, so many folks payin' to get in there and have a look at yer. It were impressive to a lot of them folks, I could hear them all talking about you and the boys, but there weren't no resemblance, just a beard like yours. I suppose they wouldn't really know what they was lookin' at anyhow. It were like a bad dream, Ned, I rushed out of there.'

'That Kreitmayer is making money off our misfortune, Kitty, he's a mongrel, stay away from there, girl. It ain't worth the disturbance to your mind, Kitty.'

The Kellys could not have known how far Kreitmayer's obsession with Ned would go. The day after Ned's execution, Kreitmayer eagerly nominated himself to be one of the few who would disrespectfully mangle Ned's body. In coming months, Kreitmayer would surgically remove Ned's brain and then his head from his body, keen to showcase casts of it.

The Great Waxworks Exhibition

will be exhibited at the

COMMERCIAL EXCHANGE, HUNTER-STREET

commencing on

WEDNESDAY, 9TH NOV.

THIS Mammoth Collection has been exhibited for an uninterrupted season extending over 20 consecutive months in Sydney, where over 250,000 persons visited it; also throughout New Zealand and Queensland, with a success perfectly unrivalled, as it is unequalled and unapproachable by any exhibition ever offered to the public, comprising—The Outlaws of the Wombat Ranges; Kelly Gang (two magnificent groups); Ned Kelly's Armour; The Melbourne Opera House Tragedy; the late Prince Imperial—how he died in Zululand; the Two-headed Nightingale; Mr. Charles Stewart Parnell, M.P., the great Irish agitator; and numerous other groups, forming the most artistic and instructive exhibition in the colonies.

Admission—1s; children, half-price. Open from 10 a.m. till 10 p.m.   7349

This advertisement from the Newcastle Morning Herald and Miner's Advocate, *8 November 1881, shows the widespread and enduring appeal of the Kelly story and confirms that a Kelly-related waxworks display was exhibited in Queensland and New Zealand.*

SHERRITT AND OLD MRS BYRNE 1878–1880

Aaron Sherritt, police spy and former friend of the Kelly Gang, had a distinct look about him. He wore large white shirts loose over his trousers, and his trousers were always tucked into the top of his boots. For quite a time, Sherritt was the lover of Joe Byrne's sister Ellen, who lived with their mother Margaret, aka 'Old Mrs Byrne'. Sherritt was frequently at their house and was well acquainted with the bushland behind the house that the Kelly Gang had utilised in the past.

Police were attempting to lure more and more people in to help them locate the outlaws, or at least help them with information about the Kelly Gang's movements, using the promise of money.

Superintendent Hare, who was at times in charge of the Kelly hunt, told Sherritt that he would give the whole of the initial reward of four thousand pounds to him if he helped Hare exclusively to bring down Ned and the gang.

The lure of this fortune was an even better inducement than the small amounts Sherritt had been earning from the other police he had been helping, and the first thing he offered up was access to what he described to the police as 'a very secret location that the gang had used in the past': the wooded bushland at the back of Mrs Byrne's house.

A collection of police stationed themselves in varying spots of cover along the hills that looked down towards Mrs Byrne's hut. Without the Byrnes' knowledge, Sherritt regularly joined them and held a surveillance spot closest to the bottom of the hill. They were there for one nervous month, living with the discomfort of the winter weather and the constant fear that the gang would arrive at the site and attack them. Lying on their bellies behind logs and rocks, each man held his place and slept in between taking turns to watch the activities below. They could not even light a fire because the risk of revealing their stakeout was too high, so they lived on tinned meat and fish in the miserable conditions.

One morning, old Mrs Byrne was in the yard at the back of her hut when something caught her eye. She moved towards the hill and then pulled up suddenly. She had spotted Sherritt but not the other men. Trying to remain undetected, Superintendent Hare rushed to grab Sherritt while the other men retreated up the hill. At the same time, the wily Mrs Byrne launched her own expedition into the hills.

On their knees in the long grass, Hare signalled Sherritt to follow him quickly. Once they made it to cover, Hare let Sherritt know that he suspected Mrs Byrne was aware of his presence at the stakeout. 'Sherritt, it is certain she saw someone there. If she was able to recognise you, I do not know. You need to get the hell away from here, now!'

Sherritt turned as white as his shirt and began to perspire. 'I'm done. That is my fate sealed.' He thought about what would happen to him. Would he be beaten to death? Would Ned just shoot him? Or did some other tortured fate await him?

'I'll visit me girl this evening. It will be the only way I can tell for sure.'

Not realising that she was being watched, Mrs Byrne kept climbing the hill, looking up every few seconds, not sure what she would find but convinced there was something to uncover. As she scrambled through the scrub, the glimmer of a sardine tin left on a rock caught her eye. In that moment, she was certain that she was being observed, and her anger propelled her pace.

Determined to catch them, she scurried up the steep slope on her hands and knees, keen to discover whose campsite it was. Perched up above Mrs Byrne, the police watched her ascending, and Superintendent Hare sent a man down to thwart her efforts.

Instructed to wait behind a rock, the officer jumped up with his weapon as Mrs Byrne arrived, and he yelled at the unsuspecting woman. Mrs Byrne screamed with terror and began to shake through the fear and shock of the ambush, growing wild with anger.

'You pox-faced, evil-hearted, no good mongrel dog! I have a right mind to get my son and his friends to hunt you down and murder you lot just like they did at Mansfield.'

The policeman laughed and told her to get out of his way and not to interfere with police work before he sent her back to her hut. Mrs Byrne had discovered all she needed to know, and she swore at the policeman all the way down the hill through the scrub until she was home.

That evening, Sherritt called out to his young sweetheart Ellen from outside Mrs Byrne's house. Usually she would spring out to meet him and plant a kiss on his cheek, but no sweetness greeted him that day, and he braced himself as he entered the house. Sherritt noticed a man he didn't recognise sitting at the kitchen table, and it made his stomach squirm. The man's eyes met his, but the strange visitor ignored Sherritt, as did Mrs Byrne. Sherritt's shoulders tightened as he moved towards Ellen, who was sitting on the opposite side of the table. Ellen was icy cold towards her boyfriend and turned her head away from him as he leaned in for a kiss. Sherritt pulled back quickly in response to the rejection and followed Mrs Byrne outside as she went to get wood.

'What a trick you have been playing on me, Aaron,' the old woman said without looking at him. He bent down slowly to pick up wood from the pile.

'What trick is that, Mrs Byrne?'

Sharply she responded, 'As if you do not know! An old woman like me uncovers the police camp, but you do not know they are there? Hogwash!'

Sherritt played dumb, but there was no point in pretending. 'A police camp, you say?'

She looked him in the eye as they dumped the wood near the fuel stove back in the cabin. 'Do not test my patience, Sherritt. Go out there and see for yourself. It's time you left. You're not welcome here. Just get going and do not return. Traitor. You'll pay dearly for this, Sherritt.'

The mystery man stood close behind Sherritt, who heard the man's breath at his shoulder before he moved swiftly towards the door. Mrs Byrne was furious, slamming it behind him as he left. Sherritt skulked away, but he urged Superintendent Hare to remain at the site. He was certain that Ned or the gang would show up, even after the police stakeout had been exposed, and Sherritt needed his regular fee plus the reward, so he could start again somewhere else. But the double-crossing Sherritt knew he was living on borrowed time.

A few days later, Kate rode into Benalla in search of information about police movements. She caught up with friends who were deemed 'suspected persons' by the police and confirmed the next delivery of supplies from local sympathisers to the gang. She stayed the night with them, and early the next morning she visited other loyal contacts, anxious to get the latest word on the whereabouts of Superintendent Hare. As soon as she discovered that Hare and his men had all returned to the Benalla barracks to replenish supplies and await fresh orders, Kate took off like lightning to get the word back to Ned.

Close to midnight, three local men went out with their drays in convoy, two of which were decoys. Under the moonlight along a bush track near Merton, the drays pulled up and the men waited quietly until four men on horses silently emerged from the scrub. Ned and the gang moved straight towards the middle dray without a word spoken. They took items from it swiftly and filled their saddle packs, tied heavy bags onto their packhorse and vanished again into the bush.

One of the drivers spotted a man up the road who had been watching the delivery unfold, and he pursued him as the spy took off on foot. Launching himself from the front of the dray, the driver tackled the man and demanded to know who he was.

The man looked like a scared rabbit and said he was a tourist there on business and was just in the wrong place at the wrong time. The dray driver swore at him and punched him in the guts. 'Get the hell away from here and never come back. If I see you again, I'll cut your ears off.'

The punched man rolled on the ground clutching at his stomach, winded.

'You understand?'

He nodded, desperately trying to get the words out so he could ward off any further harm. 'Yes! Yes!' he breathed out in a whisper. 'I'll go. I'm gone. I promise.'

Knowing that Hare was in Benalla gave Ned the chance to get to Mrs Byrne's place and check in with her. She was a reliable and constant source of news, helping to keep him and the gang alive. The news she told Ned this time confirmed everything the men had suspected of Sherritt. Ned took the fresh news back to the gang.

The police got wind of Ned's visit to Mrs Byrne and set out to try to head him off but, by the time they got there, Ned had doubled back on the police party and was long gone.

DEALING WITH SHERRITT THE TRAITOR, 1880

From what the gang could tell, Aaron Sherritt appeared to have constant protection from the police. It was months after the event at Mrs Byrne's, and he had taken up with another young woman after Joe's sister Ellen. She was pregnant and living with him at his hut, along with four policemen.

Even before the gang found out through Mrs Byrne that Sherritt was a spy, the boys had already laid a trap. Too many 'coincidences' kept happening, so they'd set up a little test.

Joe Byrne had sent a letter to Sherritt, asking him to ride his black mare in the steeplechase at the Whorouly races and indicating that the gang would be there. Joe figured that if the police turned up at the races, they would know for sure where the information had come from. Sherritt rejected Joe's request to be a rider for him, which probably was signal enough that something wasn't right.

On the day of the races, the police were on site in disguise. Sherritt turned up in an attempt to make things appear normal, but it just made him look worse as he fraternised with the plain-clothed police.

Joe's brother and the Kelly sisters attended the day and, while they were mixing with the other riders, they easily picked the foreign faces in the crowd. Kate and Maggie asked questions of the incognito police rider about where he was from and what people he knew in the region, but he couldn't bluff his way through it enough to convince any of them. The other police were on edge, looking everywhere around them as they walked through the crowds, hoping to find the Kelly Gang.

Sherritt chatted with Joe's brother, who became even more suspicious when Sherritt made no inquiries about why the gang wasn't there when they had been expected to attend.

Disappointment was written all over the traps' faces when they finally surrendered to the fact that the Kelly Gang was a no-show and that it had all been a ploy.

After that, the gang knew for sure that Sherritt was playing both sides, so the news about the police stakeout at Mrs Byrne's home was the final nail for Sherritt. At their hideout, the gang devised a plan of retribution.

'That damned traitor! Hiding out the back of Ma's place with them traps.' Joe was livid.

'He's been on the payroll for those dog bastards for months now. I can't believe he sold us out.' Dan shook his fist in the air.

'Looks like we'll be paying him a visit,' Joe said.

'I'm gonna fill that bastard with lead.' Dan was fuming.

'Nah, Dan. I'll be doing that.' Joe made it very clear that he was the one who would settle it with Sherritt. He had vouched for his mate longer than he should have, and Sherritt's betrayal was very personal to Joe. It was his sister and his mother who had been spied on and badly deceived. 'He's a damned turncoat dog, with no limits to his foxing.'

Ned and the gang sat around the fire, conspiring their revenge. They made a plan to take Sherritt's neighbour Antoine to Sherritt's hut late at night and get him to call out for Sherritt to come to the door. Sherritt would recognise the voice and feel safe enough to answer it himself.

'How many traps stayin' there?' Ned asked.

'Four, they reckon. Aaron would be in the back room with the new woman, and 'er mother is in the front room, I've been told. My wager is that them big brave traps would be under the bed in no time I reckon, with Aaron's wife as a shield!' Dan scoffed.

The boys had seen it all before, gutless troopers with no clue and no incentive to do their jobs. Sherritt meant nothing in the policemen's lives, and he was about to mean nothing to the gang. None of them could believe that money had won their close friend's loyalty so easily.

'What price a friendship? What price a life? How could he do that to my family?' Joe wondered to himself.

The visit to Sherritt was going to be a message for the police and everyone in the district and the perfect start to their rebellious plans. Now that they knew how they were going to deal with Sherritt, Dan began talking again about their grander kidnapping plan. 'But this plan, about the governor, Ned. We can't just be going to Melbourne. They'll have us surrounded in no time. And how do we get him to see our situation or assist our cause?'

It had been on their minds for months. Things were coming to a head, and surrendering was not an option. That was the only thing they were all clear on.

'After we get rid of Sherritt, the news of that dead dog will surely get back to the bastards in Melbourne, and all them special troopers that they've been braggin' about will be up 'ere in no time. They'll get that special train happening, no doubt. All we have to do is rip up them train tracks near Glenrowan. We get our own men, our supporters, to meet us there. Give 'em a signal when the train has come off the tracks, and we can herd up any surviving police bastards like beasts, the rest can rot where they lie.'

The gang was counting on Sherritt's death to provoke the police into sending the special train, which would be derailed by the gang near Glenrowan. The gang would then grab any police hostages to assist their rebellion. Their mission? To create a new colony in the north-east of Victoria.

Ned was inspired by anecdotes of the uprising of the Eureka Stockade, the rebellion fought in Ballarat the year he was born. Red Kelly, Kate and Ned's father, had spent time on the Bendigo goldfields, and he knew men who had fought at the Stockade in Ballarat in the battle for their miner's rights. As a child, Ned learned about the allegiance sworn by thousands of miners to the

Southern Cross flag at the site of the uprising: 'We swear by the Southern Cross to stand truly by each other, and fight to defend our rights and liberties.' The death of over twenty miners killed in an attack by government troops still resonated in the collective memory of the public.

Many stories from Ireland had also travelled through Kate and Ned's ancestors about the Great Famine in their homeland and the history of uprisings in Ireland and Europe. The colonial system of English landlords ensured that the life of Irish farmers was one of hunger and suffering, with sky-high rents on land and poor conditions that made it impossible to produce enough food to survive on. Matters were only made worse when those English landlords continued to export food to Britain while the Irish starved. Across the whole of Ireland, thousands upon thousands of people starved to death or died of malnutrition-related diseases, and so the resentment towards the English travelled deep in Irish blood.

The Eureka Stockade and the history of a homeland that Ned would never see but was deeply connected to through his heritage were filled with powerful narratives. Through discrimination and desperation, Ned was propelled towards the chance to create a new chapter by leading an uprising of his oppressed neighbours, family and friends. *A republic within the colony, is it possible?* he wondered. 'The Republic of North-Eastern Victoria!'

Ned and his gang assumed, incorrectly, that support from the people of rural north-east Victoria would be enough for them to win their cause and that the bloody rebellions of recent history were some kind of map to standing up for their rights and fighting for changes in society. But to create such radical change would require more than good, brave men. The supporters would also need a sufficient level of desperation to fuel and sustain their fight. Ned and the gang were desperate, but would that be enough?

TREATED LIKE OUTLAWS, JUNE 1880

When the Victorian Government introduced the new laws in 1878 to ensure the extermination of Ned Kelly and his gang, no politician imagined the gang would evade capture for eighteen months.

On Friday, 25 June 1880, when the Victorian Parliament dissolved, the new laws dissolved with it.

The government's lack of attention to detail meant that Ned and the gang had resumed their rights again as citizens: their right to have a fair trial, the presumption of innocence and, most importantly, the right not to be murdered.

Despite the fact that most people in the rural setting of northeastern Victoria had weapons, the bounty on the outlaws' heads hadn't delivered the dead bodies of the gang that the government had so desperately wanted. In fact, during the time they were outlawed, the gang had galvanised even more support and created a movement intent on revolution.

The original outlawing of the Kelly Gang had provided a legal bribe to implore the general public to kill four men, to do the dirty work for the government. Yet it yielded no success, other than Sherritt's attempt at betrayal. Ned, Dan, Joe and Steve were about to take their revenge on him for his disloyalty and rock the foundations of the Victorian Government in an effort to change the colony.

Over the following weekend, when police troopers pounded Ned, Dan, Steve and Joe with lead at the Glenrowan siege, the gang members were free men, not outlaws, but no one knew or cared.

REVENGE ON SHERRITT, SATURDAY, 26 JUNE 1880

Aaron Sherritt's father was a former policeman who had been embarrassed by his son when he and Joe Byrne did time together for the theft of some meat. Joe's family had treated Sherritt well throughout their friendship, and Ned and Joe had both helped Sherritt to fence the land around his modest slab hut before they became wanted men. But the loyalty his friends had shown Sherritt wasn't returned.

Sherritt had heard the latest gossip. He knew he was done for. Anticipating this scenario, he had already sold his little hut and land. He planned to escape with his woman and start somewhere new. In and out of gaol many times, Sherritt was a survivor, but this time his web of deceit and lies had stuffed him. Despite the presence of Constable Armstrong and three other police at his hut, Saturday night, 26 June 1880, was Sherritt's last.

Joe Byrne and Dan Kelly were outside Sherritt's house after a visit to his neighbour's farmhouse. In the freezing cold, with Dan's shotgun at his back, Antoine would do whatever Dan told him.

Joe ran over to the closest tree and pulled the stolen fowling piece up to his shoulder. Using the trunk to steady himself, he lowered his head so he could train his eye along the barrel of the weapon, pointing it directly at the front door. Adjusting his position ever so slightly, he signalled Dan.

Dan gave Antoine a good shove in the back as he whispered, 'Do it! Call out to him. Now.'

'Aaron! Aaron, are you there? Can you help me? I've lost my way. It's so dark out here.' Antoine was ashamed to be the lure, but helpless against the men.

Sherritt swung the door wide to greet the old man, exposing his figure against the vibrant flames of the fireplace behind him. It outlined his body perfectly, and Joe wasted no time. Shot after shot rang out as Joe yelled, 'You'll never put me away again, Sherritt.'

Shrapnel exploded into Sherritt, jolting his body back with the impact. Blood and bits of flesh flew out of him until he fell to the floor. Amid the screams of Sherritt's mother-in-law and his pregnant partner, Byrne continued his abuse of Sherritt. 'You will not tell anyone what you do with us now, Sherritt. You bastard traitor!'

Antoine ran for his life to escape the murderous scene at Sherritt's and as soon as there was a break in the spray of lead pellets, the police grabbed Sherritt's body by his legs. They slid him back from the door and kicked it closed. One of the policemen barricaded the door and they dragged Sherritt's body into the bedroom, mopping the floor with his blood as they scrambled for cover.

From the tree, Joe turned his attention to the police. 'Come out here, you pigeon livers, before I blast you all to visit Lucifer himself.' Byrne fired a frenzy of lead and demanded that the police surrender.

Hysterical, the women could not contain their screams as they stared at Sherritt's body and shuddered with the shots hammering the little hut. The police didn't care about Sherritt, and they quietly considered that the women were better off without him in their lives. What was more pressing to them was what the hell the attackers outside would do next. With no way out, they sat and waited.

Byrne continued bellowing at those inside the hut while he and Dan collected kindling so they could set fire to the house. 'You're all gonna burn. Say your prayers or surrender.'

But to Joe's dismay, everything was too wet to start a fire, and they gave up on the notion after a couple of failed attempts. Feeling confident that word of Sherritt's death would make it back to the Melbourne police headquarters, the pair left at first light.

Riding back from Woolshed to Glenrowan, Joe and Dan didn't anticipate just how much they had terrified the police, who stayed inside Sherritt's hut and failed to report the news for twelve long hours. The gang was relying on senior Melbourne police learning about Sherritt's death and triggering the special train and troopers to Glenrowan. Without the train, their plans were useless.

16

The Glenrowan Siege, 26 – 28 June 1880

People believed in Ned. They heard his dream for a new beginning. Mrs Byrne and Kate had both been bragging to journalists and anyone who showed an interest that a grand plan was looming, something that would make the locals, the police and all of Victoria pay attention.

The working class, condescendingly known as the larrikin class, wanted to call it a day on the corrupt systems that were sending their innocent family and friends to gaol. They wanted the unfair distribution of wealth and opportunity to stop, and they wanted a fair go at land ownership and farming.

The dodgy practices they had all been witnessing involved the upper echelon of society: police, judges, squatters and landowners; the wealthy. The antics that the working class were up against included police horse-stealing rackets where innocent men were framed and gaoled, stacked juries and perjurers rigging the legal system, and even poor farmers having their livestock captured by police or wealthy landowners when found grazing on common land. They were then charged a prohibitive fee for the animal's return. Often the farmer had to take the day off from his work, travel a fair distance to the nearest police station only to find out about the fee and be unable to pay for the animal's return. Life was hard enough without these unfair disadvantages. It was time for change.

Kelly supporters had been nicking mouldboards from tractors on farms across the region since February. The thick plates of heavy steel were what they were after. Local blacksmiths helped the gang innovate an achievement in ironmongery: bulletproof protection in a style that had not been seen before. This cracker of an idea gave the gang a bold confidence in their plans.

After all their robberies, the gang had accumulated a war chest, and the least of it included fifteen revolvers, two double-barrelled shotguns, four single-shot rifles, three single-shot carbines, four repeating rifles and a sawn-off carbine. The gang's cumbersome, heavy steel suits, all their guns and the mass of ammunition and gunpowder that Kate and Maggie had been helping to acquire meant the gang was ready, come what may.

Kelly sympathisers gathered more frequently at the McDonnell's Railway Tavern, across the tracks from the newer Glenrowan Inn, also known as Ann Jones' Hotel. The inn's Irish owner, widow Ann Jones, had only been in business for about eighteen months and, whether she knew it or not, her pub was going to be a base for the siege. The gang wanted it to seem like any other day, just business as usual for Kelly supporters to be at the public house on the day of the uprising so, to avoid suspicion, they had started to go there more often in the lead-up to the siege.

The police efforts to track the gang down up to that point had been futile and, most recently, even the Aboriginal trackers seconded from Queensland had failed to locate Ned and the gang, although they had come closer than any of the outlaws would have liked. It was only the heavy winter rains that had spared them.

The idea was to draw police from Melbourne all the way to Glenrowan, with the hope that local police would be drawn out, too. The train track had a dangerous downward bend more than half a mile from the Glenrowan platform on the Wangaratta side and that made it a great spot for a derailment.

It was anticipated that with the derailment all police resources would be focused on Glenrowan, and Ned thought it would be the perfect opportunity to target the banks in Benalla and other local places, which would most likely be unguarded. The spoils would create a great source of revenue to fund the proposed Republic of North-Eastern Victoria and any future endeavours.

This very cold, harsh winter weekend started off with the cold-blooded shooting of Aaron Sherritt late Saturday night. Meanwhile, a team of men and horses arrived at Glenrowan with Ned and Steve, their ammunition, armour and weapons. While Ned waited with Steve Hart for Dan and Joe to ride back from Sherritt's hut at Woolshed, they watched for the last train scheduled to pass through the town until Monday. As soon as it had passed, they could start pulling up the tracks. They failed, however, to anticipate how difficult that would prove to be. Both men were swearing and irritated as it became obvious that they would need to recruit assistants to get this crucial part of the plan done.

Camped in tents near the Glenrowan railway station was a group of labourers whom Ned assumed were platelayers with specialised tools and knowledge of laying the rails. Ned woke the men at gunpoint and pushed them out of their tents. In the freezing cold, the workers shuffled along the tracks, with Ned and Steve pointing their guns at them to keep the men focused. They were set to work under close supervision, but it soon became obvious that they couldn't do it.

Ned insisted the men tell him who else knew how to pull up the tracks. They told him about the local platelayers. Steve and Ned took the labourers back up to the stationmaster's house, and Steve stayed there to watch them all while Ned coerced the two plate-layers out of their warm beds. Ned and the men returned to collect the tools needed, which were stored near the station. Steve was to keep guard while Ned and his new team headed back to carry on with the task of dismantling the railway tracks.

The two platelayers knew what they were doing, but they dragged it out for as long as they could. Every metre or so, there was a heavy wooden sleeper attached to the line by a plate and a metal spike. These had to be removed across a length of about seven metres to dismantle that section of the track. After hours of hard work, the gap was created. It was just before dawn on the Sunday morning, and the men were marched back to the township and held at the stationmaster's house until transferred over to Ann Jones' Hotel much later.

Well after sun-up, Dan and Joe arrived in Glenrowan, and as the morning passed they rounded up random people who were in the wrong place at the wrong time. Women and their husbands out for a stroll, men who happened to be in the area for the day, locals and strangers alike were claimed as hostages and brought in from the street to the stationmaster's.

A number of sympathisers and some of the gang's hostages went with Ned to Ann Jones' for a Sunday breakfast while others remained where they were under Steve's watch.

The news of Sherritt's death hadn't reached senior police in

Melbourne as quickly as the gang had expected, and so the outlaws waited and waited, wondering why the special train had not arrived.

Later that day, when the train still hadn't arrived, Dan took the remaining hostages across to Ann Jones' Hotel. Women held on to their partners' hands tightly and even tighter to that of their children as they walked at a fresh pace to the public house, where their arrival filled the hotel to capacity.

Inside the quaint, wooden-posted little pub, the gang encouraged everyone to have a good time to pass the lagging wait for the special train. Ann Jones was thrilled with the captive trade as the patrons blew whatever cash they had at the bar. A concertina was played, and the hostages danced, chatted, sang songs and played card games. The gang talked about Ned's plans and continued to wait for the train.

To entertain Ned and the gang, 'The Kelly Song' was performed by Mrs Jones' son. Young Jack stood up straight in front of Ned and, as he tucked in his shirt, clearing his throat, the noise around him settled. Clapping his hands and tapping his left foot, he looked around the room, a little frightened, hoping others would join in.

A single clap or two started the boy's performance until drunken patrons got the rhythm of it and they stomped and clapped a hearty percussion for the lad. The concertina musician played an Irish tune to support young Jack, and he sang his heart out trying to impress the very man the song was about:

Ned Kelly was an Irishman,
Kate Kelly she was bold,
They never robbed a poor man,
But the banks they robbed of gold,
It's come along my hearties
And together we shall roam . . .

156

Ned smiled at the boy and tapped his feet while the audience continued to clap along. It had been a bizarre day for them all, but they tried to forget about the circumstances that brought them there as Jack carried on with his song:

We'll make for yonder mountains,
Yon gullies or yon plains,
Before we will work for government,
Bound in iron chains . . .

Ned's attention drifted away from the song when Joe leant in close to his ear. Joe covered his mouth as he spoke so that no one could hear what he said before the pair walked together into a side room. The boy continued on as the concertina carried him over a few more verses until he was done, and the audience gave him a big cheer.

Some of the hostages headed outside to a large campfire at the back of the pub. The hostages didn't feel directly threatened, but they knew they must toe the line or there would be trouble. Around the fire, the captive men talked about what the gang had told them they were doing and speculated as to whether any of it would really happen.

In the side room where Ned had disappeared with Joe, the gang had stashed many of their weapons, ammunition and the helmets. Beneath their overcoats, each of the gang members concealed their heavy armour. No one in the pub was aware of the reasons each of the men had such a bulky appearance, but they were very aware of the loaded guns and rifles the men walked around with.

Ned told Ann Jones that he was taking her daughter Jane to call out to the local policeman, Constable Bracken, so they could lure him out of his house and take him hostage, too. They imagined that the sound of a child's voice would give Bracken no reason to suspect anything untoward. The gang had been unable to find him in the hours beforehand. Bracken had been regularly involved in the surveillance of Maggie and Kate, even though he thought they didn't know. The boys were keen to use Bracken to their advantage.

Ann pleaded with Ned not to use her daughter in the trap, worried that something would happen to her. One of the hostages, Mr Curnow, a local teacher, overheard the conversation between Ned and Ann. The teacher was not a sympathiser but wanted to create the impression that Ned had his support so he could get out of there.

'I have a suggestion,' he boldly put forward to Ned. 'What say you take my brother-in-law instead of the girl? Bracken knows his voice and surely would not question it.'

Ned squinted his eyes as they darted from Curnow to his wife and the others standing near him. 'If we did this,' Curnow continued, 'would you let us go? Let me take my sick wife and the others home?'

Ann Jones was keen on Curnow's suggestion and pleaded with Ned to take it up. Ned considered it for some time and then agreed. 'But know this, Curnow, if any of you have a notion that you can trick us, you will die for it. We will come along later and check that you are in your home.' Curnow acknowledged Ned's threats and promised his loyalty.

Curnow's horse and cart were prepared out the back, and his wife and relatives entered it swiftly, hopeful that they would shortly be free of the wretched situation. Together, Ned and the Curnow family made their way to Bracken's home. Curnow and his brother-in-law walked alongside the horses, and Ned sat upon his horse with his weapon pointed at the men.

The simple trick lured the ill Constable Bracken out of his house and earned the Curnow family their freedom. Bracken raised his hands in the air like Ned told him to, and Ned followed Bracken with his weapon in Bracken's back. Ned instructed him to walk in front of Ned's horse as Ned got back in the saddle. Bracken offered no argument.

Ned turned to Curnow and his terrified party with a final warning. 'Go quietly to bed and do not dream too loud or you'll be shot.' As the Curnows headed home, Ned returned to the inn with the policeman, happy that he'd added Bracken to his list of prisoners even though there was still no sign of the train.

Sometime after one o'clock on the Monday morning, the gang considered whether they should just clear out of town. They'd finally given up on the train ever arriving and instructed two of the hostages to saddle up their horses and bring them up to the back of the pub, ready to ride out.

The gang decided to let the hostages know that their plan to derail the train had failed. Thinking the game was up, they told the crowd that they planned to surprise the police in a different way in the near future. Soon all the prisoners would be free to go but not before Ned gave them all a warning.

Ned climbed up onto a chair, his tall athletic body becoming an even more dominating presence above them all. In his long over-coat, with a rifle in his hand, Ned gathered the hostages around him and addressed the crowd.

'I have something to say, and I want you all to hear it. First, if any of you present here today tell the police of our doings or our plans or say anything about us, I shall visit you and one day have a settling with you.' He looked threateningly and directly into the faces of many people across the room.

'I am not one bit afraid of the police and I know that, if left to them alone, I would never be found. But I do honestly fear those damned black trackers. They can track me across bare stones for God's sake. It was mostly to kill those bastards and capture those useless senior police that we tore up those rails. I wanted to fill the ruts with police carcasses. Scatter their blood and brains like rain. I can't make out what has delayed the damned train but let them come when they like, we are always ready for them!'

Meanwhile, Curnow had returned to his home as instructed but, much to his wife's distress, he'd decided he had to do something to thwart Ned's plans. In the darkness, Curnow had made his way to the train tracks with a red llama scarf and a candle. If the train did arrive, he was going to stop it before the carnage.

Ned and the gang didn't know it, but the train was nearly at Glenrowan. The special train was filled with police from Melbourne, including the Queensland trackers. Five reporters were also along for the ride, and it had stopped at Benalla to collect another eight policemen and their horses before continuing on to Glenrowan. As the train approached the town, the police loaded their weapons and talked among themselves about what the gang might be up to.

In the distance, Curnow could hear the approaching train and quickly lit the candle. He picked up the red scarf and held the candle behind it, which created a red signal that he hoped would stop the train. What Curnow didn't know was that the police had set up a pilot engine to lead the special train, staying about a hundred yards in front of it to be on the lookout, as they expected the gang may have placed explosives on the track.

The pilot driver was concerned about the red light he could see at the edge of the track, but he second-guessed it as a possible trick masterminded by the outlaws. Panicked, the fast-talking train driver yelled at his co-driver. 'Red light. Red light. Do we stop? Is it a trap?' If they were going to stop in time, they needed to act right away.

At the pub, Ann was relieved that it was all coming to an end, and she was hopeful that the gang and everyone else would leave quickly. Constable Bracken had a real beef with Ned and was irritated by the outlaws' antics and his drawn-out speech. He wished he could have arrested Ned and his mongrel offsiders right then and there.

Ned continued to address his crowd, thinking that the gang and he were about to disappear into the wee hours of the morning. The crowd listened to him, but they all just wanted to go home. 'The money and spoils from Euroa and Jerilderie were far more than reported in the press and—' Ned's narrative was cut short by a high-pitched train whistle in the distance.

The whistle that had betrayed the train's presence was the pilot driver's signal to warn the special train that they were stopping. The pilot engine and the special train pulled up in time to greet Curnow and receive his warning.

Ned exclaimed in shock, 'By God, I bet that sneaky bastard Curnow has deceived us! Dan, you keep an eye on this lot, I'm going to see for myself.' Within minutes, Ned had ridden close to the scene of the whistle. Seeing that the approaching train had been spared, he realised that the plan they had masterminded had fallen apart and that the train full of police would soon be upon them, so he returned to the hotel and instructed the other men to prepare.

It was about three o'clock on the Monday morning, 28 June 1880. The train wreck and police slaughter that the gang had predicted weren't to be. The outlaws knew that, within minutes, the police would be all over them like flies on shit. In the side room, the men loaded their weapons and lifted the heavy helmets over their heads. They grabbed their weapons and went back out to the bar.

Following Ned's orders, Ann extinguished the fires that had been keeping them all warm and put out all the lamps and candles as she gathered her two children ready to take shelter. The gang walked towards the front door of the pub, and Ned yelled out a final warning to the hostages. 'Lay as low to the floor as you can, or you will wear bullets.' The patrons all fell to the floor, desperately looking for hiding holes. They nestled themselves in behind pieces of furniture where they could. The gang strode heavily out of the pub and across the front verandah. Ready for combat, they waited for their enemies to approach.

The police had established that the gang was at the pub, and the whole armed party crept towards it. In the moonlight, the nervous constables and sergeants could see movement on the verandah, and they inched closer until bullets landed at their feet and flew past their ears. The police scattered to find cover behind trees, logs and in small dips in the landscape around the hotel. The police had returned fire, but they called out to the outlaws to surrender.

'Surrender, be damned. You can shoot us for six months and never hurt us!' was the reply.

Like huge metal beasts, masked by their unusual thick, heavy armour, the iron creatures stood on the verandah of the inn shooting their attackers. Feeling invincible, Ned shouted at the police, 'Fire away, you dogs! You can't hurt us!' A smile grew under his sweaty helmet.

To the gang Ned yelled, 'Let 'em have it, lads!'

But Ned's smile evaporated when he was shot in the foot and the arm. The police were unwittingly hitting the gang's exposed limbs. And after Joe was shot in the leg, the gang retreated into the hotel while the police continued their attack.

The blasting and booming of the gang's shots from inside the hotel left many ears ringing, and everyone coughed and spluttered as gun smoke filled the lungs of the hostages and every part of the hotel.

Lead shot from the police guns pierced through the thin weatherboards at high speed, casting shrapnel and shards of timber into the air, lodging into chairs and tables and human flesh.

'Hail Mary, full of grace . . .' Hostages were praying loudly.

Men, women and children were screaming as bullets whizzed past their noses.

'Pray for us sinners, now and at the hour of our death . . .'

Flinching at every sudden movement or noise, the hostages expected each minute to be their last. It was the police gunfire they were afraid of, not the bushrangers'. Despite the cries from innocent parties, the police had no intention of stopping their onslaught. People were shocked that the police were so willing to attack the gang, knowing that members of the public were sitting ducks inside.

Constable Bracken made a run for it amid the deluge and safely joined his comrades. Joe and Steve were furiously looking for him from room to room and were in a terrible rage when they realised he had escaped.

Joe Byrne ducked as a bullet struck the clock on the mantel-piece, making it strike like a death knell a hundred times or more until another bullet ended the noise by smashing what was left of it. Already wounded, Joe was slugging a nobbler of brandy when another bullet hit him, this time in the groin. Blood sprayed out as he fell to the ground.

Ned had disappeared out the back of the hotel, but Dan and Steve were still inside with all of the hostages and were shocked when they found Joe's body and realised he was dead. They moved their mate's corpse into a bedroom at the back.

The McDonnell's Railway Tavern on the eastern side of the tracks was positioned on a mound and looked across to the station and over to Ann Jones' Hotel to the west. A confused Kelly cousin was waiting there with a barrel of gunpowder and fuses, which were supposed to be lit as a signal to Kelly sympathisers waiting in the distance that the train had been derailed. But, without the derailment, it was unclear what to do, and the horsemen were hanging in the background baffled as to how they could implement their plans now that the train had been spared. They waited for some kind of signal from Ned, expecting the gang to escape from the scene. Sympathisers watching the shootout from near the tavern grew in numbers. The group let out great cheers of support any time the gang fired, and booed when the police were sending volleys at the gang.

As the battle continued through the early morning, Ned lay down near a log out the back to ponder the sorry state of things without the police noticing him. As he nursed his injuries, he tried to figure out how he might adapt the plans that had so severely come undone. He limped up to his mare, Music, and released her into the bush, hoping his rebel horsemen would find her and take it as a sign that it had all gone wrong and that plans should be aborted.

Dan and Steve held fort inside the hotel, where most of the weaponry remained. 'What the hell to do now, Dan?' Steve was looking to Dan for guidance, but his friend simply shrugged. Dan kept low as he approached the back door to look for Ned. He opened the door a little and poked the barrel of his gun out first. When no bullets were fired at him, he stuck his head out quickly, but he couldn't see Ned anywhere.

With no sign of Ned, Dan and Steve thought he was probably dead like Joe. Their plan to clear out seemed pointless now, as they considered themselves completely alone against the small army of police outside—a situation they hadn't planned for.

A white handkerchief was waved out the door by a small family who were trying to get the hell out of there, but as they made a dash for it, someone in the police yelled out, 'It's the Kellys. Bring them down!' The poor children and their father were forced to turn around and run back into the hotel, screaming and receiving bullets. Inside the hotel, innocent people had suffered painful and eventually fatal wounds, and when the police announced that the hostages could escape, many were too frightened or injured to leave and missed their opportunity to flee.

Steve and Dan didn't know that Ned was still alive and preparing himself for another round of the battle. They looked quickly out a window when there was a lull and saw that about twenty police reinforcements had arrived from Wangaratta and Benalla, bringing police numbers to around fifty. Sympathisers booed as the enthusiastic new arrivals began an intense attack against the gang.

Ned loaded his pistol and listened to the barrage of shots being fired into the pub. He heard Dan and Steve's reply shots and the cheers from the crowd. Ned didn't know it, but his friends had removed their armour and were resigned to the shootout being their last.

Ned mustered all the strength he had left and launched himself into the fray, emerging like a tall steel monster from the edge of the bush, floating in a cold winter mist. Frightened onlookers and police screamed out, 'It's a bunyip before our eyes!' Their screams evoked a frantic storm of shots as the police opened fire on the animal before them.

Ned yelled out, 'Fire away, you buggers, you can't hurt me!'

When the police realised it was Ned, they took up his invitation and continued to ply lead into him as rapidly as they could. His body jolted a little with every bullet that collected his armour, as though he were being punched. The bullets seemed to have no effect, and the police began to wonder if perhaps he truly was invincible.

Ned's arm was severely wounded by this time, making it hard for him to shoot, and he was lame, but he still wielded his revolver, trying to pull the trigger.

Sergeant Steele crept up behind Ned, shooting him in his leg. Ned sank a little as his leg gave way and blood spurted from the wound. With his injuries and heavy gear, Ned was unable to turn quickly enough to shoot Steele, who launched himself onto Ned and made a grab for his revolver. The police held their fire as the pair grappled over the pistol. Ned fired the gun at Steele's head during the struggle, but the shot missed and Steele wrestled the gun from Ned's weak hand. He brought Ned down with the help of Senior Constable Kelly, who added his weight, and they pushed Ned to the ground and kept him there.

A voice could be heard from inside the hotel, calling for another chance to exit. Many of the hostages figured that this would be their last chance, and they ran towards police lines one after the other. Thrilled with their new freedom, they were stunned as they were forced onto the ground face first and examined one by one. The police made sure that none of the escapees were part of the Kelly Gang and treated them all as if they were suspects. The rest of the police quickly prepared their weapons for the next round and commenced yet another episode of attack on the hotel and the remaining gang members.

Among the wounded were both of Ann Jones' children, and the little family and other injured people rushed off to Wangaratta hospital, where Ann's son later died. Poor old Martin Cherry, a local man, had been hiding in the kitchen, too wounded to get himself out of there and was overlooked when the last of the hostages escaped.

Maggie first arrived on the scene and was ordered to leave by the police but did not. Kate arrived shortly after, and they both tried pushing their way through the crowd. 'Let us speak with our brothers, hold your fire! You must let us speak with them! You must!' They themselves became violent and loud, desperately calling for everything to cease and pleading with the police, 'Hold your fire! Stop this! Stop this now! Hold your damn fire!'

The Kelly girls realised that Ned had been captured, and they knew that the rest of the men simply would not give up. They wanted to find a way to get Dan and his friends out of there without the need to surrender. If the truth be told, they would rather see the men die than surrender to the dogs who were shooting them down, but how could they help their brothers escape now? The police ignored the sisters' pleas anyway. Together, Kate and Maggie watched the attack, unable to do a thing apart from screaming for it all to end over the thunderous and relentless sounds of weapons blasting the inn. Onlookers were coughing with the thick gun smoke, which was making it hard for anyone to see in front of them.

With the pounding of lead raining down on the hotel, Dan took a bullet and fell to the ground. As Steve kneeled over his friend to see if he was still alive, he, too, took a spray of buckshot that shredded his flesh and blew him over. He landed next to his mate and their discarded armour.

By three o'clock in the afternoon, mistakenly thinking that Dan and Steve were saving their ammunition and holding out for the dark to make their getaway, the police plotted to flush the men out of the hotel using flame.

Senior Constable Johnson dashed to a local stable to collect some hay. As he returned to the police lines through the edge of the bush, he came face to face with a collection of heavily armed, surly men on horses. He didn't recognise any of them but knew instantly they were not policemen. Thinking they could only be Kelly sympathisers waiting for the right moment to assist the gang, he pretended he was looking for his horse and asked them if they had seen his mare, to which they did not reply, and he hurried past them.

Johnson wanted to be a hero. He tiptoed from tree to tree and made his way to the side of the hotel with a bundle of straw, kerosene and matches. He stuffed the hay into a crevice at the base of the wall, poured the kerosene over the hay and threw the lit match onto it before running away. Flames slowly grew as the fire took off and spread under the wall. The calico lining inside the hotel sparked up, sending flickering flames up to the roof of the hotel in no time.

Kate and Maggie were looking for a way to get to their brothers. They were screaming out but were ignored by the police. Kate's arms and fists were flying at the men trying to hold her back. Her voice was hoarse, and it seemed too late for her to do anything as she watched the flames rise up before her eyes and engulf the public house.

Loud bursts of exploding ammunition sent intense flames surging towards the sky.

Maggie screamed at the police, 'You murderers! Murderers! Get them out of there! Dan, Steve, Danny!'

Kate called out fruitlessly to the boys, 'Danny, Joe! Get them out! You murderers! Get them out! Let me through. Let me in there! Danny, Danny, Danny!' Rage and confusion were mixed with shock as Maggie and Kate cursed and yelled at the police some more.

Finally, Father Gibney, a priest from out of town, took action, appalled at the decision to burn the men out. Racing to the hotel, he and another man rushed into the back of the hotel and located Martin Cherry. Barely alive, he was swiftly lifted out and given the last rites moments before he took his last breath. Thanks to the brave and determined efforts of the priest, the remnants of a few more bodies were also dragged out, including Joe, Dan and Steve's. The wailing from the Kelly girls could be heard a great distance away.

Ned was carried over to the train station, maybe two hundred yards away, where Father Gibney gave him his last rites, fully expecting him to die. News correspondents telegrammed their words and artists sketched their impressions about the biggest story of the moment, which were fed to media outlets across Australia, the United States and England. Father Gibney said to Ned, 'You must ask the Lord for mercy. Repeat after me, "Lord Jesus have mercy on me."'

Ned looked at the holy man and said, 'It is not today that I began to say that, Father.'

Another of Ned's sisters, Grace, walked over to the station where she sat herself down near Ned; pale and in a trance-like state, she said nothing.

Exposed to one horrific scene after another, Kate and Maggie ran to the charred remains of their brother Dan and precious friends Steve Hart and Joe Byrne. The sight was sickening. Joe's body was scorched on one side but still recognisable and intact. But their brother Dan and gang member Steve were nothing more than lumps of torched flesh, not even whole bodies, and the sad and sickly smell was pungent and offensive.

This heartbreaking vision and odour dropped Kate to her knees, and she covered her face with her ash-stained hands. With black and grey smears covering her youthful skin like war paint, Kate felt as though someone had reached into her chest and ripped out her heart. Her mouth was open wide and her head upturned as she sucked in the smoke-filled air and wailed from the deepest parts of her soul.

Sometime later, Kate went across to her oldest brother and sat down, placing her arms around his neck, wiping his temple as she cried and looked into his eyes, wondering if he, too, would die. He was covered in blood and bullet wounds.

Joe's body was grabbed and snuck out to Benalla by the police before the girls could do anything about it. The constables strung it up at the police station so photographers could have their way before the police quickly buried him.

Amid the foul smell of smoke from the smouldering remnants of the pub, more than five hundred onlookers had arrived from around the district. They had witnessed the Kelly sisters' abusive tirade at the authorities, and seen the infamous Ned Kelly who lay wounded. The voices from spectators, police, sympathisers and journalists dissecting what had just happened could be heard over an eerie silence.

Kelly family friend Wild Wright, cousin Tom Lloyd and Steve's devastated brother, Richard Hart, wrapped Dan and Steve's corpses in blankets.

Maggie walked towards the smoking ruins of the hotel and began threatening and abusing Senior Constable Johnson, the fire starter, as he raked out the hot remains of the inn. 'How dare you! Yer no good, murderer. Look what yer done. Sleep with one eye open, Johnson! Yer murdering bastard son! We will seek revenge on you, murderer!'

Maggie lunged towards the constable with every intention of throttling him, but Tom grabbed her and pulled her back into his arms while she yelled some more. Her face was smeared with ash and tears as she defeatedly let Tom guide her away. He whispered to her that he would remove the charred bodies before the police could deny them the right. Swiftly, Tom and the others collected the two covered corpses and loaded them onto a wagon, escaping as quickly as they could to the McDonnell's Railway Tavern, where many stiff drinks were had and threats of revenge were made before they took the bodies to Maggie's property.

On the platform of the Glenrowan train station, Ned, in enormous pain but not showing it, lay still while a doctor tended his wounds. A silk cummerbund was revealed, wrapped across Ned's torso, and the doctor could not help but wonder about the significance of such a garment.

'This seems a very special object, Mr Kelly?'

'It is a symbol from better days, Doctor.'

'Should I remove it for you? I need to treat your wounds.' Ned nodded permission for him to unravel the sash.

'It is important to you, no doubt. Who gave it to you?'

'The green silk represents the colour of the shamrock, Doctor. It was given to me by a family for saving their boy from drowning on the way to school. Fifteen years ago. A time when people thanked me for my bravery.' Ned grimaced as the doctor poured alcohol into his wounds and dug around with his bullet tweezers.

'You can have it, Doctor. I won't need it where I am going.' The doctor raised his eyebrows and swiftly placed the cummerbund into his leather bag of medicines. 'That is a kind gesture. I will look after it.'

Ned was observed by many onlookers, journalists and passers-by who wrangled their way close enough to engage with him if they got the chance. Everyone was trying to get their piece of Ned. They wanted some kind of connection with the notorious man so they could either use it for material in their reports or just as a claim to fame, a story to tell their loved ones.

In his usual style, at no point did Ned give away his sympathisers or cohorts. As the result of the terrible events started to sink in, the new awareness of his total defeat left him in a state of solemn quietness. Six troopers surrounded him. Bullet wounds bled from his foot, legs and arms. In the coming days, he would be covered in dark bruising all over his chest where the bullets that dented his armour had hit his body with a force like that of a horse kicking him.

Kate and Ned were both deeply affected by the sorrow of the dramatic events as he waited to be taken to Benalla. Looking at Ned broke Kate's heart, but at least he was alive. The family's goodbyes were painful.

'Is it true, Kitty? Are they all dead?'

'It's true.' Kate was sobbing.

'I wish I was wiv' 'em, Kitty.'

'You can't be sayin' that, Ned. We need yer alive. What a tragedy this has become. I cannot believe what I have seen wiv me own eyes.'

'Things went wrong, Kitty.'

'Be strong, brother, and we will see you in Benalla at first light.'

Ned was placed onto a wagon and taken to Benalla police station, where he was kept under watch the whole evening. Overnight there was enormous fear that the many Kelly sympathisers, family and friends would liberate Ned, so there was a strong police presence outside his cell. In the early hours of the morning, the police loaded the wounded and lame Ned, who could hardly move, into a spring cart with eight armed police guarding it and relocated him to the Benalla train station. Ned's sisters spent time with him at the station, sharing an outpouring of grief and emotion, saying goodbye before he was transported to Melbourne.

Taken to the hospital at Melbourne Gaol, Ned lay recovering not far from his mother's cell, but it would be days before she was allowed to see him.

ELLEN'S NIGHTMARE

In her tiny cell, only nights before the Glenrowan siege, Ellen Kelly had been thrashing and turning in her sleep. She had sung out many times, yelling warnings to her children. Other prisoners could hear her. It went on for a long time. Screaming, crying and yelling were not uncommon throughout the suffering of one's sentence, but Ellen was dreaming.

Imagining that she was flying across the sky, she looked below and she could see the firing weapons and the thick clouds of gun smoke rising up from Ann Jones' Hotel. Flames almost touched her soaring body and heavenly wings as she screeched like a white cockatoo.

Alarmed by her new appearance as a bird and the terrible sound she had adopted, Ellen swooped down low, as close as she could to find her babies. She could see many of them. Her daughters looked up at the white cockatoo and screamed at her with tears running down their faces. They pointed to Dan, who was full of bullet holes, bleeding alongside the carcasses of Steve and Joe.

Without warning, the scene changed and she was hovering above her oldest son in a prison cell, where he was singing 'The Wild Colonial Boy' and 'The Wearing of the Green'. She looked down at him and could see that he was lying on the cell floor with a white cloth over his head.

Ellen was screaming in her waking life. She jerked herself out of her slumber and sprayed vomit in the corner of her cold cell, sweat dripping from every pore. She grabbed her stomach, like there was a lead ball inside it. She knew something terrible was coming, she could feel it in every part of her being. It was a vision, a warning. A mother knew. She hoped she was wrong but had seen too much to fool herself. She awaited the very worst news a mother could receive. She wished she could hold her children.

Father Aylward visited Ned at the Melbourne Gaol hospital as his spiritual adviser, sitting patiently by his bed for some time every day since he'd arrived from Glenrowan. Only days after Ellen's dream, the priest had to visit her to tell her the sad news of the Glenrowan catastrophe. He was the first person to break the news of Ned's injuries, Dan's fate and that of their friends.

Ellen was an unimpassioned woman to those outside the family. So Father Aylward was caught by surprise when she burst into tears as soon as he started to tell her what had happened. 'I knew it. I knew some evil thing was about. I could feel it in me guts,' she sobbed. 'Not my Danny boy . . .' She sank her head into her hands.

Rubbing her eyes and wiping her tears, she looked up again to ask, 'What of Ned, Father? Yer say he has injuries. Where is he? Will he die, too?'

'He took a lot of bullets, Ellen. The doctors are impressed by his physical strength, though, and he will probably recover. They say it was touch and go, he lost a lot of blood. He is here at Melbourne Gaol.'

'I must see him then. Take me to him, Father!'

'I have asked already on your behalf, Ellen. They say you cannot right now.'

'Rubbish, he is my son. Can you not persuade them, Father? Make them change their minds?'

'I have tried, Ellen. I promise you. I suspect they are afraid of letting family or supporters aid him in any way.'

'But I am a prisoner myself. What could I possibly do to "aid" him?'

'Ellen, I promise you I will make sure you get to see your son as soon as possible.'

'Me life is a life of sufferin'. Yer have no notion of me pain, Father. Another child gone. Me own son, who I have not set eyes on for two years, and another lies in pain not far from me and I cannot see him. Cruel. Cruel. Cruel. This life is just a torment.' Ellen sobbed tears of loss and frustration.

'I had a dream, yer know. I saw it all just days ago. Do yer believe me, Father? Do you believe in premonitions?'

'I have not had the experience myself, but that does not mean to say I do not believe it is possible. Let's pray together.'

'Pray for Ned, I beg yer, Father. Pray that me son will live and be a free man again.'

The priest reassured Ellen that it would only be a matter of days before she would get to see her son but warned that she should brace herself for what was to come.

'They are deciding now what they can charge him with. He will have to go back to Beechworth when he is a little better for the preliminary trial. The outcome of a court case could be very bad. You must prepare yourself.'

Ellen could not bear to think of the trial against Ned or what terrible outcomes awaited him. She wished only to see her son and hold his hand. At least at this moment, Ned was alive. Ellen's sadness about Dan was painful enough; she couldn't survive losing yet another child. She hoped that someone would get messages through to her during the trial in Beechworth; she felt so far away from everything and everyone.

17

Ned's Court Case, Beechworth and Melbourne, 1880

DAVID GAUNSON MEETS THE KELLYS

Kate and Maggie heard all about David Gaunson long before they ever met him. The 34-year-old Melbourne lawyer had claimed the rural seat of Ararat in 1875 with help from the much older Graham Berry, a radical politician who would serve as premier of Victoria for three terms.

No matter what Gaunson did, he always managed to provoke negative comments in the press. He was referred to as a youthful, impertinent gutter percher. The gutter comment related to his many working-class constituents and one of his clients, Madame Brussels, the keeper of Melbourne's most infamous brothel.

In 1877, the year before the Fitzpatrick Incident, Berry, Gaunson and others formed a vocal alliance known as the 'stone-wallers' who harassed the then premier James McCulloch by relentlessly pushing for progressive land tax reforms. Gaunson's prominent role in the attack helped the Liberals to crush McCulloch in the election that year. It delivered a huge majority in the lower house, and Berry formed his government. Gaunson was pegged by those within the party as an impressive, young, 'native born' Liberal to watch and was rewarded for his role in the landslide victory with the positions of Deputy Speaker of the House and Chairman of Committees.

Giving families like the Kellys hope, Premier Berry recognised the outrageous rule that only property owners could be elected to the Victorian upper house, and he also shone a light on the fact that only eight hundred men owned all of the grazing land in Victoria. Gaunson, Berry and his radical government wanted to introduce land tax and other reforms to smash the squattocracy's stranglehold, make election to the upper house a possibility for working-class people and reduce the powers of the upper house at the same time.

Gaunson's campaign for change dovetailed neatly with every-thing Ned had been thinking, speaking and complaining about. But the change that the politicians pushed for was to take place at the core of legal, democratic process, whereas Ned's radical dream hovered outside the law.

In parliament, Berry had much to say about his upper house counterparts and the exclusive system its members relied on for power. Berry came out swinging at the representatives, and it left the powerbrokers sweating.

'The upper house robs the people of the gold in the soil and the land God gave them. Changes are necessary and are afoot.'

The men threw it all back in Berry's face. 'Block it. We will block everything you put forward!'

'There will be no changes, Berry!'

'Over our dead bodies!'

Berry showed his defiance, threatening the upper house by saying, 'Refusal to support these changes will lead to members getting what they deserve!' The white, wealthy men were up in arms as they interpreted Berry's comments as a possible threat of revolutionary violence, which was never his intention. After all, that had been Ned's domain.

The corrupt systems that Ned believed ruined his life and oppressed everyone in his class were highlighted through Berry's own attempt to wrestle power from the privileged men of parliament. Throughout 1877 and 1878, the men of the upper house dug their heels in further, never willing to relinquish their power until torchlit street protests supporting Berry showed the politicians that working-class people, however downtrodden, would put up a fight, and from that Ned had taken hope.

So, despite their resistance to Berry's reform bill, the upper house did support some changes because of their fear of repercussions. But the land tax measures that Gaunson had helped to introduce had been meddled with in the political process, and by 1879 he was distressed by the results, which had indirectly punished the working class. To make matters worse, tax incentives that were supposed to accompany the new measures never eventuated, leaving rice and barley with a new duty that only added to his constituents' burdens.

In December 1878, Gaunson was greeted by over six hundred cheering locals at the largest public meeting seen in Ararat. He addressed the crowd and talked at length about his dilemma in Melbourne.

'The opposition has shamelessly blocked the legislation I have fought for! They have boldly butchered the very reform bill that is the only hope of a fairer future for the working classes.' The crowd booed, desperate for the elite to get their feet off their necks. 'My friends, it is more important than ever that I be re-elected when the time comes to continue this crucial work.' With cheers of support, they lauded the man they placed all their hopes in.

It was rumoured that the outlawed Ned met with Gaunson privately not long after his Ararat speech and discussed his proposed Republic of North-Eastern Victoria, but the politician could not risk admitting it to anyone.

Gaunson would never have anticipated that only a year or so after that encounter he would be meeting with Kate, Maggie and their cousin Tom to discuss representing Ned in court.

'Politics. It all comes down to politics, my friends. You would be best advised to allow me to represent you.' Mr Gaunson had been talking himself up to the Kellys before the trial and, given the changes that Gaunson and Berry had been lobbying for, Maggie and Kate thought he was a good choice. Those politicians were leading a fight for the working class, they were trying to achieve real change, and from what Kate and Maggie could gather, Gaunson held power and sway with those at the highest levels of government.

'However, even if you do engage me to represent your brother, I will need to hear it from him.' Ned had been brought to Beechworth for his preliminary trial, but Kate and Maggie knew it was impossible to get to him; they had tried again and again, only to be knocked back every time.

Ned's cell was at the rear of Beechworth Gaol, nearest the governor's house so he could keep a watchful eye on him. Maggie had tried to deliver a clean, smart shirt to her brother for court but was refused entry. 'If I can't hand it to my brother and see him, you damn well take it and give it to him for me.' Maggie held the neatly folded shirt out for the guard.

'No, Mrs Skillion. We have strict instructions not to let any of you Kellys anywhere near him or pass anything to him.' The guard sneered at her.

Maggie stamped her feet and raised her voice. 'This is an outrage and a disgrace. He has every right to see his family and friends.' Maggie walked away, devastated once again.

At close to midnight, just hours before the trial was due to start, Gaunson was allowed to see Ned. A guard accompanied him, rattled his keys loudly and opened the metal door.

Ned looked at the man with a searching glance. Gaunson said, 'Good evening,' and extended his hand, discreetly passing Ned a note. He waited for him to read it. 'Well, Kelly, what do you say?'

'I say, I can depend my life on my sisters.'

The note was a letter from Maggie advising Ned that the family had decided to ditch the proposed legal representative Mr Zincke, who had often represented the Kellys, and employ Mr Gaunson to defend Ned instead. Mr Zincke was the hard-working solicitor who had also been representing many of the sympathisers. He had spoken up against the injustices being committed against them and managed to get some good results, so it was a tricky choice to make. Kate and the others just hoped it was a good move by going with the politically connected Gaunson, but only time would tell.

'Your sisters have engaged me, but do I have your full consent to step in?'

'If my sisters have confidence in you, that is good enough for me.'

Gaunson sat himself next to Ned on the bed. 'If a man is to defend you, there must be confidence.'

'I agree.'

'And I cannot defend you if I do not know all the facts. That requires more time than I have had.'

Ned nodded and waited to see if Gaunson had a plan.

'Personally, I think we need to delay the start of the trial so that I can familiarise myself with the details.'

'Agreed. But until this moment I have received no visitors. I have been kept here like a wild beast, and those I trust have not been allowed to come within cooee of me. I am on trial for my life, and it is unjust to be treated like this.'

Gaunson agreed with Ned. 'It is unacceptable, and I will challenge it tomorrow, I assure you. I do not want to keep you up any later, so I will take my leave and see you in the courtroom tomorrow.'

Deemed by the press as having just enough intelligence to be offensive, sufficient vivacity to be mischievous and just so much personal insignificance to avoid being chastised for his behaviour, Gaunson's notoriety would skyrocket with his involvement in Ned's trial.

BEECHWORTH COMMITTAL HEARING, 6 AUGUST 1880

Kate and Maggie organised a cousin to look after the children so they could be at the initial hearing in Beechworth. The freezing month of August didn't stop the courtroom from being packed to overflowing, and the press abounded.

The sisters were escorted into the courtroom before the heavy wooden doors opened at 10 a.m., and they watched from their cold, hard seats as the room was rushed with keen spectators who pushed and shoved their way in, so as not to miss out on a seat. The gallery and the chamber were quickly filled to the brim with many women, new female devotees of the infamous Ned Kelly.

The troopers appointed to guard Ned, acutely aware of the enormous crowd watching them, competed with each other to take charge of the limping, shackled and cuffed prisoner as they transported him into the dock. Ned met them with a smug grin. 'Well, gentlemen, you were not so keen to meet me just over a month ago.'

Kate had read reports in the lead-up to the trial that focused not just on Ned but also on her. One piece in the *Australian Town and Country Journal* said:

> Kate Kelly, the sister of the notorious outlaws . . . whose name has been so prominently before the public during the twenty months the Kelly gang has terrorised the north-eastern district of Victoria is about [seventeen] years of age . . . Her expression is one of extreme melancholy . . . imbued with the reckless courage that made Ned Kelly so infamous . . . Kate is a dashing horsewoman and on numerous occasions has defeated the efforts of large numbers of police to follow her . . . It is more than hinted that the immunity enjoyed by the outlaws so long was largely due to the dauntless energy and activity of Miss Kelly . . . She was repeatedly seen in all parts of the north-eastern district but none of the police could trace her.

Deemed of 'a lively temperament' in some of the articles about her, Kate wondered what her temperament had to do with her brother's right to freedom. And when journalists speculated in the press that she had indulged in many humorous gags at the expense of the police who were keeping her under strict surveillance, she hoped that people would not lose sight of how much of a violation that surveillance had been. By the end of Ned's trials, she would admit to a journalist that some days she wished she'd never been born at all, the way the Kellys had been treated.

Members of the press also wondered about Ned's new lawyer, speculating that he had taken on the case to increase his own profile. Gaunson was very good at manoeuvring himself and playing the political game, as demonstrated by his position and connections. But was he just taking on the Kelly case for notoriety and promotion of the legal practice he shared with his brother? Whatever his personal incentive was, the Kellys placed their trust in him, while Premier Berry formed new doubts about his political ally.

As proceedings began, Mr Gaunson asked immediately for

a delay. The Assistant Prosecutor for the Crown, Mr Charles Alexander Smyth, put forward that he had no objection to a delay but suggested it should be granted after the witnesses, who had all travelled to Beechworth, had submitted their evidence.

Mr Gaunson sprang back at his opponent, 'Cross-examine the witnesses when I have no details of the case?'

Mr Smyth responded swiftly, 'They have all been published in the newspapers.'

Mr Gaunson played to the crowd, looking across the attentive faces in the room with a smile as he replied, 'I am very pleased to say, Your Honour, that I never read the papers.' The crowd laughed, and Smyth was annoyed.

Mr Foster, the police magistrate who was presiding over the hearing, leaned back in his brass-buttoned coat and felt around for his pocket watch.

Police magistrates were exactly that: police and magistrates. Foster's job combined the detection of crime and the apprehension of offenders with the duties of sentencing and punishing. In the previous two years, he had been responsible for remanding many of the Kelly supporters, most without cause.

Aware of the press coverage, he considered the request momentarily. 'I'll allow it. However, it will be short.' He looked at his watch and slid it back into his coat pocket. 'Mr Kelly, you have until 2 p.m. to consult with your solicitor.'

Kate and Maggie dodged the reporters who stuck to them like glue as they followed Mr Gaunson and hoped they could be part of the meeting with Ned. The electric telegram department had made preparations to cope with an anticipated surge of newspaper messages that could send the wires into meltdown. The excited crowd left the building together as they chatted in small groups and waited outside for the recommencement.

A reporter spotted a man he thought was a potential sympa-thiser and stood in front of him. 'Sir, what will happen to Mr Kelly do you expect?'

'He will not be found guilty. No, he will not hang. Something will interfere before that could happen.'

'What is this "interference"?'

'I couldn't say anymore. Excuse me.' The mysterious gentleman walked away and disappeared into the crowd.

The reporter asked a gentleman in a suit where he was from. 'I am in fact a very well-known citizen of Beechworth, I'll have you know.' But he refused to let the reporter print his name.

'What has been your experience of the Kelly Gang, good Sir?'

'It is as true as the shoes I am wearing here today that one night I was in Finch Street when I witnessed two persons dressed in women's clothing. From their horses they leant down asking me for directions to certain streets.'

'And who were these persons, Sir?'

'Why it was the prisoner himself, Ned Kelly, and his colleague in crime, Joe Byrne.'

The reporter was shocked. 'They went to such lengths to remain incognito?'

'Well, I suppose it must be so, why else would they go to such peculiar trouble?'

It had been reported in the press that a woman's hat and veil had been left behind by Steve Hart after the gang's Euroa antics. It had been a disguise that worked well for them on occasion.

The crowd was back in the courtroom for the afternoon session. Kate and Maggie had been refused permission to see Ned yet again. Maggie needed to return home for the children, but Kate would reappear shortly. The audience resumed their places, and a sketch artist tried to capture Ned's likeness. The artist's graphic illustration depicted a proud Ned in his long smart coat standing tall in the dock, with a helmeted trooper standing guard beside him. The image would be seen by all of the colonies within days.

Gaunson sought permission for a chair to be provided to his lame client, and when Ned sat on it, an opossum rug was passed to him. Flashes of scarlet lining could be seen as Ned swung it out like a bullfighter and threw it across his lap to protect himself against the bitter cold of the freezing courtroom. Gaunson requested a further delay of one week, claiming that there were so many details to the case that he simply needed more time to digest them all. His request was futile, and the prosecution called their first witness.

Ned blew kisses to Ettie Hart, Steve Hart's sister and Ned's sweetheart. She returned the gesture as if no one else was watching. Random women in the crowd were besotted with the handsome bushranger and smiled at him intensely; they wanted some kisses of their own. Ned looked into the faces of each of the many admiring women until they blushed and turned away. He chuckled, but only for a moment. 'They wouldn't be smiling if they were in my position.'

Kate was permitted to enter the courtroom through a side door, used only by women and 'respectable folk', and was shown to a seat near Gaunson. Richard Hart, Steve's brother, who was with Kate, was refused entry and was rudely instructed that he had to go the long way around.

Kate raised her head in the direction of the dock and exchanged a look with her big brother. Not far behind Ned there was a small fire, ineffective in the austere room. Kate watched as Richard Hart warmed his back at it before he slowly edged towards Ned. He worked himself closer and closer, and Kate was surprised by his bold effort. Richard hoped to get close enough to pass on information to Ned about his supporters, but the troopers stationed at either side of the dock turned to face him. One raised his arm, indicating that Richard should come no closer, and so he retreated.

Constable McIntyre, the only survivor from Stringybark Creek, was a key witness at the hearing. Whether Ned would go to trial for murder or not was mostly down to his evidence. The deaths of Lonigan, Kennedy and Scanlon still haunted McIntyre, but what disturbed him more than anything was the way he had been branded as a coward by Ned Kelly in all of his conversations and letters since Stringybark; everyone had been talking about it, and it deeply affected him. McIntyre's guilt over the way he had taken Kennedy's horse and abandoned his colleagues had made him sick, but he'd still made a claim for some of the Kelly reward, which he was denied. During the wait for the trial, the policeman kept changing his account of what happened at Stringybark, and the bushranger's recent comments, in his letters and to anyone who would listen, had further corroded McIntyre's credibility. McIntyre's eyes were hollowed and dark, and his gaunt, pale face was covered in a woolly beard to try to mask his ill health.

The only other witnesses to be cross-examined were men who had either partaken in conversations with Ned about the shootings at Stringybark Creek or those who had overheard those conversations.

McIntyre's main goal at the trial was to eradicate any possibility that Ned could claim self-defence for any of what happened to his police colleagues that dark day.

McIntyre lowered his hand after promising to tell the whole truth and then began describing some of what happened. After a while, Mr Smyth asked him to tell everyone what Ned had said to him at Stringybark Creek.

'I asked the prisoner, "Do you intend to shoot me?"' McIntyre looked across at Mr Foster to make sure he had his attention. 'Kelly replied, "No. What would I want to shoot you for? If I wanted to, I could have done so half an hour ago when you were sitting on that log."' McIntyre coughed a little and rubbed his sweaty palms together, conscious of how quiet the room had become and how many eyes were on him.

'Kelly then told me about the police he hated. He said, "At first I thought you were Constable Flood. It is a good job for you that you are not him because if you had been, I would not have shot you, but would have roasted you on that fire. There are four men in the police force if ever I lay hands on them I will roast them. They are Fitzpatrick, Flood, Steele and Strachan. Strachan has been bragging that he would take me single-handed."'

There was a disgruntled murmur through the public gallery about Strachan's bold threats.

McIntyre continued, 'When he saw all the arms in my tent, the prisoner said, "Well, that looks as if you came out to shoot me." I said, "You can't blame the men, they have got their duty to do." The prisoner replied, "You have no right to go about the country shooting people."'

The audience responded, booing the notion of the police pursuing the gang to shoot them down, and Foster told the crowd to calm down.

'Carry on,' said Smyth.

'The prisoner then said to me, "I suppose some of you damned police will shoot me some day, but I will make you suffer for it beforehand."'

'Objection! Sir, objection!' Gaunson interjected, springing from his seat. 'I strongly object to these submissions, Sir. This is hearsay and conjecture. Anything could be invented. It is spoken about as if my client said these things, but there is no proof. No one else has witnessed McIntyre's conversations. This is a blackguardly proceeding, simply manufactured to bolster up an empty case against my client.'

The crowd supported Gaunson's protests with booing again. Kate looked over to Ned, who nodded at her. He was calmly watching it all unfold.

'Order! Order!'

The public quietened their protests.

'Overruled. Proceed, Mr McIntyre.'

Constable McIntyre's testimony and cross-examination continued for hours.

Before the court was adjourned for the day, Gaunson sought permission for Ned's family to see him in gaol. Mr Foster replied that he would have an interview with Gaunson about the matter during the evening, but at that meeting Gaunson was unsuccessful. The solicitor finally decided to telegraph for authority to the premier, who acted as Chief Secretary over these matters.

In a new day of testimony, James Gloster, a draper, was called on to give evidence. While hawking with his offsider at Faithfulls Creek Station, Gloster had been held up and taken hostage by Ned and the gang in the lead-up to the Euroa robbery. During this time, Ned had supposedly spoken to Gloster about the events at Stringybark Creek.

Mr Smyth asked Gloster to share what Ned had said to him.

'My impression was that the prisoner, Mr Kelly, talked about himself as shooting the police at Stringybark Creek in order to protect his mates. He seemed desirous of impressing upon us the idea that the police party intended to shoot them.'

'Oooooh,' the crowd gently responded but quietened before Foster had to reprimand them.

'I gave a report to the police afterwards explaining that the prisoner's conversation was filled with complaints about the police.

I understood Kelly to mean that once a man offended, even if he had paid for his crime, the police would never leave him alone. He complained that his mother had been sentenced harshly on false evidence from Fitzpatrick.' The audience were booing and raising their fists, as Foster slammed his gavel down with no effect. For a moment, Kate felt hopeful about the trial.

Smyth spoke over the crowd. 'I suppose this was his justification for shooting Fitzpatrick at his mother's homestead years ago?'

More booing erupted from the crowd.

'Order! Order!'

Gloster responded calmly, unfazed by the commotion around him. 'Well, the prisoner said he was two hundred miles away when that took place. He also said to me that if the police didn't release his mother, he would overturn a railway train.'

The audience let out a collective 'Oooooooh!'

During a lunchtime adjournment, Gaunson received a written response to his second request for Ned to be allowed visitation from his family and friends: 'Considering the circumstances of the case, I must decline to vary the order of my predecessor in office. Graham Berry.'

In a private room at the courthouse, Gaunson scrunched up the telegram from the premier and threw it against the wall. Kate moved quickly out of the way as it ricocheted. She had been speaking with Gaunson briefly and was deflated by the news, but Gaunson dug his heels in when they returned to the court for the afternoon session.

'The whole community is concerned to see that the first principles of English justice are being abided by, Sir. My client asks for no privilege, concession or favour, but I must insist that the ordinary course of the law should be followed with reference to the friends and relatives of the prisoner having access to him, as he is not yet a convicted person.' The full gallery and chamber were in support of Gaunson's argument, and loud cheers and expressions of 'Hear, hear!' could be heard. 'In conclusion, Sir, I must ask that you maintain the law by allowing the prisoner's friends to visit him. It is you who has the power to grant permission.'

Mr Foster was only a police magistrate and was not going to ruffle any political feathers. 'I could not possibly override the order of the Chief Secretary, the premier himself, Gaunson. I should be happy, however, to make any representation to the government that might be desired.' Foster wrote something in his notes.

Over the following days, nine more witnesses contributed their evidence about the death of Constable Lonigan, and once that was complete the same was delivered again for the demise of Constable Scanlon and Sergeant Kennedy. By 11 August, they had battled through five days of proceedings. Mr Gaunson summarised his case, pleaded his concerns and protests on behalf of his client to the police magistrate and awaited Foster's decision.

Fidgeting in his chair, looking down on his packed courtroom, Foster paused momentarily, looking at his paperwork before he made his announcement.

'I'm afraid the only answer that can be found here on this day is that the prisoner is committed for trial, but only for the murder of Constable Lonigan. The case will be heard at the Beechworth Circuit Court, to be held on October 14.'

There was loud booing and frantic chatter. Ned's eyes were cast downwards, and Kate shifted restlessly on the cold wooden pew, helpless to assist her brother.

Gaunson raised his voice urgently over the crowd before his last opportunity disappeared. 'Sir, I ask that my client be given permission to speak with the press today.'

Foster looked at Gaunson in amazement. 'Request denied.'

Gaunson slumped in his seat.

'This court is adjourned. Guards, remove the prisoner.' Foster lifted himself quickly from his chair and slid out the door behind him to his chambers.

The spectators were disgruntled, and noisy conversations filled the air as the attendants cleared the court and journalists hurried out to convey the news. Kate rushed towards the dock and Ned leaned down, clasping her hands as they kissed each other's cheeks and shared a few words before the guards pulled Ned away. Not to be outdone, she moved swiftly to the door that she knew they would remove her brother through and waited on the other side of it. Sure enough, the troopers brought Ned out and she grabbed his hands one more time as the party of armed police loaded him into the horse cab to take him back to the gaol. 'God be with yer, Neddy.'

Although the trial was set down for Beechworth in October, the government was terrified that a local jury would free Ned or that sympathisers would emancipate him. A summons was issued in September to change the venue for the hearing to Melbourne.

The judge appointed, and keen for the trial to start in Melbourne, was Judge Barry, who had been a strong influence behind Ned's trial being relocated. He supported the government's fears of a riot or of Ned becoming a free man again. Known as 'Hanging Barry', he was the man who had sentenced most of the Kellys to date. He had said to Ellen, as he sentenced her, that if Ned had been captured and tried with her for their alleged crimes against Fitzpatrick, he would have served up the harshest punishment possible to make an example of her son.

Barry was repulsed by what he saw as a new generation of wayward, troublemaking youth, which included both Ned and his supporters. The judge was determined to cleanse the nation of such people and settle the score with a man who was ruining the reputation of the colony. In two months' time, Judge Barry wanted to see Ned receive the harshest and most final sentence possible.

Even though Constable Fitzpatrick had been dismissed from the police force by this time, Ellen, Maggie's husband William Skillion and family friend William Williamson were still locked up in gaol. Ned remained steadfast that Fitzpatrick's evidence was foully false and that the lying constable had much to answer for.

DAY ONE OF NED'S MELBOURNE TRIAL, THURSDAY, 28 OCTOBER 1880

The press reporting on Ned's trial obsessed over his enormously loyal sisters, Maggie, Kate and Grace, so attractive in their dark dresses and veils of mourning. The newspapers' love–hate relationship with Kate had them admiring her 'dangerous smile' and the 'great natural intelligence' it revealed. But, at the same time, they made nasty comments about her class of origin and the destructive family from which she came. The press praised the Kelly sisters' love for their brother, but they ridiculed Kate's blind loyalty and her willingness to support Ned's unlawful activities. People were attracted to Kate's charisma, boldness and grit, yet at the same time they wanted to condemn her for those traits.

The hearing was set for mid-October at the Central Criminal Court in Melbourne. Mr Gaunson came very close to securing hotshot barrister Mr Hickman Molesworth for Ned's defence. Molesworth was in high demand and his father was a judge, but the barrister was expensive. Molesworth and Gaunson successfully achieved a delay of two weeks, hoping to sort out finances by then. Even with borrowed time, the Kellys couldn't get the cash to afford Molesworth and so they lost him, but Gaunson had one more move up his sleeve for what was going to be the most famous case of the year.

On the new trial date, 28 October, hundreds of people gathered at the Melbourne courthouse, pushing their way into the gallery, but police were everywhere with loaded revolvers, keeping the doors clear and excluding many of Ned's supporters. Over a thousand spectators were loitering in the hope of seeing this infamous bushranger.

When Kate, Maggie, Grace, Tom and the Wrights arrived from the Robert Burns Hotel in a horse-drawn cab, Kate felt a rush of panic as the eager crowd surged towards her. She was worried they would all be crushed in the frenzy. Then the excited masses turned, thinking Ned was coming from the gaol in the other direction, and they crushed each other trying to get to him. Kate and the others scurried into the building.

Inside, many of the spectators were more of Ned's new female admirers. Just as they had been drawn to Ned at the Beechworth committal hearing, women swarmed to see this infamous but attractive, renegade criminal in Melbourne. Ettie Hart arrived and sat herself next to Kate, both jittery with nerves. Ned looked around the room as the guards brought him in from the prison, and he limped across to the dock. His determined countenance flashed fire when he looked around the courtroom, but a look of ease came into his eyes when he saw his family and Ettie as he settled in the dock.

Ned gently blew Ettie kisses as he had done at the Beechworth trial, and she returned them to him. The other women of the courtroom glared with jealousy at her. The men seemed put out, too; if they didn't get that kind of attention from women, why should this criminal?

Judge Barry, wigged and frocked, arrived late with an air of arrogance about him, and everyone got to their feet as instructed.

After he made himself comfortable, the old man instructed those in the room to sit.

The morning commenced with lawyers from each side conducting a bitter fight over the selection of members of the jury. Ned and his defence team had suspicions about some candidates, and the prosecutors had doubts about others, so they whittled away to a composition that both sides could tolerate.

Gaunson, unqualified for this court, had withdrawn his services and appointed an unknown, Mr Henry Bindon, in an attempt to create a longer delay. No one knew anything about him, and Gaunson had asked Ned to trust his strategy. But the legal tactic employed by Gaunson backfired when the unfamiliar Mr Bindon asked for some extended time to look at his brief. Judge Barry was having none of it, and the trial pushed on immediately, leaving Ned and Bindon on the back foot.

Charles Smyth, Chief Crown Prosecutor, and Arthur Chomley, Assistant Crown Prosecutor, must have thought it was Christmas, to be up against a complete novice, but Kate was ropeable as she discussed with Maggie what they could do. 'Well, that didn't work. After all Gaunson's fancy talk at Beechworth, that Bindon hasn't even run a damned case like this before, and Ned still ain't allowed to testify.'

Maggie was aware of their dilemma and equally angered by it. Kate longed for reassurance, but she couldn't hide from the truth. 'They was only given forty-five minutes together before the trial started. Maggie, he's doomed like this.'

Constable McIntyre, the chief witness, was called up to testify first. Since the moment he had escaped from Ned at Stringybark Creek and first told his story, he had tried his hardest to make it appear that Ned shot Lonigan in cold blood. He was the only survivor of the police party, so he could say what he liked.

On the back of this *carte de visite* (a calling card or postcard) appear 'Kate Kelly?' in ink and the name of Adelaide photographer 'E.G. Tims' in pencil. A newspaper article from June 1879 refers to Kate, her sister Maggie, Tom Lloyd and Wild Wright being offered money by a photographer to go to Melbourne to have their portraits taken. It is possible that this photograph is from that session.

KATE KELLY.

This engraving was the first image of Kate Kelly to appear after the Glenrowan siege. Printed on Thursday 1 July 1880 in *The Illustrated Adelaide News* with Kate's name underneath it, the image bears a striking resemblance to the photograph attributed to E.G. Tims, and suggests that the photo above is indeed of Kate Kelly.

Ellen Quinn, Kate's mother, arrived in Australia as a free settler and married ex-convict Sean Kelly. Ellen outlived her first husband and many of her children including Anne, Ned, Dan, Maggie and Kate. She died at the age of 91 in 1923 but was reportedly older than records accounted for.

Margaret (Maggie) Skillion, Kate's older sister, worked with Kate to support their bushranger brothers while the young men were on the run. They also supported their mother while she was imprisoned for three years by keeping the homestead running and looking after Ellen's youngest children.

Left: Edward 'Ned' Kelly lived from 28 December 1854 (this birth date is assumed by Kelly descendants because neither his birth nor baptism were registered) until 11 November 1880.

Above: Jim Kelly was Kate's oldest brother after Ned. He was Kate's companion while she travelled with Flash Jack Donovan's troupe after Ned's execution, and, in 1898, he travelled to Forbes, in New South Wales, to collect Kate's children and take them back to the Kelly family after her death. Jim died in his sleep at age 87.

Left: Dan Kelly was one of Kate's older brothers and an active member of the Kelly Gang. He died at only 19 years of age and it is believed that his burnt remains were dragged from Ann Jones' Hotel at Glenrowan after the siege in 1880.

E.BRAY. PHOTO.   BEECHWORTH

Left: Alexander Fitzpatrick became a constable with the Victorian Police Force in 1877. In April 1878, he made an ill-fated visit to the Kelly homestead, now known as the 'Fitzpatrick Incident'. Fitzpatrick's affair with Kate Kelly had devastating consequences and at least two other women had children by him. Fitzpatrick was removed from the police force for misconduct and incompetence in August 1880.

Bottom: Oswald Thomas Madeley was the police photographer who took many photographs at the scene of the Glenrowan siege in 1880. In the days after the siege he devised a set of 19 photographs re-enacting the siege. This particular image, 'Group at the Kelly Tree', was taken at the site where Ned had been captured on Monday 28 June 1880.

THE KELLY GANG—From an original Photograph.
Steve Hart.   Dan Kelly.   Ned. Kelly.

This black-and-white printed postcard is believed to be of three Kelly Gang members, and is captioned 'Steve Hart. Dan Kelly. Ned Kelly.' The men are seated on horses in the middle of bushland on a dirt road most likely in the high country of the north-east of Victoria.

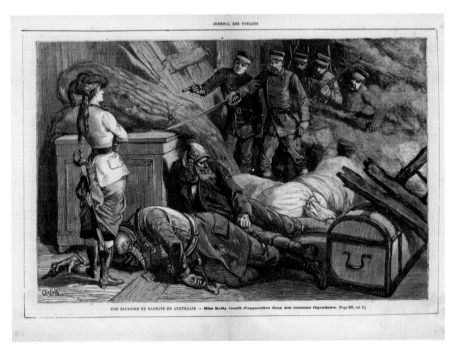

JOURNAL DES VOYAGES

UNE HISTOIRE DE BANDITS EN AUSTRALIE. — Miss Kelly venait d'apparaître dans son costume légendaire. (Page 205, col. 3.)

This engraving featuring Kate Kelly appeared in the French newspaper *Journal des Voyages*, 1883. The caption, which translates as 'Miss Kelly in her legendary costume', appeared under the headline *Une Histoire de Bandits en Australie* (A History of Bandits in Australia). This is an example of the wide-reaching appeal and fame Kate Kelly experienced and eventually tried to escape.

NED KELLY AT BAY.
FROM A SKETCH DRAWN ON THE SPOT BY MR. T. CARRINGTON.

Journalist and illustrator Thomas Carrington travelled with the police deployment from Melbourne on the special train and was present at the Glenrowan Siege in 1880. His wonderfully descriptive sketches and engravings appeared in *The Australasian Sketcher* on 3 July 1880, just days after the headline-making shootout.

A small portrait of Kate Kelly on horseback from a painting entitled *Dan Kelly, Steve Hart, Ned Kelly, Joe Byrne, Kate Kelly* by Australian artist Patrick William Marony, 1894.

A romantic interpretation of 17-year-old Kate Kelly breaking through police lines to get to her brothers at Glenrowan by George Washington Lambert. The oil-on-canvas work entitled *Kate Kelly during the last stand of the Kelly Gang* was painted in 1908, and shows that Kate Kelly continued to be depicted by artists long after the dramatic events of her youth and well beyond her death.

The authorities overseeing Ned's detainment in gaol were fearful of his escape and severely limited any visits by family members. But they did allow his request for a photograph to be taken and given to his family as a memento of his final days in Melbourne Gaol.

This photo of the Kelly homestead at Eleven Mile Creek, Greta, was taken in February 1881 to commemorate Ellen Kelly's release from gaol after serving just under her 3-year sentence. Pictured on the left is Kate with young Alice, then Ellen is seated to the right with a young girl often referred to as Grace, Jack and Ellen Jr. Reverend Gould stands to the far right.

Pictured here is possibly the only surviving photo of Kreitmayer's Kelly Gang wax figures, including Kate Kelly. In the *Launceston Examiner*, March 1882, an article entitled 'Waxworks Exhibition' describes the Kelly Gang display as 'a first-class representation . . . being very life like' and that 'Kate Kelly, the outlaw's sister, is also a good figure'.

Kate Kelly was photographed in her riding habit by A.C. Dreier to produce a series of *cartes de visite* (calling cards or postcards), which were very popular in the late 1800s. It is likely that these studio portraits were taken after Ned was hanged and while Kate was making her public appearances in travelling shows. An inscription on the back of the sepia card, auctioned in 2007, indicates it was bought at a waxworks display in New Zealand in 1881. An advertisement for 'The Great Waxworks Exhibition' in *The Newcastle Morning Herald and Miner's Advocate*, 1881, shows that it toured New Zealand and Queensland and included Kelly Gang figures.

The Apollo Theatre, which occupied the Eastern Arcade building on Bourke Street East in Melbourne, played host to Kate, her brother Jim, and Ettie Hart (sister to gang member Steve Hart and possibly Ned's sweetheart) the night of Ned's execution, 11 November 1880, to enormous crowds drawn by widespread advertising. Kate and the others faced stinging criticism in the press for their decision to make a public appearance on the day of Ned's death.

KELLY FAMILY.

MISS KATE KELLY AND HER BROTHER
WILL INTERVIEW ALL COMERS,

This Evening, Thursday, November 11,
AT THE

APOLLO HALL
BOURKE STREET EAST.

MISS ETTIE HART WILL ALSO APPEAR.

ADMISSION — ONE SHILLING.   *Commence at 8 o'clock.*

Cadow Station, established by pioneer James Collits in the 1830s, was where Kate first worked as a domestic servant when she came to the region in 1885. Pictured, top, is the main homestead, which no longer exists, and below is the servants' quarters, located near one of the station's orchards. This building still remains, and is most likely where Kate lived for the two years she worked at the property for Edward and Georgina Jones.

This widely circulated photograph of Kate was given to writer and bushranger enthusiast Edgar Penzig in the 1970s by an American family whose ancestors had lived in the Glenrowan region in the late 1800s.

William 'Bricky' Foster, also known as Bill or Will, was Kate's husband. In his later years Bricky lived a solitary life and rarely left his home. Neighbours recall that he had a framed photograph of Kate on his mantelpiece and a small tin of trinkets that he would sometimes show. He died in Forbes hospital in 1946 aged 79.

Post and telegraph office at Warroo Station, a large rural property next to Cadow Station. Hugh McDougall was the station manager at Warroo, and a friend of Kate's. He brought her to Cadow Station when he heard they were in need of a domestic servant. He sponsored Kate in this role and later in other similar roles in the township of Forbes. Hugh commissioned and paid for a headstone for Kate.

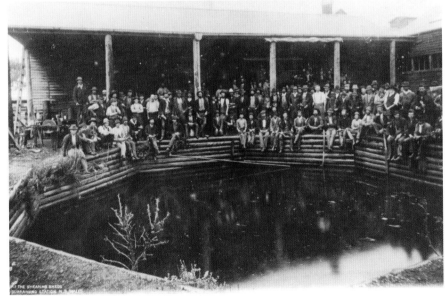

Burrawang Station, located across the river from Cadow and Warroo Stations, was about 34 miles from Forbes. In its heyday it employed hundreds of workers and produced thousands of bales of wool. Many of Burrawang's workers are pictured here on their morning break around the water supply that fed the steam engine that powered the shearing machinery they used. It's possible that Bricky Foster is among them.

When Kate left Cadow Station and moved into the township of Forbes, she worked as a domestic for a few families, eventually working for Mr Prow to help with his ten children after the death of his wife. Kate caught the attention of many admirers while running errands from the Prow house to the general store, and her future husband was one of them.

The streets of Forbes, c. 1890s. Bullock teams were a common sight and would travel across the countryside in all directions delivering supplies. A common route was from Forbes to Orange via the small town of Murga. Murga was a rest stop for bullock teams and their drivers, and also a staging post for the coaches transporting gold, goods and supplies.

The Forbes lagoon is where Kate Kelly's body was found on 14 October 1898. She was reported missing by her neighbour, and her body remained in the water for up to eight days until discovered by local man Mr Sullivan. He appeared at the courthouse on the morning of the inquest into her death to give evidence, but left before providing any information about his discovery of her body.

From 1870 to 1900 a major public works program led to the creation of grand buildings like the Forbes Courthouse. Built in 1880, it features an arched entrance portico to the central courtroom. It was the location of the district coroner's office and where the inquest into Kate's death was held.

Fred Foster, Kate Kelly's only son, was killed in action on 15 April in 1917, aged 28, while fighting in France during World War I. His service and death are recognised at the Villers-Bretonneux Memorial in Picardie, France.

Kate was buried at Forbes cemetery on 15 October 1898, the day of the inquest into her death. The inscription remembered Kate as William's 'beloved wife', but sadly made no mention of the children she left behind.

Discovered in the 1980s in the NSW town of Murga during house renovations, this .32 calibre revolver, made by Henckell & Co., Solingen, Germany, circa 1884, has the initials K.K. inscribed on the pistol grip. Opinion is divided as to whether it belonged to Kate or not. In 2007 it reached a staggering $72,870 at auction. A domestic servant who worked at Cadow Station years after Kate was given a similar weapon by the Jones family, and it's possible they gave this revolver to Kate.

Bindon knew that none of the police that were out pursuing Ned had done their duty and taken the warrants with them. 'Did you have warrants for the arrest of Daniel Kelly and Edward Kelly in your possession?'

'I did not see a warrant. I cannot swear that any of our party had a warrant.'

George Stephens, once a groom at Faithfulls Creek Station who had conversations with Ned during the Euroa hold-up, was called to the stand.

'Have you ever been a policeman?' Bindon knew that Stephens had been not only a policeman but also actively involved in the hunt for Ned as a private detective.

'Yes, I was discharged some time ago for a brief absence without leave. I do intend to seek employment with the police again.'

This witness was not some unbiased bystander who happened to be one of the Euroa hostages, like the prosecution was making out.

Despite these kinds of traps, Ned held his composure throughout the hearing. As Kate watched witness after witness testify, she wanted to scream out to defend her brother, but she knew she'd be turfed out of the court if she did.

Gloster was called on again; he had been honest in the Beechworth trial, and Kate held out a little hope that this man would help her brother's case. 'The prisoner told me that McIntyre had surrendered but Lonigan ran to a log, attempting to fire his weapon at him. Kelly said that he shot Lonigan in the head and that it killed him. He said it was a pity that Lonigan did not surrender, because he did not wish to kill any of them but only take their arms. In another conversation, Kelly said he reckoned he had stolen over two hundred and eighty horses, and if he had been arrested for that he would not have grumbled.'

Henry Dudley, also held up at Faithfulls Creek during the Euroa robbery, recounted Ned telling him, 'What would be better, me shooting the police or the police carrying my mangled body into Mansfield?'

It was a long day of little hope for Kate. The testimony and cross-examinations of nine witnesses continued until 11 p.m., much of the evidence repeated from the trial at Beechworth. By the time it was done, Kate, her sisters and the group she was there with were all drained. They gathered together outside the court and took their tired selves back to the hotel in cabs, trying to avoid nosy people and the press. They would return, to be there for Ned when proceedings commenced again from ten o'clock the next morning.

The jury was escorted under tight guard, and they remained in the custody of the sheriff's officers, locked up all night at the Supreme Court Hotel to ensure their incorruptibility.

DAY TWO OF THE TRIAL, FRIDAY, 29 OCTOBER 1880

Again, hordes of people swirled around the courthouse, trying to get in. They were keen to see Ned and hear this sensational case. Kate felt desperate about how proceedings were going so obviously against her brother. Bindon had managed to get some extra time with Ned in the morning, but she wondered if it would make any difference; the odds seem stacked against him. Ned sat in the dock wearing his black coat and white shirt, his light-coloured trousers concealing his shrapnel-filled legs.

By close to five in the afternoon, Kate was listening to Bindon make his closing arguments. 'How can it be over so quickly? How is it that me brother's life or death is to be decided in such little time? Sister, what is happening here?'

Maggie was just as concerned as Kate. 'Lord above, help us now. Kitty, this is a bloody disaster.'

Bindon tried to keep the jury focused. Much to his dissatisfaction, they had heard a lot of evidence that was padded out with anecdotes of stories and conversations that were unconnected with the death of Lonigan and reflected badly on Ned. He reminded the jury that certain things were irrelevant and should be ignored. 'In the interests and principles of fairness and justice, all evidence that does not relate to the death of Lonigan must be excluded. These matters should not have been brought forward in the first instance.' The crowd agreed and made noises in support of his argument. 'Furthermore, gentlemen of the jury, the only thing you need be concerned with is the shooting of Lonigan. I commit to you that you must remove anything else from your mind.'

The defence case focused on the fact that the police at the Stringybark Creek incident had not identified themselves as police to Ned and the others. Bindon was proposing to the jury that any member of the public would protect themselves if they were faced with a group of unknown and armed men in the bush. He was also suggesting that so many men had participated in the shootout that it would be irresponsible to single Ned out as the murderer of Constable Lonigan.

'The gang was in the bush lawfully, my friends, and let us remember that the police, also a kind of gang since there were four of them, appeared with arms in plain clothes in the form of an attempted ambush. If a fracas occurred between the bushrangers and the party of men unknown to them, it is dangerous to say that the first shot was fired by any particular man.' Bindon was looking slowly at each jury member and ignoring the contorted face of Judge Barry, who was most annoyed by Bindon's comments.

'The prisoner would not take a life unless his own was in danger.' Bindon paused, hoping this would resonate with the decision-makers. 'It would seem the police had a down on him. This is my client's belief. Lonigan lost his life in a fusillade, and the fact of Kelly being singled out as the murderer points to a desire to do away with him.'

Bindon stood tall, looking at each of the jurors individually. 'Nothing can cure a wrong decision once given. Would you take away the life of the prisoner based on the evidence from only one witness?' He stretched out his arm in the direction of Constable McIntyre. 'The others do not count, and he is a prejudiced witness at that.'

Yes! Kate was thrilled when Bindon pointed this out. There was hope.

'Can you say that Edward Kelly alone murdered Lonigan? The prisoner would give a different account, but his mouth is closed!'

Kate joined in with the applause Bindon received for highlighting how Ned was blocked from giving his testimony. Judge Barry stamped it out firmly and quickly. 'Order! There will be order!'

The audience settled again, but they felt lifted by Bindon's observations. Judge Barry bit back. 'It is incorrect to say that the prisoner's mouth is closed, as he has counsel to tell his story. If the prisoner made statements consistent with facts, he might be believed.' There was a groan from the family and friends sitting among the journalists and police.

'Furthermore, if four men went out with an intention to resist police and, on attack, one policeman was shot, each of the four would be guilty of murder and might be executed.'

There was an audible gasp from the tense spectators.

Can he really say these things? Kate was furious, her pulse racing, her eyes darting around the court.

'The police were performing their duty, and no person has a right to molest them, whether in uniform or not. The jury must remember, the criminal cannot be considered guilty of manslaughter.' Barry slammed his fist on the bench. 'It must be murder, or nothing.'

Kate slumped on the stiff wooden benches they all shared. 'This is hopeless.' She grabbed Grace's sweating hand and squeezed it tightly. Cousin Tom Lloyd was next to Maggie, and they were both looking straight ahead. Kate wanted to see their faces. She wanted to be able to look into her older sister's eyes and see that everything was going to be okay, even though in her heart she knew it wouldn't be. The tension and heat in the room were making her feel dizzy. There was a throbbing in her ears that had become so loud she was worried she wouldn't be able to hear what was being said.

Bindon persevered. 'Nevertheless, members of the jury, I trust that you will give a verdict that is very different to that which the court expects.'

It was ten minutes past five. The court was adjourned. That was it. A decision needed to be made by the twelve men, and suspense sat heavily in the room as the jury exited to make their deliberations.

THE VERDICT

Kate feared that the verdict would take a very long time, and she was unsure what to do. She and Grace considered going outside for fresh air but didn't want to deal with the masses of people or the journalists who had hassled them that morning. Maggie and Tom were whispering to each other. Kate and Grace sat silently, fanning themselves and holding the tension of the wait quietly within.

Time seemed to stretch out forever for Kate, but only twenty minutes had passed when she heard someone call out that the verdict would be announced. She held firmly on to Grace while her legs shook and she furiously said prayers in her mind.

Judge Barry looked over to the jury and asked the foreman to stand. As the man sprang up on command, the whole courtroom was deeply silent and all eyes were on him.

'What say you?' asked the judge.

'Guilty, Your Honour. The jury finds Edward Kelly guilty of the wilful murder of Lonigan.'

Kate could see Maggie's head drop. There was a collective gasp of disbelief, and many sighs and grumbling expanded to fill the room until the judge quietened everyone down. Kate's mouth was dry, she was sweating and hot faced, and she simply could not accept the verdict.

It was up to Judge Barry to determine the sentence. He turned towards Ned and said, 'The verdict pronounced by the jury is one which you must have expected.'

Ned stood and stared at the judge; his presence filled the room, and he had everyone's attention. He admitted that he had expected the verdict, due to what he saw as the unjust circumstances against him. Ned was adamant that if he had been given the opportunity to represent himself, he would have been exonerated. 'I should have examined the witnesses myself, but I thought if I did so it would seem like bravado or flashness. There is no bravado or flashness about me.'

The judge was doubtful of Ned's assertions and let him know. 'The facts are so numerous and so conclusive against you, Kelly, that no rational person could come to any other verdict.' Again, there was a collective outrage against the words of the judge, which seemed so biased.

Ned had plenty to say about the way he believed that the truth had been twisted. 'On the evidence given here, no man would have found any other verdict. I would have shown matters in a different light. Bindon knew nothing of my case.'

Judge Barry's voice of condemnation ploughed through the noise of the crowd. 'I do not doubt that you must be suffering great pain about the verdict and the sentence that awaits you . . .'

But Ned, ever defiant and boldly direct, insisted, 'I declare before God and man, that my mind is as easy and clear as it possibly can be.' There was a lot of noise from the court.

Appalled by the audacity of the young man before him, Judge Barry shouted back at Ned as if he himself were God's representative: 'It is blasphemous of you to say so. You appear to revel in the idea of having men put to death.'

'No!' said Ned, swiftly and passionately. 'I abhor death.'

The judge saw his opportunity to insult Kelly and his people. 'Unfortunately, in a new community, where society is not bound as closely as it should be, there is a class of people that disregards the consequences of crime. These unfortunate, inconsiderate, ill-educated, ill-conducted, unprincipled and ill-prompted youth must be taught to consider the value of human life. They are led to imitate notorious felons, whom they regard as self-made heroes.

'Furthermore, it is remarkable that although there was such a large reward for the detection of the gang, no person was found to discover it. There seemed to be a spell over the people of this particular district. There is something wrong when a lawless group of men, you and your associates, Kelly, are able to live eighteen months disturbing society.' Banter bounced between the two as the judge added his observation that Ned had stolen over two hundred horses in his short life.

'That has never been proven. It is held in English law that a man is innocent until he is found guilty.'

Barry raised his eyebrows, 'You are self-accused. We have had samples of felons and their careers, such as those of Bradley and O'Connor, Clark, Gardiner, Melville, Morgan, Scott, and Smith, all of whom have come to ignominious deaths; still the effect expected from their punishment has not been produced. This is much to be deplored. When such examples as these are so often repeated, society must be reorganised, or it must soon be seriously affected. Your unfortunate and miserable companions have died a death that probably you might rather envy, but you are not afforded the opportunity . . .'

Ned interrupted the judge's monologue. 'I don't think there is much proof that they did die that death . . .'

Speaking over the top of Ned, Barry asserted, 'In your case, the law will be carried out by its officers. The gentlemen of the jury have done their duty.'

Judge Barry threw a filthy look at Ned and hastened to the grue-some sentence. 'I have now to pronounce your sentence. You will be taken from here to the place from whence you came. You will be hanged by the neck until you be dead. May the Lord have mercy on your soul.'

Judge Barry's final words echoed in Ned's mind: 'To the place from whence you came . . .' Ned swiftly replied to the old man, 'I will go a little further and say that I will see you there, where I go!' There was a gasp at the power of the prisoner's words.

Barry responded in fury: 'Remove the prisoner!'

The crowd created a noisy background while Kate pondered the result. Watching her brother being removed in his shackles and cuffs made her heart sink. Ned turned to his family but was pushed away by the guards and taken back to his cell.

The shooting of Constable Lonigan was what it all came down to in the end. It was enough to end Ned's life. The argument that it was self-defence was never going to be persuasive to old Hanging Barry.

Kate supposed Ned had nothing left to lose anymore, and she knew that he wished he'd been destroyed with the others at

Glenrowan. She wondered what next steps they needed to take to save him. She could see Ned's comments to Barry had rattled him, and she'd enjoyed the fear she'd seen in Barry's face. It was a small moment of justice.

The thought of her brother hanging was painful. Ellen was relying on Kate and Maggie to keep her informed, and Kate dreaded the conversation that would have to take place.

Whether a criminal or an innocent man, a prisoner or free, her brother belonged to the Kellys, and their love for him was endless. But the newspaper reports against him were vile, and they made Kate furious. *The Northern Miner* was the worst:

Ned Kelly, bushranger and murderer, has been sentenced to death and his execution has been fixed for Monday, the eleventh of November at ten o'clock. That this fate is too good a fate for this devil's spawn, most people will think! The general feeling of the people of Australia is that the world is well rid of such a monster.

Kate couldn't believe that, after all their tribulations, her family would have to regroup, yet again, and keep persevering or they were going to lose another family member.

Finally, Gaunson's political position was helpful. He began harnessing support from The Society for the Abolition of Capital Punishment; made up of activists who created petitions, held public meetings and lobbied influential men to present talks and take the agenda to the government, the society's attempt to remove the death penalty continued well into the following century.

Gaunson and his cohorts copped a fair hiding in the press for publicly supporting Ned's right to a fair trial. Championing Ned's cause was deemed an outrageous thing for a politician to be involved in, and this allayed some of Kate's concerns about

Gaunson's sincerity. Perhaps he was genuine after all. She realised that politics was a different game to anything she had known before, and she had to trust that Gaunson knew what he was doing. He was all they had.

Secretly, Gaunson was thinking about the devastating political turmoil in recent years that had toppled Premier Henry Parkes' Government in New South Wales and how it might influence any chance of leniency for Ned. In 1865 another bushranger, Frank Gardiner, who was one of Ben Hall's offsiders, had evaded capture and started a new life in Queensland. He was pardoned in 1875 by New South Wales Governor Robinson, and there was a huge public outcry, which led to the defeat of Parkes' ministry. That experience was one of the reasons why Parkes contributed to the reward for the Kelly Gang after the Jerilderie robbery in February 1879.

During Ned's trial, the newspaper editors did not let anyone forget about the Gardiner affair. They saw the Kelly case as the perfect opportunity to remind the Victorian Government of the threat to their time in office if Ned was freed.

Gaunson knew that there was no way any political leader would ignore that threat. In his heart he knew that there was no chance at all that the Governor of Victoria would pardon Ned Kelly, but he was going to give it his best shot and follow all legal avenues.

It was time to try a new political stunt.

18

Fight for Ned's Life, November 1880

> Ned Kelly bushranger and murderer has been sentenced to death. We should never forget the fact that the first settlers in Australia were convicts of the worst class and that their descendants still retain the traditions, feelings and habits of the criminal classes from which they sprung. For this crime of bushranging there is only one effectual remedy—death.
>
> *The Northern Miner*, 4 November 1880

Despite the regular insults Kate and the Kellys were subjected to, from the moment of Ned's death sentence they worked tirelessly and with determination. They pounded the streets, garnering support from the public and getting signatures for their petition: a request to the government for mercy. Ned's only chance now was a reprieve.

Spied on by journalists, who prowled through the Robert Burns Hotel looking for the Kellys, the sisters ignored the intrusions but were always aware of the media's presence. The spies often witnessed Maggie and Kate in the front parlour, reading through pages and pages of the petition, making sure all the documents were in order and planning where each of the family members would go the next day or night to catch more signatures and encourage more supporters to help save Ned.

Kate and Jim were followed by two journalists on a Sunday morning, who watched them arrive at St Francis' Church, where they stood talking to the crowds at the gate, urging them to join the effort to save their brother. Neither Kate nor Jim would let any person pass without asking them to sign the petition.

In the afternoon, the journalists followed the pair back to the hotel and made their observations of Kate and Maggie in the front parlour before they sat themselves at the bar, writing notes and whispering to each other about the young women.

'The upper part of her face is by far the best of it,' one said about Kate to the other.

'Good forehead.'

'Her chin is rather narrow though.'

'Yes . . . best when she holds those papers up to read; conceals it.'

'Beautiful eyes, but she's terribly pale and wan.' They paused to have a sip of brandy and then wrote some more.

'Pity is all one could feel for the poor girl, though. Suppose she can't be blamed doing whatever she can to help save her brother's life.'

'Mmmm. What about the older one? Mrs Skillion.'

'Well, to put it mildly . . . not as prepossessing in appearance now, is she?'

The men sniggered, drank and compiled their articles, which they submitted under the guise of journalism, while Maggie and Kate sat side by side on the couch, plotting how else they might try to save their brother's life.

THE HIPPODROME, FRIDAY, 5 NOVEMBER 1880

Kate arrived at the gaol, stunned by the crowd of over one hundred people who were lingering and hoping to see her. She was desperate to tell her brother of the unfolding attempts to spare his life.

Kate was even more surprised when the wardens let her in to see Ned after their refusals on previous days. Kate had come alone while Maggie and Tom were meeting Gaunson at the Hippodrome in preparation for the public meeting planned that night.

The crowd at the gaol had been waiting patiently, but she had no time to speak to them—she needed to get to Ned. Her fans were not discouraged; they loitered in the hope that they would catch her on the way back out.

In Ned's cell, the pair were guarded closely; there was no privacy. 'Tonight is going ahead, Ned. There's huge interest and support, brother, don't give up. We'll fight until the end. Gaunson will speak and rally the crowds. They are thinkin' big numbers tonight, Neddy. The petition is gettin' 'round, we 'ave supporters out there.' Kate was very emotional and embraced Ned, sobbing. His hands were cuffed and his extended arms rested in front of him, so she put her arms wide around him and rested her head on his chest. 'Don't give up, Ned, it ain't over yet. I don't want to lose yer, brother.'

'Kitty, yer efforts are grand.'

They were quiet together for a few moments.

'Maggie and me tried to see yer yesterday but they refused us entry. "For what reason are yer refusing us?" I asked the rats at the gate. "Wait here," they told us. They send me wild, sitting there like old jollocks, thinking they're the kings of the blooming castle. They made us sit and wait all day and then turned us away. Damned dogs.'

Ned was riled by the knowledge of his family's treatment and his own. Kate tried to keep hope brewing. 'Tomorrow, if those jollocks let me in, I'll tell yer all about what happens tonight.' Ned nodded and Kate changed the subject. 'Will they let Ma see yer, Ned?'

'Perhaps. I'm reckonin' she won't let it rest until they do! They may have sore heads if they don't let her see her oldest son!'

It was heartbreaking for Kate to leave her brother, handcuffed, shackled and alone in the cold and tiny cell. It was a heavy and depressing scene, and Kate had to muster every skerrick of energy to keep on fighting for him.

The supporters at the gaol tried to shake hands and talk to Kate as she was leaving. 'Miss Kelly, Miss Kelly!' She thought it odd that people were so interested in her, but she was savvy about the importance of getting any help she could. 'Miss Kelly, is it true you helped Ned avoid capture? Did you truly lose the trackers out there in the bush?'

'Ah, now, I'm in a real hurry to get to the meeting. Thank you for yer interest in our cause. Please spread the word about this evening. We need yer support at the meeting. They're expecting the largest gathering in Melbourne tonight at the Hippodrome. Come and be a part of it, bring yer families, too.'

'But, Miss Kelly, Miss Kelly!'

Kate was trying to put on her best voice as she continued walking towards a horse cab. She gave instructions as she jumped into the back of it. 'To the Hippodrome, Sir!' Reserved-seating tickets had been high in demand for the event, and Kate was in a rush to get to the venue and prepare for the night's activities. She knew it was going to be huge, she could feel it in her bones.

At the Hippodrome in Stephen Street, the Friday night meeting drew a crowd of six thousand. Excitedly, the crowd gathered outside as evening approached, but only four thousand could fit inside so the rest remained on the street, eager and committed to being a part of it.

The mass of bodies before Kate stunned her. The newspapers had been making fun of Kate and her sister, and had also called for an explanation as to why Kate herself had not been arrested for aiding and abetting the outlaws. Any Kelly sympathisers were reported as criminals, lower-class scum, mere 'roughs' and 'prostitutes', but the truth was that many people from all walks of life were present at the meeting. Kate saw by the way they were dressed that there were plenty of socialites and well-to-dos.

Men and women from the general public were interested in the Kelly saga and in championing the abolition of capital punishment. People felt that the circumstances of Ned Kelly's trial and sentence were unfair, some wanted capital punishment to end, some were sick of being part of a downtrodden class of people, while others were simply curious and keen to be a part of the excitement and activity filling the streets.

None of the Kellys could go anywhere outside their hotel without a massive group of followers. Supporters and admirers, police, reporters and observers by the hundreds swarmed around the family every day. There was a hot fever of interest amid the ridicule and speculation of the press, who were spruiking the establishment's rhetoric.

Thousands came to hear Gaunson speak, to sign the petition and to show their support for the Kellys. The lower classes knew how things really happened between them and the law. They knew that the life of the average poor person was a struggle against the corruption of the powerful squatters, police and the system, all so heavily weighted against them. The downtrodden had been tormented for long enough, their hearts longed for change and their legs brought them to the streets to show it. For these people, Ned and the Kellys symbolised their own unrecognised struggles.

The poor masses wanted change in their society, and they wanted Ned to live. But the next stage of Ned's battle was looming large, and time was ticking away. Ned had only a matter of days to live.

The streets were filled with people and Kate was excited to be a part of it all. It was a ray of hope in a relentless stream of negativity.

The crowd outside felt excluded and were growing impatient as they waited to hear what was being said inside. Mischievous troublemakers played havoc with the nervous tension of the crowd when they launched firecrackers over the wall. As the fireworks whistled and spat through the air, people covered their ears. Women screamed and men laughed as the speakers on the centre stage jumped with fright and exclaimed that shots had been fired, realising their innermost fears.

A drunken woman yelled out passages of Ned's speech from his trial over and over again, while the sound of hymns being sung could be heard in the distance. The crowd swelled as more and more people tried to get in, and women shrieked as a heavy surge threatened to crush them. The police had no control.

Up on the centre stage with Kate and the Kellys, the speakers watched the crowd below, glad they weren't among them. They were uptight and suspicious about what might happen next. Activists and society people were part of the ensemble addressing the unruly mob.

Chaired by Sydney phrenologist Mr Hamilton, the public meeting was hosted by the Gaunson brothers and Mr Caulfield, an activist against capital punishment. William Gaunson, also a lawyer but less well known than his brother, was excited by the energy of the crowd and begged people to listen to what he had to say without interruption.

'In six days, Ned Kelly will hang. I ask that there be no applause and no dissent while I address the urgent need for a reprieve.' Gaunson then pulled the prosecution's case apart, to the delight of the crowd, who cheered wildly despite his request for quiet.

'The police came after the Kelly Gang and, like dogs, they wanted to shoot them down.' The crowd grumbled and booed. 'Kelly and his men had demanded surrender from this group of men disguised as prospectors who had tried to ambush them. The gang wanted to take their horses and the weapons. No harm was intended at Stringybark Creek. No harm was to be committed. But the police refused to surrender. The police refused to lay their weapons down, and they fired at Kelly and his men; from there it became a matter of self-defence. Ned Kelly is not a bloodthirsty character by any means. He abhors death, it is recorded in the court of law that he said so himself. Ned Kelly must not hang, we seek a reprieve.'

Thousands of voices rose up in unity, and the applause seemed endless. The sea of noise was overwhelming, but Kate was exhilarated by the support. A reprieve might really happen.

Gaunson soaked up the crowd's response, and as the noise settled he boomed out again, 'People!' He paused to gain their full attention.

'People of Victoria, having considered important details of the case of Edward Kelly, I move that this case must be considered fit for the exercise of the royal prerogative of mercy!' The gathering responded with enormous cheering, clapping and stamping of feet. 'I move that we earnestly pray His Excellency, the Governor in

Council, will regard the prayer of this meeting: that the life of the prisoner may be spared!'

A wild show of support rolled like a wave towards the group on the stage. Kate looked at Maggie and held her hand, thrilled. The enthusiasm of the crowd was electric. The request for royal mercy was recorded as a resolution and carried unanimously. It would be put forward to His Excellency Governor George Phipps, the Crown's representative, the following morning.

'It was not the intention of Edward Kelly to murder any such person, and without the intention it is simply not correct that Mr Kelly should have been sentenced to hang. His desire was one of theft not murder. The circumstances led to self-defence, not murder. Manslaughter is not a capital offence. Once again, the lower classes are the downtrodden. We must demonstrate that we are a sophisticated society and acknowledge that the concept of capital punishment is antiquated. If this colony is to be seen in the "modern world" as having its own place, it must move with the times. We must abolish capital punishment, now! What Kelly has been sentenced for is not a capital offence! He should not hang! This is a miscarriage of justice!' The ecstatic crowd's cheering echoed across the Hippodrome.

THE GOVERNOR, SATURDAY, 6 NOVEMBER 1880

The next day, the protestors continued to champion the Kellys' cause. Huge crowds moved through the streets of Melbourne to the gaol and then to the colony's Government House, chanting their messages and creating a spectacle for the press in the hope that it would embarrass the government into action.

In a desperate gamble, Gaunson took campaigners for the abolition of capital punishment and Kate to an unplanned meeting with the Governor of Victoria. Kate was pale from exhaustion and stress, a fragile mess of nerves inside but composed outwardly. The importance of this opportunity was not lost on her, and she was desperate to do her very best to save her brother.

Caught unaware, Governor Phipps agreed to meet with the entourage. He acknowledged Kate but felt uncomfortable about the way he had been hijacked by the group. It was easier to be detached and cold when he wasn't looking into the eyes of the young sister of the condemned man.

'Gaunson, this is most unorthodox and you know it!'

'Your Excellency, this is a dramatic and urgent situation that must be addressed, we had to meet with you.'

'There are processes for organising such meetings. You are aware of that.' He paused. 'All I can do is pass on your request for a reprieve, Gaunson, since it is a resolution from your public meeting. The petition you speak of must be delivered swiftly, and it may not change a thing. Do you understand?'

Gaunson nodded and started to speak, but Phipps shot him down. 'You are giving these people hope for no reason, Gaunson.'

The governor then turned to Kate. 'As for you, Miss Kelly, you should know that this man is peddling false hope. There is very little that will save your brother, and you must come to terms with that.'

Cut by his words, the teenage Kate fell to her knees and begged the man to spare her brother's life. 'Your Excellency, I'm begging yer to spare my brother, please. Mercy, please show my brother your mercy! A royal reprieve is in your hands. Your Excellency, please! You must, you must!'

Phipps wanted nothing to do with the girl at his feet. 'Out! Out! Gaunson, this meeting is over! Get her out of here.' This was not how things were done at Government House.

Gaunson helped Kate to her feet, and they fled the room.

The *Hobart Mercury* got wind of the story and wasted no time in humiliating the attendees of the meeting with the governor. Gaunson read the article out loud in his office:

> Gaunson organises the criminal classes of Melbourne ... as their representative he invades the privacy of the Governor ... resort[s] to the claptrap of playing on the feelings of His Excellency by the theatrical effect of a kneeling woman [Kate Kelly] the offence is beyond such punishment as society can inflict.

Gaunson was used to being ripped apart by the press, and he considered that, with these attacks, at least Ned's cause was up for public debate. He tried to calm Kate with that theory and certainly didn't mention other comments about her, including that she was a 'hyena in petticoats'.

He had laughed a little at the criticism in *The Northern Miner* that started with:

> The Gospel grinders and 'devil dodgers' ... saving 'scoundrelism' from the gallows. Gaunson ... addresses his fellow criminals and marches to Government House with a mob of ex-convicts.

But it went on and on:

> The well meaning but weak minded people who regard capital punishment as legalised murder ... The humiliating spectacle of making a hero and martyr of a pitiless professed murderer ... played out by ... the Chairman of Committees in the House of Assembly ... with all the riff raff, rapscallions and back slum scourings of Melbourne ...

Despite the insulting press coverage, the numbers of supporters marching with the Kellys grew day after day.

MELBOURNE TOWN HALL, MONDAY, 8 NOVEMBER 1880

In the early hours of Monday, a crowd of two hundred people that grew by the hour gathered in the streets near the town hall of Melbourne to support the deputation heading to Government House. This time it was Gaunson, Caulfield, Hamilton, Kate, Maggie, Jim and Wild Wright who would lobby Governor Phipps as they persevered in trying to delay Ned's execution.

The town hall crowd swelled with hundreds more people until Sub-Inspector Larner ordered his constables to turn the protestors out onto the street. The police hated these draggletailed larrikins from the back slums expressing themselves, and they could tell that the rowdy crowd was riled up. The push of more and more people from behind the growing group had them all bobbing and shuffling, trying not to lose their footing.

'Let us through or we'll belt the living daylights outta yer!' Cheers rose up, fists and arms were raised in defiance and the police stepped back further and further while they kept their guns poised, trembling from adrenaline.

'We won't rest! Even if we have to put you lousy traps on yer back!' People screamed their support and moved closer to the police, who again had to retreat.

'Riots is the message of the unheard! We ain't afraid of yer scoundrel dogs!'

The threats made Larner fret. He knew he and his men were outnumbered, and he could feel the violent energy getting stronger and stronger. He looked around to find the leaders of the mass gathering and ran up to Gaunson. 'Get this mob outta here, Gaunson.'

'That won't happen, Larner. Move your men, we are coming through. Nothing can stop this, look around you, man!'

Larner scrambled ahead. He waved his arm in the air and kept running, signalling his men to follow him further ahead of the crowd.

Kate walked among the supporters, hopeful to get more signatures for the petition on their way, but Gaunson knew that it wouldn't be safe and yanked her back. 'Stay near me!'

Gaunson had received petitions from many places all around the country, and they intended to present the entire petition to the Executive Council, a special committee of ministers and the governor, when they made it to Government House. Kate and the entourage had an extraordinary show of support from the protestors around them, but they also had over thirty-four thousand signatures to add to their case. One of the largest petitions ever presented to the Victorian Government, it was larger than the petition that would be put forward for women's right to vote in eleven years' time.

The crowd slowly snaked its way along Melbourne's streets. The Kellys walked tall and strong with their vocal supporters, whose energy sparked the air as they yelled at the police and pushed forward.

Sub-Inspector Larner and a large number of hand-picked armed policemen turned up again in the streets ahead. Too afraid to use violence for fear of immediate retribution and riots, Larner and his men attempted to stop the crowd at Princes Bridge, which proved useless. Gaunson and the Kellys jumped in a cab, concerned that the swell of people would delay them from their meeting. The rest of the wild crowd persisted all the way to the gates of Government House only to be met, yet again, by Larner and his staunch mates who were doing their best to intimidate the crowd.

The police were frustrated by their lack of effect at Princes Bridge and were determined to let no one past the gates. Kate and Maggie served the police a mouthful of outrage until Gaunson interrupted. He insisted that they all had an appointment that they must be allowed to attend. The crowd booed and hissed at the police guards as the chain of protestors bottlenecked behind the cab.

The police had never dealt with such a throng of agitated people in such numbers, and tensions mounted between the crowd and the police, even after they relented and let the cab through. Civility seemed a fragile notion while the law eyed the riffraff, weapons at the ready, anticipating that some kind of provocation would ignite the scene.

One thousand people waited outside Government House while, inside, officials tried to shuffle Kate and Maggie off to a waiting room, but they refused to be pushed around or locked away. Kate's brother, Jim, and Wild Wright had been excluded at the front entrance for looking too rough. Nonchalant, they'd returned to the Robert Burns Hotel in Lonsdale Street, followed by a huge crowd on foot. From the door of the pub, Jim yelled to them all that it was not over yet, and a huge cheer resounded before the unruly mob rushed the hotel, busting to have a drink and talk with the Kellys and their confidantes.

The Kelly sisters stuck with their men of society and politics, Gaunson, Hamilton and Caulfield, and met with the private secretary to the Chief Commissioner of Police, Captain Richard Frederick Le Patoural, because the governor refused to meet them. They wanted to present the petition supporting a reprieve for the condemned Ned. Page after page had lists of names underneath the simple but urgent request:

To His Excellency the Governor in Council,
Your humble petitioners (having carefully considered the circumstances of the case) respectfully pray that the Life of the CONDEMNED man Edward Kelly may be spared.

*The petition for reprieve was the Kellys' last hope to save Ned from the gallows.
Seventeen-year-old Kate worked tirelessly with her brother Jim and sister Maggie to collect
signatures on the streets of Melbourne. When delivered to the Victorian Government,
the petition had approximately 34,000 signatures, but failed to spare Ned's life.*

But the private secretary wouldn't accept it. Gaunson was annoyed that the governor had refused to meet them, but the aide promised that the petition would be presented in time for the executive meeting, if Gaunson and his deputation took it to the Treasury Building.

The Executive Council was designed to deal with particular aspects of government business and had agreed that at 2 p.m. they would meet to consider the petition and look at the request for a reprieve, put forward from the previous Friday's public protests. Gaunson wasn't satisfied and left with Kate, Maggie and the others.

EXECUTIVE COUNCIL DECISION

A crowd of around a thousand people gathered opposite the Treasury Building in the afternoon. Kate, Maggie and Gaunson arrived with the petition, and this time it was successfully handed over. All that was left to do was wait for the Executive Council's decision. Only Gaunson met with Premier Berry to hear if the Executive Council would recommend that a reprieve be granted. Kate and Maggie were not invited. Taken aside by a toffy-nosed assistant, Ned's sisters had to sit and wait for what seemed like forever in a 'retiring room'.

The premier asserted himself before Gaunson was even settled in his seat. 'The law will take its course.'

'How so?' Gaunson asked.

In a condescending tone, Berry dismissed Gaunson. 'I appreciate your efforts. It has been a feat of great coordination and display of sordid public interest, Gaunson. However, the executive meeting aside, those petitions all appear to be signed by illiterates, some are written in pencil and it is dotted with X's instead of signatures.'

Exasperated, Gaunson argued. 'Sir, with all due respect, many of the petitioners are indeed illiterate people but that should not exclude them from their right to be a part of it.'

'I would dare not disagree with you, Gaunson, but it also appears that many of the names have been written by the same hand; it makes it difficult to consider it a valid contribution. There are doubters, Gaunson. And, there are rumours that many in the north-east have signed simply out of the fear that if they do not they will become marked men.'

'Berry, you are aware that I represent a huge number of people who support the notion of this request for a reprieve. Thousands of people have attended our public meetings and voted for clemency, and you have witnessed it yourself, by the very numbers of people who have marched to your gates. The support is very real and cannot be ignored.'

'That may be true, Gaunson, none the less the decision has been made. The Executive Council has considered what was put before them, as they said they would, and their decision is that the law will take its course. That is final, I'm afraid.'

'We'll see about that, Berry. I'm disappointed, and who knows how the crowds will react to the news.'

Gaunson was escorted to the quiet, isolated room that held an anxious Kate and Maggie, and he broke their hearts with the terrible news. Gutted, Kate slumped in her chair and looked to her older sister, whose face went redder with every breath as she slammed her clenched fist on her knee. 'It don't matter what we do. At every turn they block us. Every turn!'

Kate leant over to her sister and embraced her. 'Let's get out of here, Maggie, we need to be telling Jim and the others the news.'

Gaunson led them out to the crowds who were still waiting, hoping to get a glimpse of them. As they left in a cab, Gaunson stood up from his seat and announced loudly and boldly to the crowd that the protest would continue the next day.

Having endured a shattering day, Kate and Maggie returned to the Robert Burns Hotel to talk to their family. The hotel was besieged all afternoon, with the public searching every inch of the premises in the hopes of a moment with their heroes and heroines.

Ettie Hart, Wild Wright and Ann Jones, the hotel owner from Glenrowan, were among the Kelly supporters staying at the hotel. Ettie Hart and Ann Jones were friends, but Kate and Maggie wouldn't speak to Ann, ever since the rumours that she was working for the police behind their backs. Because of the tensions between the Kelly women and Ann, everyone wondered what Ann was up to, but playing both sides didn't work. She would, in a week's time, be arrested and gaoled in Wangaratta.

Even though she had received money from the police for information, they determined that she had assisted Ned Kelly before and during the Glenrowan siege, despite having lost her son as a result of the shootout. Ann Jones had applied for compensation from the government for her losses of both property and child. The arrest seemed a low tactic and a clear attempt to erode her case. Ann Jones would continue to plead her innocence and eventually receive minimal compensation, but for the meantime she continued to stay at the hotel with the Kellys and their sympathisers, awaiting a result for Ned.

SUPREME COURT RESERVE, TUESDAY, 9 NOVEMBER 1880

Another day produced yet another crowd, which gathered at 7.30 p.m. on the corner of La Trobe and Swanson streets. The meeting point was the Supreme Court Reserve for an open-air demonstration.

On the back of a lorry drawn by horses, the Gaunson brothers and the Kelly siblings arrived. There were two thousand people waiting patiently to see what would happen next in the fight for Ned's life. The police, however, had demanded that no such meeting take place and tried to prevent access to the reserve. Half a dozen policemen nervously roamed the area, but the throng of people grew impatient and collectively rushed the grassy reserve.

The police panicked and called for reinforcements, which appeared in the shape of seventy men from the police barracks in Russell Street. Soon enough the chief commissioner, two inspectors and a superintendent materialised, and an extra twenty armed policemen gathered with them in La Trobe Street.

After vocal protests from the crowd about the police interference, it was announced that the crowd should make its way to the vacant block at the corner of Madeline and Queensberry streets. With that, the lorry acting as a stage for Gaunson and the Kellys slowly moved to the new location followed by the protestors.

Now the people were agitated. They could see the efforts of the authorities against them, and they wanted to push back. Gaunson rallied the crowd by criticising the press, police and politicians, and suggested that he would be suing various newspapers for defamation against his client and the Kelly family. He put forward the motion of yet another visit to Premier Berry at ten o'clock that night, a motion seconded by Caulfield. The crowd cheered its deep support.

A hat was passed around so that the cost of a cablegram direct to Queen Victoria to ask for a reprieve could be shared. Again, the crowd cheered, applauded and bellowed its support, throwing in hard-earned coins.

At the Treasury Building, Kate, Maggie, Jim, Grace and Mansfield local Paddy Quinn all attended in the hope of gaining the special audience they requested. It was a last-ditch effort to get the government's attention.

The Kellys had urged Quinn to come with them and let the authorities know what Constable Strachan had confessed to him back in 1879: that Constable Lonigan's intentions were to stitch Ned up by shooting him on sight and then laying a gun next to him.

Mr Berry greeted the Kelly entourage and allowed an interview in the executive chamber along with Gaunson and Caulfield. They pleaded their case.

Gaunson kicked it off, keen to make his case known. 'Berry, we have a new resolution from the most recent public meeting that must be conveyed with the utmost urgency. We call for a stay of execution, of course, but also we want a parliamentary commission into this whole horrid affair. And as you know, we have Mr Quinn's latest information about the intentions of the police party at Stringybark Creek. It warrants further investigation, and we need time for that.'

The premier was feeling tired by this Kelly business. It just wouldn't go away, and he struggled with Gaunson's decision to become entwined in it.

'I assure you, Gaunson, that all members of the Executive Council completed their tasks efficiently the first time around. The decision holds, and I do not hold the slightest hope for you. You are stopping the condemned man from accepting his richly deserved fate by continuing to create the notion of false hope for the family and the man himself. And beyond that, you are creating the impression that we have not given fair and just chance to your client despite every effort to hear you out and put forward every submission.'

Kate winced at the premier's cold and disconnected speech; she wanted to scream at him. All the Kellys were restless in their seats, despite doing their best to keep quiet and not upset the politician or ruin any slight hope of attaining his help.

Berry looked at their grim faces and put his final offer on the table. 'I will arrange one last special meeting of the executive tomorrow, and I will invite His Excellency, the Governor, for a 12 p.m. meeting. We will consider the affidavit you have presented but my word, Gaunson and Mr Quinn, this is not a sworn document, and if you wanted this considered you should have submitted it during the man's trial. Furthermore, it should be signed and it will be necessary for Constable Strachan to be asked about this. I hold no hope for your cause.'

Quinn piped up, 'Sir, when other prisoners have been condemned to death, they be given six weeks before the deed. Ned has been given less than two weeks, surely that ain't right.'

Patrick Quinn had done time for grievous bodily harm and was viewed by police as a dangerous and violent man. It was easy for the politicians to disregard any contribution from him, and there were many suspicious reasons that could be projected onto why his evidence had only now come to light, despite the likely truth behind it.

Mr Berry decided that the meeting had gone on long enough. 'I cannot account for the amount of time a prisoner may have between his sentencing and his death. It is very late, and I have other work to finalise. I will meet with you tomorrow. Good evening.' He exited the room swiftly.

LAST HOPE, WEDNESDAY, 10 NOVEMBER 1880

It was surprising to many that the agitation had continued for so many days and with such a strong representation of people. On this Wednesday, starting from the Robert Burns Hotel, a procession of four thousand people accompanied Kate, Maggie and the Kelly family, and their political friends helped to carry on the fight.

In the hotel a little earlier in the day, the Kellys were visited by Mr James Howlin Graves. He was a Member of the Legislative Assembly for the Delatite electorate, and Mansfield, where the murders of the police took place, was a part of his electorate.

Graves was originally from Ireland. In 1848, a group known as the Young Irelanders was rising up against the Irish Constabulary of the day in response to the Great Famine, and Graves's father was a special police magistrate for those disturbed districts. His family witnessed the failed rebellion firsthand, and Graves senior was then responsible for condemning and sentencing the perpetrators. Because of this background, there was no way that James Graves would ever support Ned's cause.

What the Graves family had witnessed in Ireland was a part of a wider revolution across Europe, sometimes referred to as 'the Springtime of the Peoples'. The witnesses to these rebellious events were exposed to the reality of the power of 'the people' and their attempts to create radical change. In Ireland, Graves senior had put people in gaol for trying to change their world, and now his son was face to face with the supporters of Ned Kelly, who wanted to fight for similar social upheavals.

The personal visit from James Graves made the Kellys realise that the government viewed Ned and his rebels as a serious threat. They feared Ned's power and influence over the public.

Graves recognised that the revolutionary elements that once played out in his homeland were being echoed by Ned and the gang in the north-east of the colony, and he identified the leading role Ned had been trying to play in an uprising against the government. Graves' surprise visit was an attempt to assure the Kellys that there was no hope left for their brother. He wanted them all to cease their efforts and dissuade the crowds.

Ignoring him, the Kelly family and friends fought on. Graves was asked to leave. Their brother's life was at stake and time was of the essence, with only twenty-four hours remaining before his execution.

In the centre of Melbourne, up on a makeshift stage, Gaunson was building up momentum, agitating the crowd. Kate stood with him, facing the thousands of supporters and spectators. Addressing the crowd one last time, Gaunson read out his planned address for the politicians when the masses reached Parliament House. He hoped to achieve at least one week's reprieve for Kate's brother, if not more.

As usual, the police presence was strong, but the crowd support was much stronger. When they arrived at the gates of Government House, Gaunson announced to the crowd that he would return to them shortly with the news from the executives and His Excellency.

However, inside, it was made plain to him that the governor was absolutely refusing to see the deputation. It seemed His Excellency had had a gutful of Gaunson and the Kellys. This was not a good sign.

The Premier, Mr Berry, however, agreed to meet with Gaunson and the others. Berry astonishingly revealed that he was person- ally feeling the strain of their attempts to change Ned's course; he pleaded with them to stop it all and emphasised that he had really done all he could. He felt that he had been a target of their attention unfairly. The way he saw it, the jury and the judge who sentenced Ned should be bearing the brunt of all these protests and meetings.

Kate was astounded by the weakness of the man. 'It is me brother who is about to lose his life, Mr Berry. We're asking for mercy. A reprieve. We're asking for yer help because yer the one who can do something.' She failed to see how putting a little pres- sure on Mr Berry warranted his complaints. It was his job after all.

This seemed to procure a strong reaction from Berry, who lost his cool. 'Now, I will tell you in no uncertain terms. The law will proceed as planned. The matter has been considered three times by men who make decisions for this country and who are deeply responsible for those decisions. It is final.'

He realised his response was harsh and loud as he looked around at the low-hanging heads and noticed the heavy silence. 'Let it cease,' he said gently. 'Allow the doomed man time to accept his fate. It is now inevitable. There is no more hope.'

Caulfield retaliated. 'Mr Berry, in the matters of capital offences, hope remains until the eleventh hour. We will keep that hope.'

With that, Berry's anger rose again. 'There is no power on Earth, Mr Caulfield, that will intervene. Tell your public meeting that the decision remains, and ask all parties to quietly disperse in the knowledge that your last hope has gone.'

The group was silent and slightly shocked by the man's aggression until Gaunson enforced their position. 'We will do no such thing.'

Berry was exasperated.

Outside, the chief commissioner, superintendent and a small army of constables flanked the gates and the grounds near the gaol and all government buildings, desperate to maintain the appearance of strength in the face of what they assumed would become a violent crowd.

The group retreated, the wind knocked out of them. Outside on the steps, Kate looked at the many supporters around them. The crowd was singing out to her, but it seemed like all hope was truly lost and she wanted some privacy to think about the situation. Heavy with defeat, she and her party shuffled into a cab to get back to the hotel, but Caulfield hung back to address the crowd, saying they all must hold on to hope.

19

The Hanging of Ned Kelly

I do not pretend that I have led a blameless life or that one fault justifies another. If my lips teach the public that men are made bad by bad treatment and if the police are taught that they may not exasperate to madness men they persecute and ill-treat, my life will not entirely be thrown away. People who live in large towns have no idea of the tyrannical conduct of the police in the country places far removed from court. They have no idea of the harsh and overbearing manner in which they execute their duty or how they neglect their duty and abuse their powers.

Ned Kelly, 'Letter to the Governor', August 1880

LAST VISIT TO NED, WEDNESDAY, 10 NOVEMBER 1880

Kate and the Kellys had exhausted every avenue possible, but no amount of fighting would see them win this battle for their brother. They had to accept it. Such a final scenario never crossed Kate's mind in her years growing up with Ned. The brother she adored, the centre of their family, the father figure and gentle man she had known and loved her whole life was about to die.

Kate, Maggie, Grace and Jim were denied access to say goodbye to

Ned as a group. They could visit briefly and on their own. Such was the government's fear of Ned's escape that, only hours away from death, he was shackled and cuffed when his family visited him. There were no opportunities for custodial mistakes or misadventure.

What could a sister bring to the brother she had loved all her life in the final moments they would ever see each other? It could not be sugar-coated. Kate thought of the story of Ned saving a young boy's life as a child; he was her hero. She knew her brother's bravery, his temper and humour, and likewise Ned knew hers. They had struggled together, right or wrong, and her loyalty could not be faulted.

Kate put her arms around her brother's shoulders; he could not embrace her with his cuffs on. She wanted never to let go of him. Kate was sobbing. He grabbed her wrists and steadfastly looked her in the face. 'We have all done our best. Look after Ma and look after each other. Remember me in your prayers, Kitty. Be brave for me and be there for the family.'

The little sister said she would be true to his requests and, after a moment of silence together, it was time for her to leave. Kate wouldn't be a part of her mother and brother's last goodbye, but she knew that Ellen would tell him that he must die like a Kelly. Kate tried to be strong, like Ned, but she felt like she had rocks in her shoes; it was so hard to put one foot in front of the other. Leaving Ned there to die felt like the biggest betrayal she had ever committed.

Now that the battle was confirmed as lost, Gaunson was notably absent. They all knew for sure that Ned was going to hang, and Kate found it disturbing that the politician made no effort to see her brother before he died. She had heard that Gaunson's brother William did, though, and she supposed that was better than nothing.

To the surprise of the police, there were no public disruptions. There were many followers and supporters hanging about the streets and the gaol, but it was a peaceful presence.

After his family left him for the last time, Ned spent much of the night singing ballads. It soothed him and distracted his mind. In between verses, he dozed a little.

For they're hangin' men and women there for the wearing of the green,
Then since the colour we must wear is England's cruel red,
Let it remind us of the blood that Irishmen have shed
Take the shamrock from your hat and cast it on the sod,
It will take root and flourish there though under foot 'tis trod.

Across town at the hotel, tossing and turning, Kate didn't sleep a wink the whole night, nor did Jim or Grace. Maggie had taken a train home after farewelling her dear Ned; she couldn't bear any more of it and needed to be alone.

10 A.M., THURSDAY, 11 NOVEMBER 1880

The sun had risen and, for Kate, knowing what would unfold that day was gut-wrenching. It felt like she was trapped in a cruel nightmare.

An author who had requested permission to interview Ned was refused right up to the eleventh hour, even though Ned wanted to tell his story. The authorities enforced their censorship of him to the bitter end. They would not encourage the adoration of the man or aid the growth of his cause. Despite all of the government's attempts to suppress Ned Kelly's story, it would, ironically, become the most well known of Australian stories.

The word back to Kate was that police were swarming everywhere, armed with their weapons around the gaol and through the city. The government and its agents were still nervous about a possible gaol-break mission or a riot in the streets. Kate gasped when she was told that a growing crowd of over a thousand people had been gathering around the gaol from the very early hours in a show of support for her brother. Those people would remain there most of the day.

And when news arrived that during the night someone had laid an iron sleeper across the train lines a hundred yards from the Lancefield Station, she knew it was in sympathy with Ned. If the sleeper had not been spotted, a train full of people would have been wrecked and no doubt her brother's cause would have been wrongly implicated. She breathed a sigh of relief that no one was harmed, since the day was set to be dreadful enough.

Kate knew that there was no public entry permitted to the gaol, but it still horrified her that some people had made inquiries about tickets to witness her brother's death, gallows-side, as if it were an entertaining show. She didn't know that a handful of Justices of the Peace had wrangled special admission cards. They assembled themselves in the gaolyard to be a part of history and to watch the heavy hand of the legal system they represented do its work.

Underneath his knees, Ned could feel the cold, hard stone of the cell floor while he prayed. Awake since five o'clock, his prayers lasted for half an hour. His ankles and wrists ached from the heavy shackles, and in awkward movements he shuffled himself onto his bed again. If he were to remain alive, his wounds would need to be re-opened, but this day was his last and soon nothing would be a concern to him anymore.

At 9.45 a.m., a gaol blacksmith entered Ned's cell and knocked the rivets out of the irons. Ned had to override his deep instinct to run; there was nowhere to go. Ned was shocked that his wish for the grace of one last meal was refused. But they allowed a different request: he was photographed and promised that copies would be given to his family and friends.

Father O'Hea and Father Donaghy gave the last rites to Ned,

praying with him and walking with him, bearing a crucifix as they weaved through the pleasant gardens. Ned stopped to admire the beauty of a flower and the blue of the sky before he was led to the place where the hangman awaited him.

'What a pretty garden.'

Ned's calmness was a little confronting to his religious advisers at first, and then they saw him hesitate a little as he drew closer to the gallows, proving his mortal limitations.

Ned was led to the spot at the gallows where he was told he had to stand to receive his noose and white hood.

'Ah, so it has come to this.' The hood was placed upon his head.

By ten o'clock, the sombre crowds had swelled up to six thousand, and there was not a single disruption outside the gaol until a woman threw herself to her knees and started an audible prayer for Ned Kelly's soul. It was a peaceful and respectful gathering, an ode to Ned. Many police stood with their revolvers ready, still expecting the worst.

Anxiously, Ellen Kelly sat in her cell. She could hear the uproar of the inmates at what must have been the strike of ten, the horrible moment itself. Exempted from her laundry duties that morning, she felt like a caged animal, helpless in the knowledge of what was happening to her son.

In the hotel room, Kate and the rest of her family sat together praying for their brother, in deep sympathy and dark sadness, willing him their love. They prayed he would not suffer. They sang him into the next world. As the clock ticked, they acknowledged the moments that passed, until the clock signalled that their brother's existence had ended. It was a cruel sign.

Ned's request that his body be given to his family was ignored and, for some bizarre reason, it was considered appropriate for the authorities to allow others to mutilate it. His sisters were not told this until the coming days when they tried to take him home. It was maddening to them, salt in their wounds.

Ned's body was whisked away to Melbourne Hospital. Ned's organs were removed and examined by an overzealous team of intrigued doctors and medical students who were keen to see the inside of this notorious and unique individual. His head was severed, his brain removed and various parts of Kate's beloved brother were divided out to men for examination and exhibition as trophies around the Melbourne medical and social scene.

Whatever disturbed mess remained was interred in Ned's supposed resting place. But with body parts thrown like offal into a pit in the ground, covered with quick lime to become ashes and dust, there would be nothing restful about it.

Even in death, the fascination with Ned and the Kellys had no boundaries. Little did his loyal and loving sisters know that it would take way beyond their own lifetimes, in fact over a century, for all of their brother's bones to be returned and interred properly after people had taken pieces of him as macabre souvenirs.

THE APOLLO THEATRE, 8 P.M., THURSDAY, 11 NOVEMBER 1880

It was distasteful to some that Kate agreed to appear on stage with her brother Jim and Steve Hart's sister Ettie the very night of Ned's hanging.

A popular and successful run of the Georgia Minstrels was surprisingly halted for the night, because some enterprising agents had swooped onto Kate and persuaded her and the others to appear at the Apollo Theatre Hall at the Eastern Arcade on Bourke Street East at 8 p.m.

The lands that constituted this relatively new city of Melbourne still belonged to the Kulin nation that included the Wurundjeri,

Boon Wurrung, Woi Wurrung and others, but it had a post-goldrush population of 280,000 people, and their insatiable hunger for entertainment often involved the gory, bizarre and unreal. There was a tantalising appeal for the unusual and the otherwise inaccessible.

Kate's extended family and the press judged her harshly for the decision, but the Kellys needed money to keep the family going and there was a story to tell. The days leading up to Ned's hanging attracted the largest gatherings in Melbourne's young history; how could the Kellys forgo the chance for the public to console them, support them and help them financially?

Kate wanted to tell their side of the story and thank people for their support. She was criticised for having made herself as notorious as her infamous brothers, but it was the press who had taken care of that, not Kate.

Her proposed appearance was creating a huge stir, a lot of publicity and opinion. Posters were up all over Melbourne, and advertisements were found in newspapers, too. It was going to cost participants one shilling each to meet her, and they did not baulk at the fee or the opportunity:

Miss Kate Kelly and her brother will interview all comers, this evening, Thursday 11 November, Apollo Hall, Bourke Street East. Miss Ettie Hart will also appear. Admittance is one shilling. Commence at 8 o'clock.

Kate found herself on the stage looking out at a crowd of people as the curtain lifted and she took a small bow. The crowd was as nervous as she was. The audience just stared at first, uncomfortable with nothing to say.

Next to Kate, her brother Jim stood like a fish out of water. Next to him was Ettie Hart, Steve's sister and Ned's girlfriend. The flowers in Kate's hand wilted from the heat of the hall. A small hum of air could be heard from people in the audience fanning themselves, along with echoes of wooden heels on the floorboards as they shifted loudly from foot to foot, against the quiet murmuring about the sight before them.

Soon a line formed and people were walking along the stage in a quiet procession, shaking hands with each of the entourage, muttering condolences and staring. As they became more comfortable, people spoke freely and openly asked questions, which Kate and Jim answered. She thanked them for their support as Jim and Kate took their place in armchairs on the stage. Their appearance was the most unusual theatre piece the people of Melbourne had ever seen.

The audience members were offering their kind thoughts to the family who had known and loved the country's most infamous bushranger and whose world had been shattered by the extraordinary circumstances of their loss, that very day.

Kate understood poverty, she understood what it was like to have nothing in her belly and, conversely, she was beginning to understand this strange concoction of fame and celebrity, politics and the press. The bizarre combination of recent events and dilemmas sent her young head reeling. Her suffering was real, but nothing could bring back her dead family members. Nothing could extricate her mother from an unjust prison sentence, or soothe its harsh effect on her family's lives.

Kate looked at Jim, who exuded sadness. Inside, he was burning for revenge. The tall, strapping young bushman struggled with the attention and fidgeted nervously. Having followers with him each time he left the hotel over these last days had been an unusual pressure, but he was adapting. He would always be more comfortable alone on his horse in the bush, but he wanted people to know what the law had done to his brother. Someone started a rumour that the money raised would help the family leave the country so they could start again. Anything was possible.

Ettie Hart was equally bruised as the Kellys. She, too, had suffered the loss of her dear brother, Steve, his friends and her beloved Ned. At home in a treasured tin, Ettie had her own keepsakes of Ned. In coming months, her love poems about her deep loss and sadness would accompany newspaper clippings and small mementoes that would stay hidden and never be spoken of for generations. She loved Ned, and in a different world they might have had a happy life together.

During this public display of mourning in front of two thousand paying spectators, both Ettie and Kate were approached by agents with big ideas and propositions. Ettie was asked to work at the Robert Burns Hotel to draw a crowd for them. She took it on but left soon after, disappointed with the reality of life in a public house as a cheap attraction. She needed time to deal with her grief.

Most dedicated in his pursuit of Kate was the flamboyant agent and showman, Flash Jack Donovan. This man was known as the sharpest dresser in town, the latest fashions always hanging from his slight frame. Ever the showman, he was distinguished in any crowd by his top hat, waistcoat and Albert watch. It had been said that the wheeler and dealer, who once was a boxer, could, if given the right opportunity, convince a royal princess of the purest blood to 'exhibit' for him.

Donovan was making his money in Bourke Street from his permanent and travelling sideshows. His voice could reach a large distance and conjure up images of freaks and fantasy that crowds found irresistible. He created suspense and desire so that people would push and shove each other out of the way in the fear of missing out on the astonishing attractions inside his tent. They would force hard-earned shillings into his palms while making their hurried entry.

Donovan was sizing Kate up in the flesh; he watched her moves and manners, and the effect she had on those around her. He saw the desire and satisfaction emanating from the audience members as they approached her and touched her hand, gushing as they spoke to her. Kate had something people wanted.

He considered the brother Jim. Donovan could tell that Jim was protective of his sister and realised that he would be part of any decision she made, so he must win them both over. Donovan was lining up gigs mentally: Sydney, Adelaide, Melbourne, maybe New Zealand, too. The money ticked over in his mind's eye.

Donovan had a reputation for starting his deals with a fair split of fifty-fifty but he always ended up shifting arrangements so he received two parts for the performer's one. Not long after, he would make a move for all of it, offering nothing to his victim before the deal inevitably collapsed.

Donovan selected his timing and smoothly glided in to approach the pair, introducing himself to Kate first. 'I am sorry for your loss, Miss Kelly, and a lot of people here feel the same way.' He launched his pitch. 'There is enormous interest in your story, Miss Kelly. People want to hear about Ned and his gang and how you have helped your brothers. They want to see you on your horse. They want to be close to the things Ned owned and the people who knew him.'

Kate was holding back tears for her brother.

'Everyone needs money, Miss Kelly. I can help you achieve that. We would have sell-out crowds, of that I am convinced. Look at the number of people here tonight. Look how many people walked with you in the streets to protest. We are talking about thousands of interested people. Not forgetting how many people gathered outside the gaol today for the terrible and unfortunate event.'

Kate remained composed. She refused to cry in front of these people.

'Here is my calling card. It shows all my details. Do you know the premises I use just near here? It is a most successful venue. I have organised many events and travelling shows in my professional life. Don't miss this opportunity, Miss Kelly. I would arrange it all, of course, and would reward you and Mr Kelly handsomely. There is a venue in Sydney I would like to arrange and I'm sure Adelaide, too. There is much interest, Miss Kelly. I hear that you desire funds to leave the country and this may be the perfect arrangement for you ... and me.'

Donovan knew if he didn't snag them, someone else would, and he wasn't prepared to let that happen.

'What a pleasure it is to meet you, Mr Kelly. It is a shame that it is in such sad circumstances.' Jim, only 21 years old but so much older than his years, took a good look into the eyes of this Flash Jack Donovan, and he didn't like what he saw.

'Mr Kelly, Miss Kelly, would you commit to me this evening? Become part of my sideshow and come to Sydney, where I know the crowds will also gather in strong numbers?'

'When, Mr Donovan?'

'Jack, call me Jack. We need to act quickly, Miss Kelly. If I have your word this evening, we could be there within a couple of weeks. Why, you could start right away at my premises.'

'Is there that much interest, Mr Donovan? Jack.'

'Why of course, Miss Kelly! It is of international significance, and indeed I have no doubt there will be reports in the newspapers in New South Wales tomorrow about your appearance here tonight and of the sad events earlier today. Possibly in each colony, in the mother country, even in America. I want to help you be a success.'

Jim knew that when Kate made up her mind, she stuck to it. He could see she wanted to do it. Despite how Jim felt about Donovan, he naturally agreed to escort his sister. He couldn't allow her to travel on her own. He saw the way people looked at her. He knew that she didn't even realise the effect she had on men. He had seen it in their faces when they met her.

And so, a deal was struck. Kate Kelly would be the star attraction of Flash Jack Donovan's Bourke Street sideshow. They would do a regional tour and then travel to Sydney.

Donovan was elated with his jackpot. He praised himself aloud as he left the building: 'The ole boy still has it!'

The Apollo's tenants made one hundred pounds that night and wasted no time in booking another evening with the Kellys for the following night. It was bound to bring even more attention once word got around throughout the following day. But the police stopped the endeavour. The government was desperately trying to smother and extinguish any public interest regarding anything to do with Ned Kelly.

As additional insurance, the police threatened the family, saying they would not return Ned's body to them if the show went ahead. The cruel and unethical blackmailing of the Kellys was in fact complete bluster, as there was never the intention to provide the grieving family with their brother's body—the Kellys just didn't know it yet.

20

Kate and Jim's Travelling Shows

MELBOURNE, 1880

Despite the show being described in the press as a horror that one must look away from, Donovan put Kate centre stage in Melbourne, and he billed the relics and metal scraps they'd managed to retrieve from Glenrowan, plus the things he'd added to the collection, as genuine articles. True or false, he didn't care—who would know? He made his living promoting freaks of nature, like his five-legged calves, tattooed women, world boxing champions and talking dogs. The fact that the talking dog lost his voice right when it mattered never concerned him. His acts didn't need to live up to their reputation once the money was paid.

Donovan made sure it was known that he was a nasty fellow if you locked horns with him, and this seemed to have been an effective complaints policy to date. Most of the gang's armour and weaponry had been plundered from the ashes by the police at Glenrowan, for evidence and souvenirs, leaving Kate with only melted gun barrels and bullets as trinkets to show for it, but what she did have mattered to her, and it included Ned's saddle.

The man who acted like a millionaire, even when he was stone cold broke, took to work spruiking his starlet without blinking an eye when the police came to warn him off with threats of shutdowns. He would gamble on anything, and there was no way he was missing out on the chance to make a small fortune from the famous Kate Kelly.

Donovan knew that people would come from all around to see Kate and that it wasn't just 'larrikins' who were interested in the Kelly story. The spieler had a knack for impressing people from any class, and so businessmen, gentlemen and their society wives were lining up alongside average Joes, prostitutes and workers, eager to hand over their shilling and get in first. Despite the constant visits from police, Donovan added money to his coffers in Melbourne daily.

Jim somehow agreed to Kate travelling alone, and she went with Donovan and his troupe in a convoy of drays, carts and horses into the countryside. The carnival team weaved north through to Wangaratta, Wagga Wagga and across to Temora, then further west into South Australia, stopping at many country towns as far as Kapunda. On the road, Donovan kept Kate hidden away from punters like a priceless jewel, and it added to her allure. If anyone wanted to see Kate, they had to pay for the pleasure.

His shameless and sensational spruiking at the tent entrance lured the rustics into his amazing tent to see 'The World's Aggregation of Marvels'.

'Roll *up*! Roll *up*! Come and meet the daring Kate Kelly, in the very riding outfit she used to help her bushranger brothers with their amazing escapades hiding out in the bush. Miss Kelly will even ride the very same horse, her fearless companion, Oliver Twist.' He paused to take money and push people into the tent, then started up again.

'See the saddle that belonged to the outlaw Ned Kelly. Meet Ned Kelly's attractive sister Kate Kelly. The girl whose charms caused a police officer to make violent love to her and started her two brothers' careers in crime!' Donovan had no boundaries, and the crowds flocked to him. If Jim had had the faintest notion of what Donovan was saying, the salesman would have been knocked to the ground and Kate whisked away, but instead Donovan filled his moneybags without Kate seeing a penny. Then the troupe headed back to Melbourne, where Kate, Jim and their horses were scheduled to depart by steamer. Donovan had a lucky feeling about Sydney.

SYDNEY, SATURDAY, 20 NOVEMBER 1880

Kate and Jim arrived on the *Katoomba* steamship, gliding across Sydney's glorious sea-green Woolloomooloo Harbour under a turquoise sky. Sandstone buildings and the city's streets appeared slowly as the ship moved in, filling Kate's eyes with a scene she had only imagined before.

With a population of around 224,000 people, Sydney wasn't as big as Melbourne, but with its multitudes swarming from the harbour back to Haymarket, it was indeed a city.

Its surrounding land had long been home to the Eora nation, a group of about twenty-nine clans, whose chants of 'Warra, Warra!' from the shore at the English ships that arrived in 1788 did nothing to prevent the invasion that followed. Nearly one hundred years of white settlement had changed their lands and ways of life permanently.

Nine days after Kate and Jim's infamous brother was hanged, Ned was still world news. For the Kellys, the pain of losing Ned and Dan sat in their hearts and ran through their heads at night.

'This is a once-in-a-lifetime opportunity! We'll do as many shows as we can. Bigger crowds, more publicity, more money!' Donovan's greed was insatiable. Kate was past wanting to spend any time at all with him, and she had grown tired of his excuses and changes in their deal. Kate and Jim were not becoming wealthy, like Donovan had promised, but they knew that he was. Jim wouldn't stand for his sister being ripped off, nor was he afraid of putting pressure on Donovan to extract some cash for her. Donovan coughed up a tiny sum to keep Jim off his back.

Donovan had engaged the services of James Pringle and James Gregory Tompkins for the Sydney gigs. Pringle was an agent and Tompkins was the lessee of the proposed venue at the rear of Keeshan's premises in King Street. The venue was accessed via Lees Lane, also known as 'Star and Garter Lane'. Facing King Street on one side of the lane was Keeshan's Star and Garter Hotel, and on the other, Mr Jackson's tailoring shop. Chinese lanterns lined the laneway all the way to an empty shed, which was being fitted with gas lighting for the proposed exhibition.

The Sydney agent was already trying to poach Kate and Jim and cut Donovan out of the equation. Pringle wanted to look after them in Sydney because he knew he stood to make a lot of money if he could ditch the showman, but his nervousness about the unpredictable Melbourne personality and a violent story about Donovan's bulldog made Pringle hesitate.

It was well known that Donovan's bulldog Jerry had won many fights. One brisk Melbourne morning, Donovan was walking past a chemist's store, and a large dog came running from within. The dogs latched on to each other, and a bloody match ensued. Donovan assumed arrogantly that his dog would emerge the victor. At the end of the battle, alas, his poor Jerry lay dead in front of him.

The chemist, who emerged from inside his store, was the owner of the dog who had launched the ambush. He was not alarmed, and it appeared as if setting the dog on Jerry had been deliberate.

The tall and pasty-looking man said to Donovan, unemotionally, 'Looks like my dog has killed your famous bulldog.'

Before the man had a chance to blink, Donovan had picked his dead dog up by the tail, swung it like a hammer throw and landed it through the huge glass window of the store. Donovan simply said to the man, while walking away, 'Yes, it seems your dog has killed my dog, so now you may as well bury it, too!'

It was probably volatile actions like this, combined with Donovan's lifelong propensity for ripping people off, that led to him being found floating face down in Melbourne's Yarra River in 1909.

Donovan had money on his brain, and he had barely arrived in Sydney before his sights were set on a gambling house frequented by high-rolling businessmen and criminals. Obsessed with his new mission to multiply his earnings at the card table, he all but vanished from Kate and Jim's world but not before he cashed in on a couple of bumper shows. Pringle and Tompkins were simply pawns in Donovan's plans; he wasn't going to be cut out of anything, and he manipulated the situation, yet again, so that he was taking all of the money but they were taking all of the risk.

Pringle organised the accommodation for Donovan, Kate and Jim in Campbell Street, Haymarket, at the Freshwater's Packhorse Inn, which had stables for their horses. The pair had brought the horses, Kate's Oliver Twist and Ned's trusted and loyal mare Music, rescued by Kate after it was found wandering around the train tracks after the siege at Glenrowan. Before Kate found the horse, she had been horrified at the thought of the slaughter of Music, who, like Kate, would have followed her brother anywhere and done anything for him.

Kate and Jim arrived ahead of Donovan at the Packhorse Inn amid a rowdy scene. Kate had not expected such a crowd waiting to see her. She didn't fully understand yet that she was an enigma throughout the colonies, the public's newest and much sought-after celebrity and muse.

Hundreds of swarming fans knew who she was, they called out her name and they remained below the window to her room, hoping to get a glimpse of the famous Kate Kelly.

Only minutes after Kate and Jim had pushed their way through the crowd to get inside the hotel and up to their rooms, they received a visit from a Detective Williams and his offsider, plus a solicitor and a magistrate.

The cocky detective was very forward in his admiration of the seventeen-year-old Kate's good looks. Jim didn't like it and, as he was never backwards in protecting the women in his life, he acted swiftly. All he had to do was position his large self near the excited young detective and look down at him from a very close range. The young man moved well away from Kate, having got the message loud and clear.

The magistrate accompanying Detective Williams was there to deliver a strong message from the New South Wales Government. 'No performances will be tolerated here. Victoria may lower its standards enough to allow it, but we most certainly will not. We've come down here to see you today so that you are left with no confusion about our position. If you cause the kind of disturbance we have heard of in Melbourne, we will waste no time in suppressing you by law. Do you understand Mr Kelly, Miss Kelly?'

'What a shame you wasted yer time today, Mister.' Kate was having no part of it. 'And just so there be no confusion about my position, my brother will show yer the door. Good afternoon then!'

Jim leaned across silently and opened the door, eyeballing each of them as the shocked quartet exited. The detective's swagger was a little dented. He tried to address Kate again from outside the doorway, and Jim piped up, 'Miss Kelly isn't taking any visitors this afternoon, thank you for yer time!' With that, he slammed the door.

Kate looked at her brother, exasperated. 'They knew we was coming, Jim! Outrageous! Traps and their spies everywhere! Never to leave us be, are they?'

'Who does he think he is?' Jim was quiet but cranky.

'Pringle and Tompkins told Donovan it was all booked, Kitty. It'll be all right. It ain't illegal to perform your horses.'

Kate was furious. 'This treatment of us ain't on. Damn traps. Where the bloody hell is Flash Jack now?'

Kate sat on the bed and looked out the window across the wide streets of Haymarket, and she watched the collection of admirers who were waiting to see her. This city was a less busy place with a different feel to Melbourne. The people were friendly enough, it seemed to Kate. Well, they were all singing out to her and wanted her to stop and talk to them, so she supposed they were friendly. It was surprising to her that so many people had come to see her when she was so far away from home. How could anyone know of her here, so far away from Greta?

She was concerned about the police, though. 'What mischief are they up to, these traps, Jim? It's suffocating. Having their eyes on me always. It be endless.'

Kate felt overwhelmed by the police visit and was weary from the trip. Still, she was determined they would perform, regardless of the police harassment. She remained defiant.

The word spread like wildfire that Kate Kelly and her brother Jim were staying at the Packhorse. The crowd was growing, not shrinking like Kate had hoped. The corner of Castlereagh and Campbell streets became blocked by swarms of people of every sex, age and social rank.

The Bulletin

86 Years Ago: November 27, 1880

KATE KELLY'S TROUPE

THE Kelly troupe made their first appearance on the night of the same day as that on which their relative was executed. The *locale* was the Apollo Hall, Melbourne, where some speculating miscreant exhibited them to the tune of a shilling a head admission. Kate Kelly assumed a bouquet.

Last Saturday night the Kelly gang stuck up the whole of Campbell Street, Sydney. This street was positively blocked with every rank and sex, all eager to feast their eyes on the fascinating spectacle of a rough bushman and his helpless sister. *O curas hominum!* What trifles form the cares of men; and ditto as regards the women. Unless prevented by the authorities these talented artistes show this week, and we venture to remark that their opening night will bring a greater crush than an Irving Shakespearian reading or a Sims Keeves and Santley concert.

EVERY woman in the community was shocked at Kate Kelly's unfeeling conduct on the night of the day on which her brother was executed.

THE Melbourne spiritualists claimed Ned Kelly as a medium.

A GRAVE-DIGGER was on the jury at Ned Kelly's trial.

THE BULLETIN, November 26, 1966

Kate Kelly and her brother Jim had only just arrived in Sydney but caused a huge sensation in the streets near their accommodation. 'These talented artistes' performed until the police shut them down. (This 1966 article reproduced the original from 27 November 1880.)

Kate and Jim decided they should entertain the crowd, since the throng of people seemed to be expecting something. Getting on her horse made Kate more at ease. She and Jim trotted out onto the street, where people cheered and applauded at the very sight of them, and it made the horses move sideways and whinny. People moved quickly to make a large circle on the street where the Kellys could parade their horses. Kate moved her horse slowly around the edge of the ring, smiling as they sang out for her attention.

'Miss Kelly, Miss Kelly! Over here!' She snuck a little wave to the voices calling from different directions as she pulled her riding gloves on. Even well-to-do society players were vying for a taste of one of Kate's smiles. 'Holy snakes!' a gentleman exclaimed after a couple of glances from the talented artist upon her horse.

Pringle and Donovan arrived to visit Kate and Jim. Both of the showmen were overwhelmed with excitement when they came upon the cause of the enormous crowd. Donovan pushed his way through the masses, sucking the energy from the crowd and letting it fill him up with adrenaline. Pringle was less accustomed to working a crowd and just tried to follow Donovan's path to the centre. They rushed along the inside of the huge ring of people, welcoming the onlookers. Donovan was in his element and, as he prepared to work his magic, he directed Pringle to hand out leaflets promoting the coming opening night. Donovan got busy campaigning like a true professional. His motto was 'Never waste an opportunity!' and he lived up to it daily. 'Tell your neighbours, bring your friends and family! Don't miss this rare and sensational event!'

Jim was less inclined to enjoy the attention, but he truly admired his sister and her skills. 'Miss Kelly, Miss Kelly!' People called to her with their hands outstretched.

Brother and sister met each other in the middle of the ring and manoeuvred their horses so they faced one another and began a short routine. The entertaining game involved Kate trying to pass her brother to the other side of the ring. Beautifully poised, Kate grabbed the reins and shimmied with Oliver Twist from left to right while her brother, also comfortable in the saddle, mirrored her moves. The crowd loved the tension of their quick moves and cheered loudly when Kate passed her brother, smiling.

The pair circled back to the middle while the crowd yelled out for more, and the Kellys repeated their routine again. It had been a long enough day for them both and, feeling weary, Kate signalled Jim, who rode towards her, slid off his saddle and held out his hand for her as she dismounted and bowed to the crowd. She was lifted by a sea of cheering and applause.

Jim took the horses and walked with Kate as she worked her way around the ring, and they edged back towards the hotel, hoping that people would be satisfied and leave them alone. Jim was a modest man but the city crowds loved the idea of this rugged bushman, and they watched him as he took the horses to the stables round the back.

The impromptu performance was a great success, and Pringle was very excited about what was to come. Donovan reminded the crowd about the show the following night, and Pringle left, filled with excitement about the venture. 'This is going to be remarkable, Miss Kelly! You are so popular!' And with that, Donovan was gone again, high on the thought of coming riches; he waded out into the Sydney nightlife, keen to see what the city had to offer him, oblivious to the warnings Kate and Jim had received from the law.

Later, there was a gentle knock on Kate's door.

Jim opened it a little. He couldn't believe his eyes. It was Constable Fitzpatrick's sister, Jane, and she forced her way in.

Jim stood back to watch, saying nothing. He waited near the door that he had no doubt would be in use again in no time.

'What the devil are you doing here?' Kate asked in an icy tone. 'Is it not enough that my brothers are dead? What more do you want from us?'

'It's been a long time since I've seen you, Kate. Did you know Alexander was stationed here for a while?' Jane strutted around the room and looked out the window at the lingering fans.

'On the hunt for my brothers, no less? You have a hide.' There was venom in Kate's voice. 'I heard he got booted from New South Wales. He's an embarrassment, you should be ashamed of yer brother. He couldn't lay straight in bed, some kind of policeman.' Kate's eyes followed the woman as she sat herself down in a high-backed velvet chair as if she owned it. 'Yer not welcome to stay,' Kate barked at her, but Jane stared at Kate defiantly and removed her gloves, one finger at a time.

'You are doing very well for yourself, aren't you now?' Jane sniggered as she flopped the gloves on her lap and interlocked her fingers like she was praying. 'The famous Kate Kelly.'

'What concern is it to you how I might be faring? Your brother, your family, you, have expressed no consideration for my welfare before now.'

'It seems to me, Kate, that since the death of your brothers, life has been very rosy for you. You must be making a lot of money from their misfortune.'

'You are outrageous!' Kate launched herself at Jane, but Jim grabbed his sister before she made it to the chair.

Jane jumped to her feet, thrilled that she had evoked such a reaction but frightened nonetheless. She yelled at Kate very quickly, 'How is Alice? I wonder what people would think if they knew the truth about your daughter? A handsome payment would keep me quiet.'

Kate was eager to mess up the woman's face with her fists.

'You are a disgrace! Get out!' Jim said, holding onto Kate as Jane shot out the door.

'I'll be back another day for the money. How much is my silence worth to you? Your family ruined my brother . . .'

Kate escaped Jim's clutch, and Jane ran for the stairs as Kate threw herself through the door but lost her footing. It was the only reason Kate couldn't get a hold of her blackmailer. Jim picked Kate up and pulled her back into the room.

'Why'd yer stop me, Jim? Why did yer do that?' Kate was on the edge of the bed, sweaty, red-faced and sobbing with frustration and anger.

'Kitty, she ain't worth it. Yer know it. I know it. She won't be back. She was cocky but terrified.'

Jim took the lid off a brandy bottle and handed it to his sister. Kate gulped and gulped and gulped until Jim snatched it off her. 'Steady on, sister.' She shot him a look, wiped her face and cursed the Fitzpatrick name.

The small hurricane that wreaked momentary havoc in their space had blown back out the door and left Kate feeling shattered. Just another surprise ingredient in the soup of madness that had become Kate's life. It exhausted her.

THE DETECTIVES

In the heart of Sydney's city streets, a large African man named Lewis, with his big voice, was yelling from the corner of Pitt and King streets:

The daring Kate Kelly on her horse Oliver Twist. Kate Kelly's brother Jim on the horse of Ned Kelly, the infamous bushranger. The true relations of the outlaw performing here tonight. These are no wax replicas, no oil paintings. Come one, come all. A sight never seen before. Relics from the Kelly Gang, even the saddle that belonged to Ned Kelly himself.

Donovan himself joined in further along the street; spruiking was what he loved. 'Step inside, my friends; there you will see the renowned Kate Kelly! The sister and brother of the famous Ned Kelly, the real deal here. No waxworks! You'll never see this again. Get your ticket before they sell out and the talented Kellys leave the colony.'

He took their money and directed hundreds of patrons up the lane as the crowd swelled across the footpath, pushing past each other with urgency.

'This way, madam, follow the crowd through the gates. I commend you on your choice of entertainment this evening.'

The crowds were rushing in to see the spectacle. Twelve hundred people a night. Young men, old men, women, girls and boys, the police had to control the crowds and guide them to keep them orderly, trying to prevent people from flowing onto the streets.

The show commenced around 7 p.m. and continued until midnight. The police watched the shows, regulated the crowds and made their reports back to headquarters.

Tension and excitement from the masses of people pulsed through the air. But already the business owners on either side of the exhibit were lodging their complaints to the police, demanding that the gates be closed and the attraction be brought to a halt.

Kate would make her entrance on Oliver Twist, and the crowds went crazy for her. Jim would ride Music, Ned's trusty grey mare, and the pair would parade together. Kate would then perform by herself, receiving applause and causing great excitement.

The pair walked around the edge of the crowd with their horses and greeted their new fans. Members of the audience would shake Kate's hand and talk to her, calling out to her and to Jim, reaching out to touch them. The siblings would answer questions and talk about what happened to their unfortunate brothers and outlaw friends, and complain about police behaviour.

Everyone wanted to touch the horses, the saddles or anything that had been a part of the Kelly story. The Kelly relics were fascinating to the crowd. People touched the melted trinkets as if they were touching Ned himself. They had all dreamed of what it might be like to be a bushranger, a part of the action. The idea of robbing banks, camping out, riding horses and living rough in the Australian bush in the southern colony sounded amazing to these city folk.

The very notion that the beautiful young Kate was equally skilled as her brothers and that she had played such a helpful role in their survival also impressed people. It was hugely marketable. The boys and men wanted to be like the bushrangers and coveted Kate. At the same time, the girls and women all wanted to be like Kate and coveted an imaginary romance with characters like her wild and dangerous brothers. There was much appeal in the idea of it all, but Kate's reality was far removed from their fantasies.

One big part of Kate's reality was the police, and she just couldn't shake them. They were threatened by the huge interest in Kate and the massive crowds she attracted.

'There is huge interest, Detective,' a constable reported one morning. 'The crowds over the last two nights were enormous! This could easily become a permanent attraction if we don't take action. It's a moral crime.'

The detective had already determined his course of action for the day. He and his subordinates rushed out into the street, keen to swoop on Pringle and Tompkins, delivering both men a summons to appear in court the following day. This time, Detective Williams had Sub-Inspector Anderson with him.

'Oh now, Detective,' grumbled Tompkins, 'I'm only the simple lessee of the premises. How can I control any of this, Sir? I don't have that kind of power, Sir.' Tompkins was getting great money from Pringle, and damned if he was going to let these clowns ruin it for them all.

'It's a disgrace, Tompkins, and you know it. We've seen the youths, the larrikins and the disorderly classes lapping this up. It's injurious to public morals. It has to cease. Immediately. I'll see you in front of the magistrate tomorrow. We're going to shut you down. We'll make this request official.'

'Oh! That's a bit harsh ain't it, Detective? It's entertainment, Sir. That's all.'

The detective and the inspector were already halfway out the door, yelling back at the man without turning around. 'Tompkins, we're shutting you down!' The policemen hurriedly made their way to Pringle's office.

Feeling pretty impressed with himself, Williams slammed the summons on Pringle's table with a smirk, saying that he'd already seen Tompkins and delivered the same to him.

'It can't happen tonight, Pringle. I know you are the commissioning agent. It's got to stop. No more. There's been a letter, signed by the local businesspeople, addressed to the inspector general on the subject, Pringle. This is serious. The crowds are out of control, and I won't have this rowdy class creating disorder on my streets. I had to put two constables and a sergeant out there again last night. No more shows.'

Pringle said innocently, 'Well, Detective, that's a real shame, but there is nothing I can do about it. It is Tompkins who leases the premises. I am merely the agent. I knew there would be horses but nothing more. I doubt I have the power to make the show stop, Sir! I signed an agreement to sublet the premises, and there is nothing illegal in that. Besides, it does seem to be what the people want! You saw the numbers these last nights. It's so popular!'

Pringle and Tompkins had anticipated a reaction from the police when they saw how many people were turning up, so both were playing innocent with the police to avoid any culpability.

It just made Williams cranky. 'I hope we understand each other, Pringle.'

The detective moved in close to Pringle, gritting his teeth as he spoke. 'Ned Kelly was a murderer. A notorious criminal who has recently been executed. His sister, Miss Kelly, although without charge, has been credited with assisting her fugitive brother and being an accessory to his gang, aiding their longevity. And she is trying to profit, as you are, from her brother. It is in poor taste, and it is unacceptable that your show continues in any capacity. We are shutting you down, Pringle. Be at court tomorrow, or you'll be in the lock-up if I have anything to do with it.'

Pringle remained defiant and unperturbed. *On with the show!* He smiled to himself. *We'll get one more night in at least!*

SHOW STOPPER, WEDNESDAY, 24 NOVEMBER 1880

Detective Williams knew what Pringle and Tompkins were up to—he was no fool—but he was confident he was going to put a stop to it all.

After a string of money-making sell-out shows, Donovan remained unperturbed by the threats from the police, mainly because it was not him who had been bailed up. He would push on until forced to stop, and he couldn't see how any of it would fall back on him anyway, so he had nothing to lose. All he wanted was more cash to take to the card table when all of this was said and done.

When Kate and Jim trotted into Lees Lane in the late afternoon, the crowds had already started gathering, and a loud cheer greeted the pair as they pulled up their horses and dismounted at the gates.

Donovan was instructing Lewis down at his usual spot on the footpath when he heard an argument of some kind and was surprised to see the bottleneck of fans. It was not until he was a little closer that he could understand the cause of the unfolding commotion.

Detective Williams was marking his turf. He had sent his constables to block the gates and deny admission to Kate, Jim and the whole crowd. Kate and Jim got back on their horses, looking around for Pringle or Donovan to figure out what to do with all these people. The crowd started to boo the men in uniform for ruining their entertainment, but the police weren't budging.

As Kate and Jim rode back towards Donovan, he yelled out to Kate that she should make her way to the site of the Royal Victoria Theatre just around the corner on Pitt Street. Commonly known as the Old Vic, it had been the largest theatre in Sydney until it burnt down in July that year. He turned on his heel and waved to the crowd to follow them. 'Come along one and all. We're heading to the site of Old Vic!' The crowd was excited by the possibility that all was not lost, and they followed Kate and Jim, eager to see what would happen next.

Excitement rose up from the crowd as large numbers surrounded Jim and Kate, bottlenecking at the laneway to where the Old Vic once stood. *Now what?* Kate wondered, and she threw a look at Jim as the police spotted Donovan and ran towards him, yelling that everyone must move along. 'What in heaven's name is going on here? You can't gather here!'

The crowd booed the constable, and Donovan moved in close to reason with him. 'Our entry has been blocked behind Keeshan's, so we can't access our usual place of exhibition. These people want what they came for.' A cheer went up again from the crowd.

'No! You certainly cannot exhibit here. You must clear out at once. It is not suitable to have horses out here with all these people. Move away before we arrest you all.'

The horses were becoming distressed, so Kate and Jim walked them back towards Lees Lane, leaving Donovan to tame the crowd once more. Some patrons gave up and walked away, while others stood their ground to hear what would happen next. Thinking it might be worth a shot to head back to the gates, Donovan signalled to the crowd to follow him once more.

By the time they made it back to the lane, Donovan knew it was pointless. He rushed over to Kate and Jim, and the three of them decided to call it a night. Donovan announced to the audience: 'Sadly, my friends, the police have ruined tonight's entertainment. There will be no show tonight.' The crowd booed again, disappointed and let down. People slowly dispersed, while Kate and Jim turned their horses away and waved goodnight to the crowd.

The headlines of the *Australian Town and Country Journal* and the *Evening News* announced the end of it all: 'The Kelly Show Stopped—Prosecution of the Owners of the Premises'.

Detective Williams was unaware that Donovan was in town trying to secure the site of the Old Vic as an alternative venue, despite the debacle the night before. He never knew when to stop.

Pringle was reading aloud from a newspaper to Kate and Jim at the hotel. He didn't take any offence from the reporter's comments at all. He knew that the police and the press were in cahoots.

'If anything could be calculated to fully eradicate the last remains of mistaken sympathy with what may be called "Kellyism" it would be the conduct of the brother and sister of the late outlaw.'

Kate gasped, and Jim shook his head. 'But it ain't true.'

Kate sighed. 'So many people have come along on other nights, and they loved us! They are wanting to know our story.'

Pringle kept reading: '. . . feel aversion and contempt for a woman who would trade on her brother's relics and her relation-ship to him . . . great damage and common nuisance . . . to the evil example of others . . . offending against the peace . . . highly injurious to public morals . . .'

Kate was mortified. 'What a disgrace to write that about me family and me like that.' She looked for guidance from Jim, but he was over it. He just wanted out of it all. Out of performing, out of Sydney, out of the press.

In contrast to Kate and Jim, Pringle was enjoying the press. He thought it was great publicity and, despite the knowledge that he had to go to court that day, he had every intention of pushing on with the whole shebang.

'Tompkins and myself will get through this legal obstacle, and we'll come and talk to you this afternoon. Donovan thinks if we could use the Old Vic site we could really pull some crowds. This could be sensational!' Pringle left feeling exhilarated by his antici-pation. He wanted to get his appointment with the magistrate out of the way so he could carry on making some serious money.

Pringle was alone in his enthusiasm. Kate and Jim held strong suspicions that the magistrate would bring it all to an end. If that was the case, what was next for Kate? The thought of returning to the glum and depressing homestead in Victoria and the familiar surrounds that would constantly remind her of her grief disturbed her, but that's where Jim was headed and he wanted Kate to come home.

'I can't go back there, not yet anyhow. Jim, I never wanted this kinda limelight or attention, that's for sure. But it don't matter what we do. I don't appreciate what they're saying in the papers, it's humiliatin'. But it's our chance to tell our story. No matter where I go, or what I do, the press follows me. And when I am at my lowest, they want to push me down even further.' Kate knew that she was damned no matter what she did. 'They're never gonna leave me alone, Jim. Never.'

A knock at the hotel door prevented Jim's reply. Kate was reluctant to open it, afraid of any more surprises or unwanted visitors.

It was Detective Williams. This time, he and the inspector were delivering a summons to the Kellys.

'Kate and James Kelly, we are charging you both with creating a public nuisance.'

Kate looked at Jim in shock as he got up from his seat and walked towards the door. 'You're surely joking,' Kate said loudly.

'No, Miss Kelly. Both of you need to come with me right this minute to attend the Water Police Court.' Neither of them could believe it. They had been paid to perform to huge and adoring crowds, had sold-out shows and now were being arrested.

The two Victorians were escorted out of the hotel. At the court, the Kellys were pushed past Tompkins and Pringle in the hallway. Both men were alarmed to see their clients. The Kellys were placed in front of the magistrate and dealt with as a matter of urgency, ahead of the hapless agents. The provocative attitude of the agents with the detectives the previous morning hadn't helped their cause but neither had Kate's defiance.

It was a brief encounter with the magistrate, who reminded them both of their first meeting, the night of their arrival into

Sydney. 'You were warned, Mr Kelly, Miss Kelly, that it would be unacceptable for you to exhibit yourselves. We asked you both not to create trouble for yourselves. That was, after all, the nature of my visit to you. I trust you do recall what we discussed?'

The Kellys nodded in unison at the judge peering down at them. They didn't need any more trouble. Kate was keeping her mouth closed and nodding when needed. 'Yes, Sir,' said Jim.

'You have been arrested and are charged with creating a public nuisance. I will permit bail and provide an adjournment if it is agreed here and now that you will not attempt to exhibit your-selves any further while you are in Sydney. You simply must not, or I will throw you in the lock-up without hesitation. Is this clear enough to you both?'

'Yes, Sir,' they both replied.

'Bail is set at forty pounds.'

Kate cringed. That was a lot of money. The agents could cover that one as far as she was concerned.

'Another date will be set for a further hearing.' The judge paused momentarily, looking at a schedule belonging to an assistant, and commanded him to insert the details. 'We shall see you both in one week, the second instant in the month of December. Wait outside, the detectives will provide you with the information you will require and you can pay them your bail, assuming of course that you can afford to pay it? If not, you will go straight to the lock-up. Understood?'

'Yes, Sir.'

Next, the agents were thrust into the room with the judge.

The judge slammed Pringle and Tompkins. They were allowed bail after a scathing lecture. Like the Kellys, the agents had to pay forty pounds and proceedings were tied over for another day. No more exhibitions.

LATEST TELEGRAMS.
[FROM OUR OWN CORRESPONDENT.]
INTERCOLONIAL.
KATE KELLY ARRESTED.

Sydney, Thursday.

Kate and James Kelly made an attempt to exhibit themselves last night, but were stopped by the police.

The exhibition which Kate and James Kelly intended to hold has been officially prohibited, and the pair made their appearance at the Water Police Court this morning, and were charged with creating a nuisance. The case was adjourned, bail allowed on condition they did not exhibit themselves.

Later.

A man named Tomkins was brought up at the Water Police Court to-day, together with a man named Pringle, to whom the premises rented by Tomkins were sublet, for allowing relatives of a criminal lately executed in Victoria to exhibit themselves, thereby causing a nuisance. The case was adjourned for a week and bail allowed on the distinct understanding that there should be no attempt to exhibit the Kellys during the week.

Sydney, Thursday.

It wasn't just Kate Kelly's Sydney agents who were arrested—Kate and her brother Jim were both charged with creating a public nuisance because of the enormous crowds that came to see them, as this article from 25 November 1880 describes. Kate Kelly headed back to Melbourne soon after.

Aware that they had only just avoided gaol, Kate and Jim called it quits. 'Time for us to be going. Yer won't see me heels for dust, boys. You lads can fork up the bail money, we reckon. You've made plenty of money out of us.'

Pringle wondered where the hell Donovan was. He was bitterly disappointed with the outcome and fuming that he was stuck paying everyone's bail when it should have been the sly showman coughing up the dough.

Jim was relieved but Kate felt dejected. They returned to the hotel, where they packed up their humble belongings and filled the large trunk with the exhibits from the show, ready for a swift exit the following morning.

But Donovan returned from his 'business meetings' with exciting news for Kate and Jim. He had intended to book the site of the Royal Victoria Theatre as a venue, but instead he had leased a block of land located at the corner of Pitt and Bathurst streets. He was thrilled with himself.

Boldly defying the police and ignoring Kate and Jim's tales of their day in court, Donovan was determined the show would go on. At that very moment, labourers were on site, erecting the marquee that would be their new venue.

'The people want to be entertained and we shall entertain them!' Donovan exclaimed confidently, but Jim was having none of it.

'Kitty, that's it for me, I'm done. I'm headin' home.'

Donovan grimaced at Jim's news but Kate wanted Jim to stay. 'Jimmy, stay a wee bit longer, won't yer? Just a couple more weeks.'

'Don't ask me that, girl. No. This ain't no way to live.'

'Ah, Jim, don't be like that now. I understand yer want to go home but I can't, Jim.'

'All right. But think about what yer doin', Kitty. Yer need to come home.'

'Splendid!' Donovan interjected, breaking the tension between the two.

Donovan had convinced Kate and Jim to carry on with his plan, but he had underestimated the police. They were unrelenting and continued to shut down all the shows. Each time they tried to perform the police closed ranks on the crowds outside the marquee. Kate and Jim would enter the huge tent on their horses only to find empty benches. After another two failed shows in mid-December, Kate and Jim called it quits.

Grateful to have avoided police apprehension, Kate and Jim took whatever cash they had managed to extract from Donovan and set sail for Melbourne. They arrived on Friday, 17 December, and from there Jim returned to Greta, and Kate sailed on to Adelaide.

Donovan was nowhere to be seen. Once again, he had hung Kate out to dry, but she was over him. And once Donovan got wind that his starlet had split the scene, he took himself and his fistfuls of cash to the doorway of a gambler's den for the next five nights. By that time, Kate was back in Melbourne, saying goodbye to Jim and preparing for her journey onto Adelaide.

A well-known boxer, Eddie Seymour, was the resident thug on the door at the Market Street gambling den. Seymour warned Donovan not to ask for credit and told him that if he was allowed in he must agree to leave without a fuss when his funds dried up. Donovan pushed past Seymour in an addictive fervour, and the door was bolted behind him.

By the end of the first night, Flash Jack Donovan wasn't feeling so flash. His temperament had been tested, but he held it together as he peeled off over two hundred pounds of cash and donated it to the table. The following night, he was sure he would make his money back. He didn't blow his top, even as he lost a further two hundred pounds.

After the fifth night, he had lost all but ten pounds, and he felt as though his head would explode. Despite a last-ditch, desperate effort, the winning house sucked the last tenner from the Melbournite. His final roll of the dice landed suddenly, showing sevens.

Donovan screamed with the fury of a murderous lunatic as he realised that he was about to be escorted from the table, penniless, and would never be allowed to return. He abused his tormenters as they yanked him each step of the way, and he was thrown out the door. He heard the metal bar lock into place behind him as he tumbled down the stairs. Donovan had fallen into the same trap that he had set for so many others. He had ripped Kate and Jim off and blown every penny of the profits.

KATE IN ADELAIDE, 21 DECEMBER 1880

Parallel to Adelaide's white society, the Kaurna people called the Adelaide Plains and most of the Fleurieu Peninsula their home. They had experienced the destruction of their homelands and the strange behaviour of the many new, mostly white or Asian faces over-running their land. They struggled with the imported diseases, massive impacts on their water and food sources, and desecration of their sacred sites while the new inhabitants committed themselves to 'progress'.

Adelaide would one day be known as the city of churches, but at the end of 1880 the 'progress' this white settlement had resigned itself to had led to it being a city of hotels. It was also home to just under 268,000 people and had an infant death rate 40 per cent higher than anywhere else in the country as they struggled to contain the spread of disease in the city's overcrowded accommodation and the population's detrimental alcohol abuse.

There were, it was generally considered, too many drinking establishments in Adelaide, and as a result every art was used to entice men to drink. It was considered somewhat peculiar to drink water and if that liquid was ever offered, the source of it had to be questioned. It was safest to drink alcohol, and it had become an extraordinary part of Adelaide's culture. Abstaining was considered suspicious.

The latest fashion was to have a whiskey toddy before bed, sherry and biscuit in the morning, and wine and biscuit in the afternoon. Nobblers could be commenced by mid-afternoon, and beer was always had with lunch. Many young men were being hurried to their destruction, and it was a common expression that a man might find himself drunk, drowned and buried, all in one day. A popular ditty revealed it all:

> The brewer's in the counting house, he's counting all his money.
> His wife is in the parlour, eating cream and honey.
> The drinker's in the taproom dressed in ragged clothes.
> Soon he'll be made to see the cause of all his woes.

Robert Fitzallan Long, the publican at the Galatea Hotel in Adelaide, was reasonably good at coming up with new ideas for business; however, it was an understatement to say he was shocking with finances. So, this brewer, despite the folk poem of the day, wasn't counting lots of money. He had been declared insolvent twice since 1877, and his wife had one foot out the door of their marriage.

Long was trying to be creative and earn more money. He had organised lucrative fundraisers at the Exhibition Hall and Grounds in Adelaide, as well as music events in the concert room, also known as Long's Music Hall, attached to his hotel. He happened to have been in Sydney when Kate was performing there, and he was surprised but thrilled when she accepted his invitation for her to come and be a drawcard for his hotel in Adelaide.

He offered Kate good money, five pounds a week plus expenses. She didn't realise that he wanted her to do bar work to attract customers in the flooded market of inns.

Originally opening in 1845 as the Star Inn, Long's public house with stables and a music room had taken the new name in honour of the ship, the *Galatea*, which brought the colony's first royal visitor, Prince Alfred, to South Australia in 1867. The Galatea Hotel may have been grand in her day but that was not the case by 1880.

Kate was feeling weary, but not weary of wandering. She wasn't letting her creeping weakness interfere with her plans. Travelling as a passenger on the South Australian steamer, Kate had a cabin booked under a false name after her precious daughter, Miss Alice King. Kate sailed with the Australasian Steam Navigation Company, whose boat was one of many regular vessels heading on to London delivering passengers, mail, copper, wheat and wool. It was one of a steady stream of ships that would dock at Adelaide on their return from Europe, making foreign worlds seem closer.

The nautical giant landed off Glenelg on Tuesday morning, 21 December 1880, in time for Kate to take the earliest train, only twenty minutes into Adelaide. Despite disguising her name, Kate's arrival made a splash in the papers the day after.

Long greeted Kate like a wolf sizing up Little Red Riding Hood, but he had no idea what a feisty spirit he was dealing with. There was no way in hell Kate was doing bar work, which she made perfectly clear on her arrival at the Galatea Hotel.

'I'm not working in yer bar, old fella. I've nought interest in such things,' she told him.

Long was horrified by the 'old fella' reference—he was only thirty-five—but to the teenaged Kate he seemed old.

'Put me on a horse and let me speak with people. They'll pay, it's happening everywhere. You saw me in Sydney, you know what I mean. It's just the traps you'll need to worry 'bout.' This bush girl knew she had a deal and was prepared to not only make him stick to it, but also make him do it her way. Kate had learned a lot over the last month.

'You'd better be givin' me that money up-front I'm reckonin' now.'

'Jeeeesus H. Christ!' The pommy bartender blurted out. Long was bowled over, but he couldn't help liking this sassy, no-nonsense girl–woman with her fragile frame and confident mouth.

He fumbled some cash and handed over a few notes. 'It's not good business for me to hand over all the money up-front, but I'll meet you halfway. How's that?' Long thought that was fair, and he expected her to agree with him.

'No. I'll be takin' ten now, an' you can give me the last five at the beginning of the last week.' This determined young lass was willing to stick it out for three weeks, no more. He hadn't planned to appear so easy to manipulate, but he found himself simply handing over exactly what she ordered.

Kate was looking after herself from now on. She had lost so much and been through plenty more than she would have liked in her short life. Her grief and tiredness allowed a quiet recklessness to shine through.

Long could sense she was edgy. Unpredictable. He sensed it keenly enough not to argue with her, not too much anyway.

The Galatea Hotel was rough. Adelaide was stricken with poverty, and many people were homeless and broke. Long was in and out of court all the time charging thieves, fraudsters and drunken vandals who had stolen things, presented false cheques and broken windowpanes or other furnishings at his public house.

There was seemingly no end to the stealing, and Long had found many people on his premises without permission, including one man whom he discovered under a bed one morning. The man claimed to have fallen asleep the night before in a drunken state, but Long knew the man must have broken in since he had no recollection of the vagrant.

Long was something of a ruffian himself. Over the years, he'd chased many a thief down. He'd had to rough-handle plenty of drunken men and sailors over the years. He'd broken up fights and physically thrown people out.

The publican himself would be charged with drunkenness and

indecent language, even assaulting an officer, on many occasions in his life. However, his father was a solicitor in Sussex, England, and the junior Long tried to stay in good stead with the social set of Adelaide, always assisting their fundraising. He was a combination of contradictions and managed to walk on both sides of the line, the wealthy and established, as well as the poor and rough, and it would play for and against him on different occasions.

In the nearby streets of Rosina and Currie, as well as along Hindley Street itself, many Chinese workers and drifters, sailors who were unemployed or off duty and up to mischief, along with prostitutes and people of doubtful to bad character lived in filth and squalor. With ships always in and out, suspicious activities flourished from the docks into the back streets and the heart of the city.

Houses of multi but derelict storeys were filled with rubbish. Chinese workers spewed poisonous opium smoke through their noses until they lay comatose on dirty stretcher beds. Dead bodies could lie where they were stabbed or otherwise destroyed, sometimes for many days before someone bothered to report them. It was the type of environment and circumstance in which diseases and plagues could easily germinate. Over four hundred people each year were dying from tuberculosis in Adelaide, and the city's planners were nervous about how to control disease.

The unseemly sight of poor white people in the streets had to be controlled by the elite, and so the introduction of the *Destitute Persons Act* was intended to remove them from sight in the drought-ridden capital, and it was hoped that it would get rid of baby farming, too. Young helpless babies, mostly illegitimate, were handed over to random women for a regular fee or lump-sum payment, and they often ended up dead from human neglect. The shame of illegitimacy and the incapacity of women to earn a living while raising a child led to desperate decisions and loss of life.

It was frequently unsafe, for many reasons, to be on the streets here. Only a few months earlier, out the front of a house in Rosalina Street, a rough-looking crowd had gathered on the promise of a fight between two local thugs keen to settle a debt. The dirty and disorderly congregation was disrupted by the arrival of Sergeant Irwin, who dispersed the crowd of misfits. The sergeant walked around the corner to the Galatea Hotel to get the latest gossip from Long and was horrified to discover that Long's hotel was full of men and prostitutes cavorting together.

Irwin searched the premises for Mr Long to no avail. He was shocked when he witnessed a woman pulling and pushing a man in a dark corner of the back parlour, but when the sergeant confronted her, she explained that she wasn't beating him up, she was simply trying to reach past him for the glass containing her brandy.

Finally, Long presented himself to Irwin.

'Long, you should not be allowing prostitutes to assemble in your bar like this. It's a moral disgrace!'

'Oh Sarge! They're not prostitutes. Besides, they must go somewhere!' Irwin may as well have been slapped with a wet fish by the way his face contorted.

'Surely, Long, you're not telling me that you are letting your business be turned into a brothel?'

Long remained silent.

'Shut it down, Long . . . Now! I'm charging you.'

'Oh! Sergeant Irwin, with what?' Long couldn't hide his disappointment.

'Allowing prostitutes and disorderly persons to congregate at your hotel.'

'Come on now! Will yer cut me some slack here, please? I can't help it. Look what part of town this is.'

Long's day in court came and went without a drama. Testimony was given, and much to Sergeant Irwin's utter disgust, the case had no legs.

'Based on the facts being insufficient for a conviction, this case is dismissed!' The presiding judge wanted to go to lunch.

Long was deeply relieved and looked forward to reporting back to his wife, who had been most unimpressed with the circumstances that drew him to court. He hoped that he might be back in the good books with her again.

Despite the darker side of his clientele, Long's socialite contacts were thrilled with his previous entertainments and activities for the public, and no doubt they were ecstatic about meeting Kate Kelly.

Long always tried to keep one diamond-wearing socialite, whom he called 'Sparkly', onside because she was a great contact for him. He reasoned that if he could get her to see Kate, many others would follow. Sparkly was thrilled with the way the publican always found new entertainment to keep her and her important friends linked with the latest fascinations. And she was suitably impressed with Kate. 'Just when I wondered what on earth could be next, you amaze us yet again, Mr Long! Kate Kelly! Here in our very own Adelaide. Why, how extraordinary! Oh, I can't wait to see this little bushranger's sister. Well done, Mr Long! What faaaabulous amusements you provide us.'

The bragging rights of seeing Kate in the flesh quickly became a valuable asset in particular social circles. Long organised private audiences with Kate, and the novelty of it was enjoyed immensely. The stigma of Kate's lowly position was temporarily forgotten by punters, the opportunity to meet her too irresistible, as it brought the paying customer ever closer to the romance and terror of the outlaws.

Long had been warned that the police could forfeit the licence of any public house in which a Kate Kelly exhibition took place, but the fact that all public performances were forbidden created extra allure. The police were saying one thing but the public wanted another, and capitalism would win if Long had anything to do with it.

On high alert, he kept a small stash of cash handy in the hope that, if needed, a payment or two would keep nosy, overzealous constables at bay, but he knew that the Waxworks and the Academy of Music had agreed to exhibit Kate, and he had his own music hall, so things were looking very promising. Some of these venues would also show the great equestrian company the English Circus, but Long didn't see these as competition to his famous attraction.

It was possibly not a coincidence that, shortly before Kate arrived in Adelaide, Mr Kreitmayer of waxworks fame had also taken a tour of figures and relics through the region.

In Melbourne, Kreitmayer had increased his morbid but lucrative stock by adding a Ned Kelly head cast; the bloodied riding boots of Joe Byrne, taken from his corpse at Glenrowan; and a cast that Kreitmayer had made from Joe Byrne's body. The disturbing treasures were now on offer for his Adelaide patrons. Kreitmayer's extravagant purchase of Ned Kelly's armour was the new drawcard displayed alongside the successful wax reproduction of the scene of the Kelly Gang at Stringybark Creek. And now, in Adelaide, similar disturbing treasures were on offer in Mr Kohler's waxworks display at the Academy of Music, Kreitmayer's latest competitors.

The Adelaide press gave a scathing summary of the kinds of people intending to see Kate's performances and the wax display, and the *Port Adelaide News* criticised Kate for how she was earning money:

... if she has with her ... Ned's photos ... a suit of his clothes, one or two of his pistols or ... his front teeth, or a handful of hair choppings, she should ... make her fortune ... Rejoice, O South Australia, that you have those in your borders who can appreciate and love these things. Will there be a flocking of prostitutes to give vent to the softer womanly emotions?

But Long knew the truth of both the inducement he had paid Kate and the many classes of people interested in seeing her, from whom he was making a small fortune. He just had to keep the traps away and make sure Kate didn't see the nasty reports.

The combination of the touring objects and Kate's presence in Adelaide created a sensation. Many people enjoyed a private audience with Kate, despite police warnings about her appearing in public. The people who flocked to the hotel were not disappointed either. Simply gaining a glimpse of Kate was enough for most. Where would they ever have that opportunity again?

By the end of Kate's first week, the crowds at the Galatea had been enormous and Long was more than happy. As with every destination for Kate, the police were aware of the new visitor. They let Long know that the time he had just enjoyed could not continue.

So a halt came to the Kate Kelly entertainment when Long had to explain that, after the third week of their sly activities, it would be no more. It was January 1881, the traps were keeping a tight watch, and it was nearly time for Kate to disappear again anyhow.

Long tried to be diplomatic, he needed no more trouble with the law and he didn't want to lose his licence, so they would have to be content to keep the last couple of engagements he'd booked and then Kate would be on her way again, back to Victoria. Unfortunately for them both, Kate managed to come undone on a horse and that sealed the end of their partnership.

Kate was simply mounting the restive horse she had been

working with in recent weeks when someone in the crowd let off a firecracker. Kicking its back legs high, bucking and jumping with fright, the spooked horse took off across the paddock, throwing Kate off as it went. With her left foot caught in a stirrup and her body flung to the ground, she was towed ten yards on her head and upper back until she managed to get her foot free.

Kate was lying motionless on the ground, and the crowd thought at first she might have been dead. A couple of men rushed over the fence and hurried to her side. Checking her over and calling out her name, one of the men in a large cowboy hat put his hand under her nose and yelled out with relief, 'She's breathing. She's alive!' The crowd put up a loud cheer, but Kate was out to it.

After a splash of water on her face and a few anxious moments had passed, Kate was back in the real world but could hardly move. The kind men helped her to her feet, and one of them swooped her up in his arms and carried her to his sulky, swiftly returning her to the hotel. Lucky not to have been more severely wounded, Kate's shoulder and neck were black and blue, and she had to spend the rest of her last week sore and sorry in a guestroom at Long's hotel being cared for by his wife.

After that, Kate made her way back to Melbourne, where she had photos made of Ned from the gaol negative she was given. She had one image of Dan reproduced as well, so she had a keepsake. Looking at Ned's photo made her feel like he was still with her. Her head was filled with inescapable memories of her brothers and the nightmare of her losses. No one else could ever understand how the whirly-whirly of shocking memories and terrible images went around and around in her mind, nor could anyone know how deeply her thoughts filled her with anxiety.

Kate found it hard to imagine what it would be like when she returned home, and she was unsure if she would be able to remain surrounded by all the places, memories and glaring absences. Recently, she had heard that things had failed to settle down in the north-east, but Greta was where she knew she should rest and recover.

Within weeks, Ellen would be freed from gaol. Kate looked forward to the day she could collect Ellen and return her home.

21
Life After Adelaide

ELLEN'S FREEDOM, 1881

The Kelly sympathisers of the north-east were still nursing their grief and anger. The Royal Commission on the Police Force of Victoria had been announced in 1880 but was only established and conducted in 1881, and the press deemed that Kate's homeland was a place of disturbance and danger. The reminder of the devastation and loss at the site of Ann Jones' Hotel would remain a sore wound for a long time.

On 7 February 1881, almost three long years after Ellen had been locked away for a crime that, according to the Kellys, had never happened, Kate greeted her mother at the sadly familiar doors of Melbourne Gaol and escorted her home to Eleven Mile Creek.

Mother and daughter boarded the train in their dark mourning dresses and veils that kept their faces hidden, the journey both a relief and a burden at the same time. They were on their way back to the place they called home, which would always seem empty without Ned and Dan and their network of dead or gaoled friends.

Kate brought with her two potted cypresses and two pots of flowers, sad symbols of the family's losses, to be planted where Dan lay and where Ned should have been buried, if the family had been given his body as requested, instead of it being mutilated, dismembered and lost to them. The ghosts of the people they had both loved, all their regrets, joys and sadness, remained in Greta.

It was as if the women were walking through two lives, the lives before and the lives after their losses. The view that flashed past them of the hot February landscape of 1881 only served as a reminder of the years Ellen had lost behind bars and the loss of Kate's innocence and youth. The *clickity clack* of the train played a rhythm for mother and daughter, who sat beside each other with little to say. It was all too painful to talk about.

Kate had done the trip many, many times during her mother's absence, having gone to Melbourne for court cases, gaol visits, business deals and decoy runs. She hoped that bringing her mother home was the full stop to a chapter she would never have chosen to write for herself.

The pair alighted from the train at Glenrowan, and the searing February heat met them like a slap in the face. Locals milled around the platform looking for newly arrived loved ones and they signalled greetings to Kate and her mother, recognising the grieving Kelly women in their black frocks as they hurried past, eager to escape from public view.

When Ellen saw the burned remains of Ann Jones' Hotel, a horrid site of death and tragedy, it felt like a punch in the guts. Kate's skin pimpled up with goosebumps and her stomach turned as she threw her arm around her mother's shoulder, steered her in the opposite direction and stepped up the pace as she fought back her tears.

Ellen, tough as old boots, said nothing, but in Kate's mind the tormenting carousel started again. The sound of screaming and gunshots, and the image of her brother's charred carcass caused her heart to rush and her hands to sweat, and when she couldn't get enough air she thought she might crash to the ground as the world around her spun. The sight of her brother Jim snapped her out of it. Like a lighthouse of safety and comfort, he stood tall and strong beside his horse and cart. Kate was flooded with great relief as she rushed towards him, guiding her mother, who was trembling, so overwhelmed by it all.

Ellen hugged her son like she would never let go. Of her gorgeous trio of adult sons, he was the only one who remained. She looked up at his face and stared into it. 'So good to see yer, sonny.'

'And you, Ma.' He could see the mixture of torment and relief in her eyes, and he wanted to comfort her. 'Don't worry none now, Ma. I'll always look after you.'

When they arrived at the homestead, Maggie, Grace, Ellen Junior and Jack opened their arms wide to receive their mother, but it brought bittersweet comfort, their lives so deeply steeped in loss and trauma.

A photo was taken to commemorate Ellen's return, and it was a stark memento. Sitting on a chair out the front of the basic hut, a relieved Ellen was surrounded by little Ellen Junior and Jack, one of them giving a bottle to a pet goat. On the left was a smiling Kate with a small Alice, snuggling against Kate's knee and wondering who the old woman was.

Ellen always considered the homestead her true home, and the tough Irish woman hoped she would be able to remain there for the rest of her years. Ellen had to start again; they all did. Kate, however, would not be able to suffer it for long.

THE ENGLISH CIRCUS, 1881

In the first half of 1881, Kate's brother Jim and their friend Wild Wright found themselves in court, individually, for horse stealing. There was deep history between the Kellys and Wild. Jim Kelly and Wild had been caught stealing horses near Wagga Wagga back in 1877, and Jim had ended up in gaol for it, which was the only reason he had not been a part of the Glenrowan siege; he had only just got out and had been lying low.

Ned and Wild had been done for horse stealing in the early days, too, around 1874. Ned was riding a horse lent to him by Wild, who failed to let Ned know it was stolen. Not long after he had ridden it into town, Ned was arrested and soon after was handed a three-year gaol sentence, while Wild only got twelve months. Ned had seethed over it.

When Ned finished his sentence, the pair met at a pub in Beechworth to settle the debt with their fists. They agreed to fight like it was a prize match, with rules, to prevent a complete bloodbath. Both men were tall and powerful, but Ned was fuelled by the injustice of his three years of hard labour and he gave Wild a flogging. The fight was rumoured to have continued for twenty rounds. The old score was settled once and for all, and the physical clash of the two adversaries ended where a loyal and committed friendship began.

During Jim's trial in 1881, Kate fronted the court in Beechworth alongside Steve Hart's brother, to show her support for Jim, who managed to avoid gaol for the time being. Come August of that year, Jim and Wild both became the focus of a Wangaratta constable's attention over Wild's 'uproarious exuberance' after a huge night on the drink at the English Circus travelling show in Wangaratta. Jim was equally drunk, but he was always the quiet one and tried to calm the situation. On the other hand, Wild lived up to his name, and it always got him into trouble.

Hauled into the station, Wild didn't make it easy for the police or himself, so he was thrown into a cell and put in front of a judge at the first opportunity. Told to cough up five shillings or spend another six hours in gaol, Wild had sobered up enough to thank the judge for his leniency. He quickly paid the fine and skulked away with faithful Jim by his side.

Kate was the reason her brother and Wild had been at the English Circus. The company's advertisements boasted about its fine equestrian perfomance and pronounced it the best travelling circus of its time. Kate had become its latest addition.

The troupe had already made appearances in Tasmania and South Australia. The show was in Adelaide at the same time as Kate earlier in the year, and it would have seemed a natural fit to seek Kate out for their well-loved equestrian performances. After the Victoria leg, the circus would make its way into New South Wales with its mammoth marquee and alternating program of arena events and novelty acts. New attractions and performers were added to the bill every couple of nights.

Ready to drift away from home again, Kate accompanied the performers to Albury and Bowna, playing to full houses alongside Benhamo, a famous clown; mesmerising trapeze artists; and Madam Duvalis, whose steel teeth attracted much attention as she used them to lift eye-wateringly heavy objects. On her horse, Kate entertained the crowds: country folk who admired her skill and control. Children and adults alike cheered for more from this entertaining horsewoman, who was so impressive on her steed and so gorgeous in her riding outfit and her long, dark locks.

As the circus approached the towns of Young and Grenfell in September, The *Burrangong Argus* wrote, 'This company were [sic] very successful on a former visit, since which we understand there have been important additions made to the horses and riding staff.'

English Circus !

THIS FAVOURITE EQUESTRIAN COMPANY having recently visited South Australia, Tasmania, and Victoria, and pronounced the BEST CIRCUS now travelling,

WILL APPEAR AT GOULBURN

FRIDAY & SATURDAY,

SEPTEMBER 23 AND 24.

Brilliant Programme of Arenic Novelties.

CHANGE OF BILL EACH EVENING !

Million Prices : 3/, 2/, and 1/.

☞ The Mammoth Marquee will be erected on ground in BOURKE-STREET, near MONTAGUE-STREET.

Doors open at 7.30 ; commence at 8.

790   Business Manager, T. KING.

After Ned's death, Kate Kelly took to the road. It is possible that she performed in the equestrian act of the English Circus, advertised in this article from 22 September 1881, most likely under an assumed name.

The troupe carted themselves across regional towns such as Boorowa, Burrangong, Gundagai and Coolac and back to Albury, where crowds were keen to see them again and again. By the time the circus reached Goulburn, the press had reported successful performances but suggested that their horses looked fatigued and worn out. Performing night after night and travelling across the countryside were exhausting for them all. And, despite the high visitation and entrance fees that ranged from one to three shillings, some of the circus workers had to sue the manager for their wages. There were always other performers who could take their place, and the troupe carried on without them, and without Kate, as the circus headed to Braidwood.

Kate was offered other work, often as domestic help, as she passed through these small towns, and so she spent time near Grenfell and Albury along the way.

But changing her location couldn't change what had happened in Kate's life. Her troubles simply travelled with her, tormenting her until she realised that her memories and suffering were inescapable, and she returned to Greta.

CONSUMPTION, 1883

The enthralled general public and press continued their hot pursuit of Kate well past the capture and execution of her brother, and beyond the time of her public exhibitions.

Perhaps, then, it should have been no surprise to Kate or anyone who knew her well enough when it was incorrectly reported that she had landed herself in Beechworth Hospital in April 1883 and that medical experts thought she would die imminently. Not satisfied, the press took it one step further and reported that the nineteen-year-old Kate Kelly had died while in the hospital's care.

It wasn't the first time the newspapers got things very wrong about Kate. The press had incorrectly declared Kate dead after her fall from her horse in Adelaide in 1881, and a year before they had accused her of the murder of Sergeant Steele, even though he was upright and breathing at the time. Without apology, the press published corrections on both occasions, acknowledging that Kate was not a murderer and was still alive.

In truth, Kate had become very ill during the early months of 1883. Her thirst and appetite had faded, and her thin frame became lighter and more fragile, until there was very little left of her. The relentless coughing that stole her energy became an ever more painful activity, and she knew it was serious when she produced blood that nearly choked her during fits.

Ellen listened and fretted as Kate coughed night after night. Kate tossed and turned as her fever made it harder and harder for her to sleep and then even harder to get out of bed in the morning. Finally, her mother insisted that she must go to the hospital.

At Wangaratta Hospital, Kate was admitted and diagnosed with the highly contagious tuberculosis, also known as TB and 'consumption'. Popularised romantic notions of TB led to the perception of it as a 'disease of passion'. With many people believing that it inflicted an 'inward burning' and a 'consumption of one's life force', its victims were considered to be sensitive and creative souls, making it almost poetically fashionable in the upper classes. Meanwhile, the poor masses, like Kate and her friends, suffered the real consequences of the life-threatening disease, which had nothing romantic to offer them.

Caused by bacteria that are spread in the air when someone coughs, sneezes or laughs, TB affects the lungs. Kate was tired and run-down, and her grief had caught up with her, manifesting in her poor health.

Kate's dear friend and cousin Bridget Lloyd, who had been married to Wild Wright since 1873, was also diagnosed with TB and had reluctantly claimed a bed at the hospital alongside Kate. Mrs Jones of Glenrowan, the previous owner of the destroyed Ann Jones' Hotel, had also been admitted, but recovered swiftly. TB had taken many people's lives, and both Bridget and Kate were very sick, remaining in the hospital to fight off the serious illness for over a month.

Wild Wright, friends and family visited Kate and Bridget regularly as they slowly improved.

⁓

Two and a half years had gone by since Ned had been hanged, but the press was still continuing their love–hate relationship with Kate. They wrote in admiration of her powers of endurance as 'a fine specimen of the native-born bush girl' as newspapers reflected on the Kelly Gang and her involvement, but then they lamented her lost potential for not directing her energies 'rightly'. The obsessed press, such as the *Freeman's Journal* in New South Wales, the *Bendigo Advertiser* in Victoria, and the *Darling Downs Gazette* in Queensland, questioned why Kate had not been arrested for helping the gang all those years ago. Regardless of the simple life she was living and the losses she had suffered, it seemed that the press would never be done with her.

Articles about Kate Kelly continued to appear in the press from the late 1870s into the 1900s. This engraving of Kate first appeared in the Illustrated Australian News, *3 July 1880, and is attributed to David Syme & Co.*

Once Kate was well enough to leave the hospital, she went home and focused on her recovery. Her grief and traumatic thoughts still haunted her as she tried to heal, both emotionally and physically. She still had a long way to go before she would be strong and healthy again. This gave her cause and time to wonder about her future. What was she going to make of her life?

22
The Disastrous Fitzpatrick

ESCAPE BY SEA

When rumours began circulating in March 1879 that Kate was in negotiations with the owner of a small ship, supposedly making plans for Ned and the gang to escape by sea, Constable Fitzpatrick was transferred to Sydney. His task was to identify the gang if they arrived at the docks.

While Kate was working hard to stave off police surveillance and help her brothers evade capture, Fitzpatrick arrived in New South Wales, away from all the Kelly action in Victoria and away from where the Kelly Gang could have kidnapped or killed him. He was thrilled.

Within two months of the constable's placement, the Police Department in New South Wales was inundated with complaints and reports about Fitzpatrick's capers.

Despite being married, he'd taken up with young Suzy, housekeeper to the very successful tobacconist, Maurice Casey. Fitzpatrick spent his time inducing Suzy away from her work, which drove Casey wild, let alone the matter of Casey's stolen jewellery, which was still being investigated. Had Fitzpatrick persuaded Suzy to steal the valuable items from her boss's wife? Casey believed so, since she'd been pleasant and reliable until she met Fitzpatrick. When Casey complained, Inspector General Fosbery lost his cool with Fitzpatrick; it was the last straw.

'Fitzpatrick, what were you doing at Maurice Casey's residence last night? He made a complaint that you were intoxicated and making a scene. Casey says you were disturbing the peace in front of his family. You're a disgrace! You are a police officer. This is serious. Especially when added to the list of your escapades since you have been in our colony. That's it. No more cautions. Get out of my sight!'

Fitzpatrick had made no progress at the Sydney wharves other than furthering his criminal connections with the lower classes, and so Fosbery had decided to cut him free. Sending an urgent telegram to the Victorian authorities, the inspector general demanded that Fitzpatrick be removed from Sydney, and he sent police officers to swiftly collect Fitzpatrick from his seaside post. They were instructed to make sure that he gathered all his possessions and that he exited the colony, never to return.

Fitzpatrick's many and varied indiscretions were surprisingly not enough to have him dismissed. On his return to Richmond, he was unwell and as such was limited to general mounted duty and drill for nearly three months. After this, he was stationed under a very strict Sergeant Mayes at Lancefield, where Fitzpatrick tried to start a new life but again, he managed to bring himself undone.

Fitzpatrick had been instructed to attend an assault case. The assaulted man had multiple, serious injuries. Despite the beaten man's shocking condition, he was able to identify the perpetrator, so that Fitzpatrick could arrest him.

'That bastard belted me. He says I owe him money but I damn well do not. I have paid my debt and now he insists I owe him a percentage for the service, in addition to what he has already accumulated from me.'

The giant, heavy-set, angry-looking man who had committed the assault was inside a drinking house, and the accuser was at the door with Fitzpatrick, pointing him out.

Fitzpatrick took one look at the huge man at the bar, who glared back at the constable with a look of defiance and the threat of violence written all over his face while he sank a shot of whiskey. After a moment's consideration, Fitzpatrick said to the victim that he would not conduct the arrest he was sent to perform.

'What do you mean you won't arrest him? For the love of God, man! You are a policeman! It is your duty! You *must* arrest him and take him to the station. You *must*! Look at what he has done to me!'

The injured man had blood all over him. He was a tough man himself and that was the only reason he was still standing after the hiding he had copped. He stared at the useless constable, gobsmacked.

'Unfortunately, I cannot arrest him,' Fitzpatrick said without shame.

'So, what must happen then, if you will not arrest him? What must I do to seek justice, you pigeon-livered fool?'

Fitzpatrick shrugged his shoulders and walked away, which made the man want to jump on him and belt the weasel.

Somehow, the injured man got himself to Lancefield Police Station, where he located the sergeant on duty. The infuriated man yelled at Sergeant Mayes in distress and demanded that a proper policeman be sent to perform the arrest that Constable Fitzpatrick was too cowardly to take care of himself. The shocked sergeant sent two other police officers over to finish the job that Fitzpatrick never really started and then he hunted Fitzpatrick down.

'Never in my entire career, Fitzpatrick, have I seen a man so useless, so cowardly, so stupid. I have never witnessed a man so unwilling to perform his sworn duty!'

With two previous cautions under his belt, this incident was the final nail in Fitzpatrick's coffin. His time in the Victorian police force was over. He was officially dismissed on 27 August 1880, just after Ned's preliminary hearing at Beechworth, and the news brought no end of delight to Kate and the Kellys. The family thought that Fitzpatrick's disgrace would prove that his testimony against Ellen and Ned was untrustworthy; they truly hoped that Ellen's sentence, and that of the others implicated on the same night, would be revoked and the debacle would be exposed, but it was not to be.

FALSE PRETENCES

In 1894, years after Fitzpatrick's dismissal from the force, he was listed as a traveller in the guest register at the Saracen's Head Hotel in Melbourne. He was still married when headlines brought attention to his latest shame: 'Fitzpatrick of Kelly Fame'.

Fitzpatrick had managed to gift himself a few nights of accommodation, meals and drinks through a lot of deception that was now catching up with him by way of a pending court case after his arrest at the hotel.

At Melbourne City Courthouse, Hanna Ryan answered the judge. 'Yes, Your Honour, he swindled accommodation, meals and cash from me, by means of a fake cheque.' She was looking at Fitzpatrick, who was absentmindedly staring at the ceiling.

'And the prisoner took accommodation at your establishment?'

'Yes, Your Honour. He and another man had arrived at my hotel, Saracen's Head Hotel, Your Honour, in Bourke Street, in May. May 16, Your Honour. He told me he needed to send a telegram to his mother in Melbourne's Surrey Hills. I sent that telegram for him, and he wrote a cheque for me for one pound. He said to me, "Here, you take this cheque and cash it for me, take from it what I owe you." And so, I gave him back twelve shillings and six pence.'

'I see. Go on.'

'Well, the bank didn't like the cheque, Your Honour, on account of it being dated 1874 instead of 1894, Your Honour.'

The judge looked at Fitzpatrick in disgust. 'Some kind of trick that is. What happened then?'

'Well, Your Honour, I asked him to fix it. The Colonial Bank had sent it back to me and by then I asked him to pay his account for the other days, it was four days later by then, Sir.'

'And?'

'So he fixed the date and then wrote another cheque for two pounds and ten shillings for his board and residence.'

'Did you accept that cheque, too?'

'Yes, Your Honour. He assured me he had an account and apologised for any inconvenience.'

'What happened after that? By the way, Mr Fitzpatrick, this is not looking good for you. And more so, due to your previous occupation, however inept you were at it.' There was a chuckle from the gallery. 'Mrs Ryan, continue.'

'Your Honour, the bank sent both the cheques back again, and this time it was not the date that was the issue. Your Honour, the bank informed me Fitzpatrick held no account with them. They said he had an account many years ago but no longer had any funds with them.

'By that time, Your Honour, I had accepted further cheques, and he had continued to stay at my establishment. It was at that time I contacted the police and they arrested him.'

'The total amount he has defrauded from your business?'

'A sum total, Your Honour, of nine pounds and eight shillings. This amount includes board, lodging and other expenses.'

'Thank you! You may be seated.' The judge shuffled some papers and wrote some notes before he looked across to Mr Tucker, Fitzpatrick's solicitor.

'Has Mr Fitzpatrick anything to offer? I warn you, though, sometimes it is best to say nothing, to avoid the risk of making a bad situation worse.'

'Nothing to add, Your Honour.' Fitzpatrick's solicitor heeded the warning and shut down any chance of Fitzpatrick digging an even deeper hole for himself.

'We will resume for the final judgment and sentencing of Mr Fitzpatrick in the Melbourne Court of General Sessions in July on the twentieth instant, for a judgment on the presenting of valueless cheques, in other words, False Pretences.'

When the judge had adjourned the trial, Fitzpatrick's solicitor addressed him bluntly. 'You must make the most of the next two nights, Fitzpatrick, as they will most likely be your last taste of freedom for a good while.'

Fitzpatrick looked shocked.

'You are guilty of fraud, Fitzpatrick. It's fraud.' Tucker couldn't understand why Fitzpatrick struggled with the situation. It was so clear that he had done wrong.

'The judge will sentence you to gaol when we return. It is just a matter of him deciding on the period of time and which gaol.' Fitzpatrick lowered his head for a moment and wondered how long he might end up in prison for.

Two days later, the judge was swift with Fitzpatrick's sentencing. 'This Court finds you guilty! You are sentenced to a period of twelve months in prison. You will be remanded immediately and dispatched forthwith to Castlemaine Prison.' *Bang!* The gavel ended it all.

⌒

At the Castlemaine Prison of Victoria, the man who used to be known as Constable Fitzpatrick was in the prison yard with his cellmates. His time in the police force was but a long memory ago, more than fourteen years. He almost considered himself lucky to be imprisoned and have permanent shelter and food, which he knew was a much better proposition compared to what he was facing on the outside, unless his wife took him back.

In a typically dishonest way, he had claimed to be Irish. It was written so in the prisoner's records. Name. Religion. Nationality. Offence. Fitzpatrick's father was born in England, his mother, Scotland. He himself was born in Victoria. It was a pretence he had maintained throughout his life, especially towards the Kellys. His nationality was really Australian. A fraud on many levels for his whole life, he had finally been convicted of it. When Kate heard about it, she thought it was a fate richly deserved. The thought of him still made her feel sick.

The hardest thing in gaol was the lack of grog. His shaking and sweating would eventually pass, but the stabbing feelings in his guts were the most painful reminders. The enforced sobriety didn't seem to have brought him much clarity, though, and he became quite unhinged. The other prisoners heard him talking to himself at night, ranting on about how he had been hard done by and blamed for things that 'weren't his damned fault'. He wasn't thinking about how he had wronged Kate or Ellen Kelly; he was still stuck on his dismissal from the police force, and he could not understand why the letters written on his behalf had not been enough to keep him employed.

Frederick Standish, the Chief Commissioner of Police in Victoria, had written back to the misguided people who had lobbied for Fitzpatrick's reinstatement to the police service, and his words still shattered Fitzpatrick. 'I cannot hold out any hope of his being reinstated to the Victoria Police Force. During his time his conduct was generally bad and discreditable . . .'

As if that hadn't been bad enough, Sergeant Mayes had put it in much stronger language, and Fitzpatrick went over and over it in his mind: 'Fitzpatrick was not fit to be in the force. He was the associate of the lowest people, he could never be trusted out of sight and he never did his duty.' Fitzpatrick had twelve long months to ponder his fate from the wrong side of the law.

His consistently selfish actions managed to leave a trail of suffering and damaged lives, not just while he was a policeman and not just for the Kellys. Perhaps it was the alcohol or maybe he was just no damned good.

Despite how the Kelly family felt about Fitzpatrick, his comments to the journalist B.W. Cookson about Ned in his later years were words of admiration: 'He was a superior man. Under better circumstances he would probably have been a leader of good men instead of a gang of outlaws.' It was too late. So much damage had been done, and Kate was glad their paths never crossed again.

Fitzpatrick must have promised to reform himself after his gaol term or somehow persuaded his wife to take him back, because he lived for another thirty years and died at his wife's home in 1924. Cirrhosis of the liver and a heart attack were the causes of his death, and his resting place is the cemetery at Box Hill in Victoria.

Part 3
REMEMBERING KATE

Kate came to an inland town in New South Wales where she went into domestic service and then married a resident of that town under an assumed name. Having been acquainted with her before she left her home, I had some interesting talks with her about the stirring days when the boys [The Kelly Gang] were out. She was a good woman.

Hugh McDougall
'Letter', *Darling Downs Gazette*, 1910

23

After Kate's Death

THE INQUEST, SATURDAY, 15 OCTOBER 1898

'Sir, he was here just now. But he has since disappeared.' Garstang was talking to the coroner about the disappearing Mr Sullivan, but the coroner, Mr C.P Sowter, was unfazed by the absence: 'So be it.'

Susan Hurley looked at the faces of each of the men in the courtroom; no one else seemed to care, but she struggled privately with the lack of accountability. *Sullivan found Ada*, she thought. *He should be here, he should tell us what he knows.*

Garstang gave his evidence and brought attention to the fact that four of Kate's rings were still on the fingers of her left hand and that a brooch remained pinned to her dress when she was found, which, for the police, suggested she had not been robbed. Garstang, sitting as upright as possible, leaned towards Sowter and put forward his cold appraisal. 'There was no suspicion of foul play from the disposition of the clothes on the deceased's body, Sir.'

Sowter nodded and wrote things down, and Garstang continued. 'Nothing in the woman's pockets either.' So, Kate had not used stones to weigh herself down, as was sometimes the case with people who committed suicide. '... There were two empty beer bottles nearby...'

Susan wondered if someone else was with Ada in those final hours.

There was silence for a moment and then Garstang added, as if he were boasting, 'I was the first one to touch the body, Sir.'

Sowter nodded his head and waited for more information. 'Anything else, Garstang?'

'Well, for the record, Sir, I made a diligent search to ascertain the woman's whereabouts, since I first received the information that the deceased had left her infant without any person to care for it. Let the record show that I continued to search for her until yesterday, about 12.30 p.m., when Kennedy and I went to the lagoon after Sullivan gave us his information.'

Sowter waved Garstang off the stand with a flick of his left hand and scribbled something with his other. 'McDonnell! Your turn. What do you make of it all?'

Doctor McDonnell and Garstang brushed shoulders as they exchanged places. 'Well, I made an examination of the body yesterday, and I should think the body would have been laying in the water for somewhere between four to eight days. Owing to the advanced stages of decomposition, it was impossible to form any definite opinion as to a cause of death.'

'No opinion, you say?' Sowter peered at the doctor.

'Well, the body was too decomposed to tell if there was any violence, Sir.'

The good doctor had distressed Susan over the cause of Kate's death. *Did he really just say that?* '*Impossible to form an opinion?*'

What the hell does that mean? Did someone do this to Ada or not? Why can't he tell? Susan nervously picked at the skin on the back of her hands. She was feeling sick in the pit of her stomach, but everyone else seemed perfectly calm and unperturbed. Susan was horrified and thought to herself, *So, we don't really know if anything untoward happened to Ada?*

She examined Sowter's sharp features and tiny eyes, which were still small even though magnified behind his glasses. She was not impressed. While Sowter shuffled papers, he looked down on everyone from his wooden bench of judgement.

'You treated the deceased some years ago, did you not, McDonnell? Was it for mental derangement?'

'I may have treated Mrs Foster, but I do not recall the particulars.' McDonnell's time with Kate had included his unsuccessful attempt to keep her son William alive in 1894, and it seemed that the sadness she had endured over the loss had no impact on the doctor since he could not recall his interaction with her. But even earlier than that, in 1890, McDonnell had treated Kate after the birth of Gerty, when her depression had consumed her. Kate could see no way out of her darkness at that time, but the doctor had no recollection of her suffering.

Sowter had heard enough from McDonnell and addressed Susan. 'Looks like you were the last person to see Mrs Foster alive, Mrs Hurley.' Sowter directed her to the witness box as he spoke.

Susan was unsure about what Sowter was implying as she placed herself into the seat. 'About 2.30 p.m. on Wednesday the 5th of October, I last saw her alive. I reported her missing the next night. She was sitting in her house, slightly under the influence of drink when I last saw her. She asked me to take her baby.'

Sowter raised his eyebrows and looked up from his paperwork directly into Mrs Hurley's eyes while they both paused a moment.

'Continue.' He stared at the ceiling while she spoke.

'She said she didn't like the baby because it was on the bottle. She wanted to get away for a couple of days and get straight. She said if I took the baby, Mr Foster would pay for its keep. She never mentioned suicide to me, I never heard her threaten suicide.'

'And the drinking?'

'I have seen her under the influence but only since the baby was born, in the last month.' Susan sat still with her heavy heart as she stared at Sowter.

'And the children, where are they now?'

'I am caring for the infant and the other children.'

'You can sit down again, Mrs Hurley.'

Susan wiped her eyes with her handkerchief and made her way back to her seat, not looking at anyone. Since the birth of her baby Ethel Alma, Susan had noticed how she felt things more deeply than before, and this whole terrible matter was nothing but tragically sad to her. She missed her friend, felt desperately for the children left in her care, and she really wanted to know the truth about what had happened.

Bricky was sitting away from Susan, and as he watched her return to her seat, he was called on to make his statement. Susan's eagle eyes followed him, sure that he was hiding something as he seemed so keen to avoid her.

As Bricky revealed his side of events, Susan was angered even further.

'Wob, wob. When I arrived I bought some things for the children. But, wob, wob, when I left, seeing her condition, I only left six shillings on the table.'

Sowter asked Bricky, 'What was your wife's condition?'

'When I first left home for Burrawang, she were in her bed recovering from her confinement. I, wob, wob, remonstrated with her about her drinking. She promised to reform. Wob, wob, wob. She has been addicted to drink. Wob, wob. I have frequently heard my wife threaten to commit suicide when under the influence.'

Susan's mind rattled in opposition to Bricky's version of things. *What's all this about Ada being suicidal and drunk all the time? She never mentioned suicide to me. Not once. Yes, she was drinking but that's just since the baby was born. Home alone, no help with the baby. She was down on the infant but that's probably milk fever or such, I've seen it before. That milk fever does something queer to you. Doesn't mean she killed herself.*

Mrs Hurley felt as if she was the only one sticking up for her neighbour. So many thoughts about the inconsistencies in all of the evidence were running around Susan's head with nowhere to go. None of the men in the room were going to pay any attention to what she thought, even if she did decide to voice it. She was very aware of being the only woman among them. *They've made their bloody minds up, haven't they? They're gonna say she did it to herself, I can tell. They already said that in the newspaper, and Bricky's suggesting it, too. How convenient!*

Susan was still torturing herself with these thoughts when Sowter announced his verdict.

'Ahhhhmm.' He cleared his throat. 'This decision is final and is based on the evidence sworn here today. It will be recorded as such: The deceased, Mrs Catherine Foster, was found drowned in the lagoon on the 14th of October 1898. However, there is no evidence to show how she came to be drowned.'

He continued on with other legal jargon, but Susan wasn't interested anymore. His annoying, well-to-do accent faded into the background as she sat stunned, trying to figure out what it all meant. She could not reconcile the emptiness of the inquest, the hollowness of the information and the indifference to Ada's life.

So, we know nothing. Nothing. How can he say she drowned if the doctor says he can't determine the cause of death? She might have even been dead before her body was in the water. Who the hell would know?

Angry, Susan burst up from her seat. She had no desire to speak to any of the men, and she rushed out the door before anyone could talk to her.

Susan made it home and into Ted's arms. Mr Hurley had, so far, remained a quiet onlooker to the drama affecting their once simple lives. Ted had gone along with the neighbour's children living in his house and his wife being entwined in this terrible mess, but it was hard for him to see her so disturbed by the whole sorry dilemma of Kate's disappearance and death.

It had been nine long and distressing days for them both, and for the Foster children in their care, the gloom would continue. They no longer had their mother.

Ted was aware of the added stress on his wife looking after the two babies. He was also a little concerned about his precious daughter Ethel Alma having to share her mother's attention. He had never pictured that they would suddenly be responsible for six children, four of them not even their own. It was testing everyone as they all grieved Kate's absence for different reasons. The children still didn't even know that their mother had died.

In the bedroom, away from the children, they spoke in hushed tones about the deliberations over Kate's demise. Mrs Hurley was red-faced and weeping, recounting it all to her husband, unable to conceal her disgust and confusion. 'I just can't understand it. No one is answerable. To me, the matter is unresolved. They are just guessing everything. Bricky is saying it is suicide and, despite his abuse of her, he remains above suspicion. Then we have Sullivan, who could have committed any type of offence in this saga, and we shall never know. And to make it worse, the doctor says he simply cannot tell how Ada died, but the coroner says she drowned. It's deplorable. What a mess!'

Ted, a large but gentle man with a handlebar moustache and kind eyes, allowed his young wife the space to express her grief. He admired her level of concern about a life that had ended so dreadfully. At least Susan cared. 'So what of the children then, Susan? Did Mr Foster talk to you?'

'No, he avoided me. I am none the wiser, but I know he cannot raise four children alone, Ted.' He nodded.

Susan continued. 'We're going to have to tell the children that their mother is dead. She's probably buried by now. The police said the funeral was happening straight after the inquest was done with. Bricky won't tell them, and it is carrying on longer than it should.'

'Well, if you think you need to do it . . .' Ted said.

Susan snapped back at him, 'I don't want to do it, Edward, but someone has to let them know the truth so they know why they have been left here unattended, for goodness sake.'

'Don't get testy with me, woman.'

They fell quiet for a few moments.

'I'm sorry, Ted. It's been an overwhelming day.'

Ted patted her on the shoulder and left for the pub. He hoped that it would all be dealt with by the time he got back for his tea.

Susan watched her husband leave, cranky that she had been dumped in this situation. Her first priority was to feed the babies, who she could hear crying out for her attention. Susan's kindness had been keeping baby Catherine alive, but her body simply wasn't up to it. Kate's infant had been on the bottle from the start, and she wasn't going to latch onto Susan's breast. No matter how much Susan wanted to give the baby its best chance, she knew that she was up against it.

In that moment, Susan tried to calm herself and the babies. She picked up baby Ethel and put her on the breast, which quietened one screaming voice. When Ethel was settled enough to keep feeding, Susan reached for tiny Catherine, who was underweight and uneasy. She fed her with a bottle of goat's milk, but it was a struggle for the little girl.

The day had truly been an ordeal, and Susan looked forward to putting the babies to bed and seeing the end of the day, but she had an onerous task hanging over her head.

THE CONVERSATION

After feeding the babies and burping each of them, Susan laid them down to sleep on her mattress with rolled-up blankets by their sides. The conversation needed to be had with the other children. Susan was just going to have to get it done with.

Gathered in the sleep-out, on a large mattress on the floor, Kate's three older children rested. Susan walked into the room slowly and sat on a wooden chair as she greeted them.

'There is some serious news I must tell you. You all need to be very well-behaved about this news, and once I tell you we won't talk about it again. Do you understand?' The little children instantly became uptight but they nodded their heads.

'Your mother has not come back because she has died. Today she was buried. There is nothing more I can tell you. You must speak to your father if you want to know anything else. Do you understand what I have told you?'

There was a quiet pause. Of course, they didn't really understand it. 'Dead?' Gerty asked.

'Yes. She died and now she is buried. She will not come back.'

The older two looked at each other, confused and disbelieving.

'But you said she went away and was coming back,' nine-year-old Fred said.

'Yes. I did say that. That was what was supposed to happen. But it didn't. Something went wrong, and now she has gone to heaven.'

Three-year-old Elsie had no idea at all what 'dead' meant, but she understood that they were saying her mother was not coming back. Eight-year-old Gerty put her arm around Elsie and pulled her in close to her side. 'I'm here, Elsie. I'll look after you.' Elsie made small whimpers and sucked her thumb as she put her head on the pillow and pulled a blanket over it.

Susan was lost for any other words but was relieved that she had dealt with the matter. 'That's all there is to say about it, I'm afraid.'

'How is she dead?' Gerty asked as she started to cry.

'She drowned.'

'Ma said she knows how to swim, Mrs Hurley. She wouldn't drown.'

'That may be the case, Gerty, but I'm sorry to say it is true.'

'How do you know for sure she is dead, Mrs Hurley? I don't believe you.' Fred was angry.

'Fred, you are going to have to be a big man about this. Your mother has passed away, and she is not coming back. It is very, very sad, but we cannot change it.'

Susan was feeling overwhelmed by the conversation and, although she knew that the children had every right to be shattered, she had little left to give.

Fred challenged Susan some more. 'I don't believe you. Why would you say such a bad thing about my ma?'

Gerty and Elsie sobbed quietly, but Susan needed to escape from it. She pushed her tired body up out of the chair and walked to the kitchen to prepare Ted's tea, ignoring Fred.

Susan cried as she chopped the spinach from the garden that would be added to the stew that would nourish them all that night. She and Ted had been stretching their meagre supplies as far as they could to keep everyone alive. Susan desperately wanted the day to be over so she could rest her eyes, soothe her busy head and heal her broken heart.

24

Kate's Funeral

As lonely and tragic as Kate's demise by the lagoon was, the inter-ring of her body was perhaps even colder and sadder, with no one familiar to her there to send her off or remember her.

The cemetery was a large flat paddock browning in the spring heat on the western outskirts of town. Multitudes of headstones, varying in sizes and stages of decay, held testament to those beneath them. An expansive sky revealed the ever-changing pinks and blues of the afternoon.

Two witnesses stood by the deep hole in the ground as George J. Thomson took care of Kate's burial. The position allocated for Kate's body was with others of the Church of England, her husband's religion, but she was placed deliberately far away from the rest of the respectable members of Forbes society, who were buried with dignity, respect and recognition. Not far from Kate was the grave of bushranger Ben Hall.

As the last of the dirt was thrown to lock Kate's body away forever, the afternoon sun sank in the west, lighting only a slither of sky. Galahs stretched their wings, enjoying the sheer thrill of flight and of being alive, a gift that had been withdrawn from Kate Kelly.

The men who had taken care of this final goodbye turned their backs and walked away in their red clay-stained clothes, their shovels over their shoulders. The disturbed soil resting in the rectangle that held Kate's remains would settle in coming weeks and remain a bare patch of ground, her identity unrecognised. It would take time for Kate's resting place to be respectfully marked with more than a simple cross.

An elaborate, sculptural headstone was organised by Hugh McDougall at his own expense. It read: 'In Loving Memory of Kate Foster nee Kelly. Beloved wife of William Foster', but there was no mention of her children. Kate's death certificate indicated that she was thirty-nine, and her headstone indicated that she was thirty-six, but if 1863 was this elusive woman's true birth date, as is commonly believed, she must have only been thirty-five.

Hugh remained at Warroo for the rest of his working life, and witnessed the changes in rural Australia from the 1880s through to 1924. He married and had three children. Kate's old friend sent a photograph of the new headstone to Jim Kelly so he could see that Kate had not been forgotten. Another photo would be taken, this one of Bricky holding his hat against his chest, standing alongside the monument, a reminder of their ill-fated partnership, sheepishly looking at the camera.

In the weeks after Kate's burial, Garstang sent a message to the Greta West Post Office via Glenrowan about Kate's passing and hoped that the Kellys would collect their mail and the important message before too much time had passed. What must happen to Kate's children?

25

News of Kate

Jim Kelly had arrived at the Greta West Post Office to collect mail and pick up supplies. It was just another monthly trip to town to get what was required for the property he and his mother Ellen shared. Perhaps that was what made it such a shock.

Jim had to sit down. He reached out for some support and leaned on the wooden slats of the wall inside the post office building.

'Sorry for the sad news, Mr Kelly.' The young man behind the thick timber counter floundered a little as he watched Jim become pale. Jim's legs failed him, and he leaned into the wall with his back. He couldn't catch his breath. He was not expecting this kind of news. *Not Kitty! No. When in damnation would this suffering ever end?*

Jim kept looking at the telegram. How could it be? Kitty dead? Drowned, of all things? It felt like someone had just belted him with a fence paling but then his thoughts turned to his mother. His shoulders tightened. This news could kill the old lady. *Jesus, Mary and Joseph*, he thought, *this could be the last straw.*

Jim's tough life had etched lines and sorrow into his face. Worn and weathered across his sun-thickened skin and dark eyes, his wiry black eyebrows knitted together as his forehead wrinkled up, quizzically. How could Kate's children have no home? Where was her husband?

Everything about this news was overwhelming and confusing. How must he tell the woman who had already lost so many of her children that her cherished daughter Kate had gone, too? Ned, Maggie and Dan—Jim and his mother had felt every one of those losses deeply. This was no different.

After what seemed an eternity, Jim gathered the mail from the counter. He nodded to the clerk and made his exit. Outside, he walked back to his horses, tied up at the nearest cluster of trees along the street. He leaned over the tray of the wagon and lowered his head. He was weeping. The man who had seemed unbreakable throughout all of the Kelly hardships and tragedies was gutted by the loss of his little sister. Jim succumbed to his deep sadness while alone with his horses under wide and leafy trees.

He needed a few moments before he could climb back in and head home to complete a task that no one could envy.

Back at the homestead, Ellen was moving around the place slowly when she heard her son and the horses arrive home. She removed a large black kettle from the kitchen stove, a wood burner that gobbled up firewood all year round regardless of the heat or the cool of the seasons.

She grabbed a fat brown ceramic teapot and swirled some hot water into it, placing the lid back on to warm it. She let the hot water heat the pot, then cast the water out the back door. Quickly, she threw a few teaspoons of black tea-leaves in, with one extra for the pot. Deftly, she poured the boiling water into the pot, placed the kettle back on the stove and replaced the ceramic lid almost as one motion. She slid a pink woolly crocheted cosy over the top of the tea-laden vessel and sat it on the kitchen table. She spun it three times by the handle and wiped her hands on the apron tied around her tiny waist. Her wrinkled hands reached behind her to release the strings of it, and she placed it on the sideboard. She reached for two large cups just as her son entered the doorway.

'Ah, Jimmy. Tea is brewing. Busy in town?' Rinsing the cups with hot water, she had not looked at Jim yet but she could feel his tense mood before he'd even muttered a word. Turning gently to place the cups near the teapot, she looked for an explanation in Jim's face as he lowered his exhausted body into his usual seat. She pulled her chair out and sat without looking away from Jim. 'What is it, son? Something has happened, I can see it in your face. Just spit it out, Jim. Make haste with it, don't torment me now.'

'Ma, it's Kitty. She's gone.'

His mother breathed in suddenly and loudly. 'No, no, no, no, no!' Ellen was turning her head from left to right. 'No!'

'Ma! She's passed away. She's gone.'

'It can't be true. I don't believe it.'

Jim slowly reached into his pocket, pulling out the only evidence he had. He showed Ellen the folded paper. 'They sent us this tele-gram. I don't recognise the name. Kitty drowned.'

'Holy Mary! No, no, no!'

The shocked mother's heart was racing. 'Read it to me, Jim. I can't bear it. What do they say about my baby girl?'

Jim took his time to recite the contents to her as requested. He needed to read it again to believe it himself. The news of Kate was old. Their precious Kitty had died some weeks before. 'It must have taken them a while to find out how to reach us, I suppose. And I haven't been to town since last month.'

309

'Where must the children be then? Who is this Mrs Hurley caring for them, Jim? The husband, where is he?'

Jim shrugged his shoulders. 'I will rest the horses and ready the wagon. I'll leave in a couple of days.'

'You are a good, good man, Jim. God bless yer. Yes, if they need a home, they must have one. Bring them home, Jim.'

Time stretched in the silence between them as they sat.

Ellen's forearms reached out across the worn wood of the table, her fists were clenched with a handkerchief squeezed in one. She was a tiny thing, and her fine features became gently twisted as her shoulders moved in time with her sobbing. The news was sinking in. A little whisper underneath her tears, 'No one could ever understand the suffering of my life.'

It was quiet in the house, until the word got around and other family members came to visit, sharing their sympathies with the old lady and staying with her when Jim set off on the journey to Forbes to meet his nieces and nephew for the first time. His mission was to collect them and bring them back to a family and a place they had never known.

26

Jim Arrives in Forbes

Jim always said that every long journey started with one single step, and he was determined that if he kept going a little bit every day, one day he must surely arrive at his destination.

For a distance of around three hundred miles, Jim, his horse team and wagon cut across country, wheeled through towns, trotted along dirt tracks and rested by creeks and rivers. Through the hot, dusty days and dark nights, the dedicated family man considered the sad story of his sister's premature death. He wondered about her children. He had many questions about how she had drowned, and he constructed a few theories about why the husband seemed to be so ghostlike in Kate's life.

The trials of grief challenged him as he travelled. He was at once angry and sad, and then sometimes hoped he had got it all wrong, that maybe Kate was still alive. But he would arrive back at the same sad place after hours and hours of thinking. His deep regret, resentment even, was parked in the middle of his pain, for it was not just one death he would think about, it was the death of many that he was reminded of. The death of Kate could not be thought of without remembering the death of Maggie and then memories of all the other deaths in his family and among his friends. This circle of death and tragedy seemed to hold an endless presence for what had been his entire life.

Just when he imagined he would never arrive, on his sixth day of riding, Jim approached the banks of the Kalari River and he knew he was close. He had only a few more miles to travel before he was in the township of Forbes. As the tree-lined lake came into sight, Jim walked his horses slowly over Johnny Woods' crossing along the low-lying end of Sherriff Street and along the water's edge until he pulled up at the goldfield flats. It was there by the lake that Jim Kelly set up his camp.

After a full sleep stretched out in his cart, Jim awoke to the laughing songs of the kookaburras scattered in the tall trees surrounding him. Splashing his face in the lake's water, he looked around to assess the place his sister had called home for such a long time. There was an appealing pink sunrise above him, but its beauty was reduced by the thoughts of Kate that plagued him. He put the billy on the fire. A hot black tea was what he needed before he ventured out to find the Fosters and this Mrs Hurley whom he had heard about.

Mid-morning, Jim figured that he must seek out this Garstang fellow and get the facts from the police. But it was a dreaded and unnatural feeling for Jim to be seeking a policeman's help.

Jim never rushed anywhere, apart from when he came to Forbes. He had spent too many years in the bush to be fooled by the illusions and pressures of time that people who lived in towns were ruled by. Jim would take a long, slow walk to the police station by the lake's edge. He wanted to use the time to think about Kate and what he would say to these people about the children's future.

From the lake, his long legs took him across town, through the wide main streets filled with bullock teams, horses and carts, and back along Sherriff Street, where he followed a sign and found himself near the lock-up keeper's residence. As he approached the police station next door, he called out to a constable, who emerged from the verandah. 'Where might I find Garstang?'

'Follow me!' The young policeman led the Victorian down past the courthouse and pointed across the road. 'He's the one with the scar.'

Standing with a gathering of local men outside a coursed stone church with a pointy roof and even sharper steeple was Garstang.

As Jim approached, the group disbanded and Jim called out. 'Garstang?'

'Who is asking?'

'Jim Kelly is my name. You know something of my sister's passing. Kate Foster.'

Garstang stopped dead in his tracks. 'Ah, Mr Kelly. Yes, I am Garstang. Senior Constable Garstang, actually.'

Jim was unimpressed. 'Can we speak frankly, Garstang, about what happened to my sister?'

Garstang nodded and indicated a seat in the park a short distance away. They strode over to it.

Jim stared deeply at Garstang and listened to everything the policeman offered up, patiently making his own assessment of who Garstang was and how much of what the man was saying he might believe. Jim trusted no one, especially the police.

Garstang was mid-sentence when Jim decided he wasn't interested in hearing any more. He didn't believe that Garstang had tried hard enough to look for his sister. Jim got up from his seat to remove himself from any potential violence he might cause. He wanted to punch the annoying man. Jim interrupted Garstang and asked for directions to locate his sister's children so that he could get away from the Englishman. Garstang was offended but obliged Jim with the directions he needed.

Jim pondered what Garstang had told him while he walked to Mrs Hurley's. *Kate was all alone when she had the baby. Poor dear. Milk fever. Delirium. Suicide. This is terrible. My poor sister deserved better than this. Poor Kitty, if only I had been here.*

He went to great mental lengths trying to imagine what Bricky Foster might say for himself about all this. Garstang had said that Bricky was away at work, but he last saw her the day she disappeared. What did it all mean?

Jim wished with every bone in his body that he could have protected his sister from the kind of ending that she never deserved. He wondered if anyone ever did get the kind of ending to their life that they wanted. Maybe these things are simply out of our hands?

SUSAN HURLEY AND JIM

Jim spotted the house, walked down a front path skirted by dirt and stopped at the front doorstep. He made three sharp knocks and stepped back. A few moments later, Susan Hurley pulled the door open towards her. She looked with suspicion at the unknown man before her, rocking baby Catherine in her arms.

'Can I help you?'

'Mrs Hurley?'

'Yes.'

'My name is Jim Kelly. Kate Foster was my sister.'

'Oh, Mr Kelly! I'm very sorry about your sister. Very sorry.'

'As am I. Can we talk?'

Susan looked the tall man up and down. The police had told her they had contacted Kate's family in Victoria. She was relieved to see him.

'Yes. Come in.' They walked down a short hall.

'The children are all very ill. They are in bed, I'm afraid. This is Catherine, your youngest niece.' Susan gestured to the infant she was carrying.

Jim looked at the baby's face and noticed how unwell she looked. 'What is ailing the children?'

'I couldn't say, Mr Kelly. But they have all had fevers for a few days. They are exhausted and upset. They miss their mother, I suppose, Mr Kelly. Are you going to take them?'

'I have to speak with the father yet. Do you know where I can find him?'

'I think you should try the Foster family home, down near the flats. Other than that, I haven't seen him since the inquest. Unless he has returned to his work at Burrawang.'

Susan showed Jim through to a small room where the three Foster children and Susan's young William were all in the bed on the floor together. Red-faced, snot-nosed and dirty, they were too unwell to greet their uncle. He said hello to his young relatives and explained that he was their mother's brother. 'Uncle Jim you can call me. We'll get to know each other when you aren't feeling so bad.' To him, they all looked malnourished and deathly, which disturbed him. *What has been going on here?* he wondered.

Jim and Susan walked out to the kitchen in a small separate building where she offered him tea but he declined. Rocking the child, Susan spoke frankly out of earshot of the children. 'Mr Kelly, I have done my best with the children, but I am glad you are here and I hope you will take them with you. As for baby Catherine, though, she should stay with me.'

Jim was caught by surprise. 'What are you saying, Mrs Hurley?'

'I'm saying that Ada wanted me to look after her.'

'You mean Kate, not Ada.'

'I knew her as Ada, that's who she'll always be to me, Mr Kelly. She wanted me to take the baby. She gave me the baby to look after, the day she disappeared. Ada even offered to have Bricky pay for the baby's keep. She asked me to write her a note about it.' Susan pointed to a piece of paper on the kitchen sideboard.

'We have a lot to consider, Mrs Hurley. I don't know how I would travel with a baby anyways. We can talk some more in a few days. I'm camped down on the flats, I'll be there if you need me. I need to find the husband.'

Mrs Hurley walked with Jim around the side of the house and watched as he walked down the street before she returned to the children.

Later, as Jim boiled his billy and watched the sky change colour, he thought about what the day had revealed. First, that he would not be leaving any time soon with the children so sick; and second, that it may not be all of the children who would be travelling back with him. Mrs Hurley had made herself clear. *That child don't look like it will live anyhow*, he thought.

Jim figured that while he was stuck in Forbes, he should put himself to use. The time that Jim had spent in prison had taught him the craft of shoemaking and repairs, so while he waited for the children to recover and let the horses have a good rest after their strenuous journey, he could make some money and ask around about Bricky. Kate's brother would spread the word around town about his shoe-repairing services.

Jim was deeply tired, worn out by the travel and the sadness of it all. He'd heard he could get a good soup and damper at the Carlton Hotel, so he decided to fill his belly and then sleep.

BRICKY AND JIM

Around lunchtime a few days later, Jim was walking among the horses along the dry, brown bank of the lake. The horses were having a drink and waving their mouths across what was left of the yellowing grass, when Jim noticed a visitor had arrived at his camp.

From the short distance away, Jim could see a large man with braces and a hat who raised his arm and took a seat on a log near Jim's wagon. Jim grabbed the horses' attention with a soft *click, click* of his tongue, and they slowly followed him back to meet the stranger. He had a feeling it was Kitty's husband.

Bricky was nervous. He'd heard all about these wild brothers of Kate's when the couple had first got together. What kind of man was Jim? Forbes was only a small place, and already the rumours were milling around about the shoe repairer down by the lake. Once disparagingly known as one of the criminal brothers of Ned Kelly, now Jim was being looked down on as the sad brother of the woman who had drowned herself in the lagoon.

As Jim approached, Bricky stood and extended his large hand. They mirrored each other where they stood, and Bricky introduced himself as Jim's brother-in-law. Both of these men had worked hard, laborious jobs and were comfortable in the bush, but Jim had a tougher edge and quite a few years on Bricky. He'd had the harder life.

Jim said, 'Looking from over there, I thought it must have been you. I suppose word gets around! No doubt you heard where to find me.'

They both chuckled a little. Small towns were no surprise to either of them. The two men sat down beside a small fire, and Jim boiled the billy again. He looked into the eyes of the man whom he believed had abandoned his sister at her time of need. It put a bad taste in his mouth.

Jim was not the kind of man to mince his words and, like Kate's widower, he was economical with them, so each sentence counted.

'Why was my sister alone, Bill?'

'Wob, wob. I was away working.' Silence. Bricky didn't look away from Jim.

'Wob, wob. She was on the drink, Jim. Wouldn't stop. She said she would quit it but she never.'

Jim watched Bricky intently.

'When she was, wob, wob, like that she would talk about destroying herself.'

Jim shifted in his seat, and the wrinkles around his eyes creased as he grimaced, angry about his sister's isolation and Bricky's assertion that Kate had killed herself. Jim considered what Garstang had told him. The doctor thought it was milk fever, that Kate had a delirium, even though he hadn't put it on the record at the inquest. But Jim also knew that the coroner never said it was suicide. He wasn't sure what to make of it all, yet.

'The children, Bill, they need to come home with me.'

Bricky was not surprised by the suggestion. Jim had ridden a very long way, and Bricky suspected that he was there to do more than pay condolences.

Bricky considered just how much of a mess of it he had been making by himself. He knew he couldn't raise the children on his own but, at the same time, they were his children, not Jim's.

Jim could see Bricky's hesitancy. 'Bill, we can offer them a home. A woman's care is needed. We don't have much, but we would care for them properly. My sister would want it this way, Bill. That I know for sure.'

Bricky could see that Jim was not going to be persuaded away from his quest. There was a slight fear in Bricky when he thought about his children being taken, but he was no fool, the children would probably be better off with the Kellys. That didn't mean he would agree to it, though.

'Wob, wob, wob. They are my children, Jim. They are, wob, wob, not Kellys, they are Fosters.'

'Well, Bill, they are half Kellys and half Fosters. From what I have seen, you are not caring for them anyhow. Mrs Hurley still has them.'

Bricky was quiet.

'Think about it, Bill.'

After their talk, Bricky felt worse than before he met with Jim. He went back up to the pub to sink his blues to the bottom of a bottle of spirits, but he couldn't stay there amid the smirks and whispers.

He took himself back to the empty house where his wife was last seen alive, and all through the night he tossed and turned, sleepless and unsettled. He knew he should hand the children over, but he was unwilling; it was too painful. As for baby Catherine, Mrs Hurley had told Bricky the same thing she had said to Jim. If she lived, Catherine should be Mrs Hurley's daughter. She believed that was what Kate wanted. So much was happening to him and around him. He seemed unable to control his own life, and he couldn't make head nor tail of it.

When Bricky woke the next morning, it had become clear to him. He would visit the children and say goodbye, then go bush.

LEAVING FORBES

Days had turned into weeks. It was time to go. The children were still sick, tired and dirty but well enough to get moving. Each of them looked bedraggled and exhausted. Elsie wanted her mother and nothing would compensate, but this new uncle and the distraction of moving to a new home were putting her mind on other things at least.

Uncle Jim loaded the girls into the wagon. He lifted Elsie and twirled her into her seat in an effort to cheer her. As the horses snorted and swished their tails, their ears twitched to the new sounds of the children. Jim held out his hand for Gerty as she reached up and pulled herself into the springy high-backed driver's seat and slid along. Gerty leaned in to her young sister, holding her hand and putting her arm around her as they settled in for the long ride, and wondered about what lay in front of them. *Where were they going? What would their new life be like?*

Mrs Hurley looked smart in her neat cotton shirt tucked into a dark, tight-waisted skirt that caressed the ground as she swayed. She had hold of the baby sister, Catherine, so her family could say goodbye to her. Susan's sense of relief that the children were going with their uncle was evident on her soft but distressed face. The toll of recent events made her appear tired and pale. Each of the children had given the sister they would never see again a soft kiss and farewelled her.

Fred was trying to be the man he thought he was supposed to be as he stood next to Jim, imitating the way his uncle stood, tall and strong. His uncle directed him to the cart. Fred was going to have to start the journey in the hard wooden tray of the wagon.

Jim was kitted out in his usual oilskin pants, complete with long gaiters, and his wide-brimmed hat. He reached over to place the long leather whip down the side of the wagon, ready for use as they travelled. It was a new beginning, and a long, daunting trip lay ahead of them.

As Jim picked up the reins, he gave them a soft flick and clicked his tongue to get the horses moving. He leaned forward and gave a little wave and tipped his hat at Susan, who raised her palm in return. The children waved goodbye to Mrs Hurley and the little sister she was cradling. Kate's children continued to stare back at Susan and waved until they had to turn their heads away.

Susan had a deep feeling that baby Catherine was not going to survive much longer, despite her efforts. Whatever virus had affected the older children, it seemed to have ailed the baby as well, and she was already malnourished to start with. Somehow, Susan's own baby Ethel had so far stayed healthy, despite William getting sick.

By 15 December 1898, baby Catherine had passed away. The cause of death was described as *debilitas*. Too weak to have carried on without her mother, she was added to Kate's resting place. Susan had done her best.

Bricky reported the death, his last parental duty to the baby.

27

Bricky Alone

Bricky was still a young man, only thirty-two, when he lost Kate, but the circumstances of her death would attract a permanent stigma. Did Bricky Foster kill his wife? Did Kate really commit suicide? Suspicion would remain and uncertainty would plague conversations about Bricky, even beyond his lifetime. Bricky had to live with the gossip, rumour, speculation and judgements from all who would ever hear of his wife's story.

Even though he had been avoiding Kate and the irritation of their relationship in the months before her death, it was still a shock to him that the people who constituted his family, who had been hovering in the periphery of his life, had evaporated. After the visit from Jim, he found himself completely alone. There was an empty space where his wife and children had once been.

Bricky returned to Burrawang for work and mateship. He stayed there, away from the gossip and speculation of townsfolk, for at least another year or so. But before long, he was in trouble again. By November of the year after Kate's death, 1899, Bricky was on the wrong side of the law when he and three other men faced criminal charges over an alleged violent attack on William McCabe, another worker at Burrawang.

The first charge for all of the men was 'feloniously and maliciously wounding' and the second was 'common attack'. Bricky's association with this kind of violence only added to the rumours about what he may have done to his wife and his role in her death; mud sticks.

The same solicitor represented Bricky and the three others, with their defence being that Mr McCabe had in fact started the whole thing by assaulting a guy called Johnson, who retaliated. The solicitor argued that Bricky had nothing to do with it and that two of the other men were simply trying to break it up when McCabe had turned on them all.

The case was thrown out of court and written off as another typical example of the rough life of men working in the bush, but Bricky was relieved not to be in any further trouble.

As the years moved forward without Kate, Bricky moved back into his family home and found himself alone again. In his later years, he preferred to keep his own company, though, and rarely left the house.

So deep was his self-imposed isolation that, even as the river water crept in during floods, lifting itself higher and higher, he would remain in his home. The flooding was an anticipated yet unwelcome guest every few years. As the muddy water and floating debris of sticks, leaves, carcasses and snakes slithered into his house, beneath the door and through the floorboards, Bricky would simply put on his gumboots.

He set about fixing chains from the ceiling and testing that they were strong enough to hold his bed and the weight of his body. Once the bed was secure, he would lift himself above the rising, transient ocean of water. As night approached, he would flop onto his mattress and keep a little fire in a large kerosene can, using it to warm himself and shine light on the tins of sardines that would sustain him. He wasn't going to budge.

Sometimes Bricky was seen in the yard by neighbours, painting walls and fences with paint he would mix from fat and white clay from the river. He was known to have kept the little shack spotlessly clean and immaculately tidy. On the mantlepiece inside was a large photo of Kate. The framed image of his beautiful wife and a tiny tin of trinkets were the only reminders of the life he used to know.

Bricky had hoped in his youth that life with Kate and his family would be good, but instead he was left with painful and tormenting memories that he mostly preferred to forget.

VISITOR

Twelve years after Kate died, Bricky was minding his own business in his modest home when he heard a strange voice calling out from the back door.

Everything about the voice and the scenario was unusual, and he tensed immediately. He pulled his braces over his shirt and edged cautiously towards the door.

'Mr Foster, I'm looking for Mr Foster.'

It was a thin young man dressed in modern clothing foreign to Bricky's eyes. Bricky sized the wiry man up and down through the gauze door.

'Wob, wob. What do you want?' Bricky barked at the man and moved forward. He pressed his body close to the doorframe and stood tall to intimidate the visitor. Nothing about the stranger felt good.

'Mr Foster, I wanted to know what you think about recent reports that Dan Kelly is still alive? I'm a journalist from the—'

'Wob, wob. You get outta here! You useless little, wob, wob, worm! You, wob, wob, wait 'til I get a hold of your little, wob, wob, chicken neck. I'm gonna, wob, wob, wring it 'til it cracks!'

The journalist cleared out as fast as his scrawny legs could carry him. The size of Bricky's hands had not gone unnoticed, and the city slicker was imagining the damage that the bushman could do to him, sweating as he rushed to avoid that outcome.

Bricky tore out the door and up the side path, but his big frame and older body had no chance of capturing his tormentor. However futile, Bricky pushed on, carried by his rage and determination to strangle the little shit. 'The Kellys is, wob, wob, dead. Wob, wob, leave 'em alone, yer little weasel!'

The shaking journalist started his small motorbike and he fled on his getaway vehicle quick smart, keen to remove himself from the violence promised to him. Bricky stood and waved his clenched fist in the air, wishing he could have flattened the rodent who had just disturbed his day so dramatically. It made him think of Kate and her family all over again.

For forty-seven years, Bricky remained on his own. He saw his children only a handful of times again. The absent father even outlived them. His son, brave Fred Foster, died in France in 1917, killed in action at only twenty-eight years of age. Fred served in the 17th Australian Infantry Battalion, and his service and sacrifice are remembered at the Villers-Bretonneux Memorial. The parental contact provided on Fred's enlistment into the light-horse brigade of Benalla was his father's name, care of Bricky's sister Evelyn, aka Mrs D. Scott.

Kate's oldest daughter became Mrs Gertrude (Eileen) Cavanagh, and she died when she was only thirty-four, close to her mother's age when she died. The tragedy and torment of Gertrude's early life were too difficult for her to overcome, and she ended her suffering with a self-inflicted gunshot. The fallout of trauma and its far-reaching tentacles cannot be underestimated.

And Bricky's youngest child, Ethel Maude, who became Elsie Hibbert, reportedly died a year before her father, in 1945. The loss of Elsie's baby Grace in 1916, the year of her marriage, left a heavy sadness that the marriage could not survive.

Before Bricky died, when he was ill and in hospital, his brother Arthur visited him and they made peace after a lifetime separated by their love for Kate. Bricky's life, which had been filled with unexpected events, disappointments and secrets, gently came to an end in 1946. There was no need to hide away from his past or think about the way Kate died anymore. And with Bricky's passing, the only evidence of Kate's life with him and the children in Forbes disappeared, leaving behind only folklore and their headstones. At least that was the case until a Henckell .32 calibre revolver turned up.

28

The Gun

In 1862, the year before Kate Kelly was born and well before the exploits of Ned and the Kelly Gang, the Escort Rock hold-up took place in Eugowra, New South Wales. Also known as the hold-up at Goimbla Station, it was a violent attack that left police wounded and was the largest gold robbery in Australian history. The bushrangers Ben Hall, Frank Gardiner and others removed a treasure of over two thousand ounces of gold and three thousand pounds in cash from the gold escort, which at that time was owned and run by Ford & Co Coaches.

The criminals raided the spoils, spilled the blood of the police guarding the gold and disappeared into the bush, where some of the gold was later recovered, left behind by the bushrangers because there was just too much of the heavy metal to carry.

A few miles from that site was the town of Murga. Like the Victorian ranges where Kate had ridden for years while helping her brothers, the heavily treed hillsides and mountains in beautiful blue and green hues of the Nangar Mountains created a picturesque background that highlighted the town's remoteness.

Located halfway between Forbes and Orange, it boasted one hundred permanent residents and an outrageous number of daily visitors, both human and animal. The town's existence and purpose at that time were linked to the discovery of gold in Forbes, and Murga's tiny population had multiplied in response to the new services needed on the goldfields.

It had become a horse-changing station for stagecoaches, which later included the famous Cobb & Co coach services shuttling between Orange and Forbes. Carriages would haul extraordinary riches in gold and cash over gravel and dirt through bush and scrub to Sydney, and the tired horses would be swapped at Murga. It was not unusual to see teams of horses and bullocks, carts, sulkies or wagonettes and coaches passing each other in both directions or pulled up next to one another. A record was set one night with over eighty bullock teams camped in the single-street town.

Ned and his gang would eventually steal their share of gold, but they would never see the quantities that were transported out of Forbes through Murga in its heyday. On one occasion, the newspapers bragged about an 11,510-ounce gleaming bounty being transported. The police skited that an extra five thousand ounces had to be left behind in Forbes because there was simply no room in the enormous security chests designed to transport the gold.

Murga had its own visits from Ben Hall and his gang over the years, and on one occasion the bushrangers entered the Intermediate Hotel, asking to speak to the owner of the house. But when the wife of the owner advised the gang that she was alone, Hall and his men sculled their drinks and paid her for them before exiting the establishment. The gang then walked across the road to perform their raid on the hotel and shops on the other side of the street, starting with the butcher who they bailed up at his back door as he was about to make a run for it with his cashbox.

By the 1890s, the population of Murga had dwindled, but the two modest wooden hotels remained. Beyond that, there was only a scattering of homesteads and cultivated fields.

Just outside of town was a small farmhouse belonging to a friend of Bricky Foster. Under a wooden panel of the front steps, a .32 calibre revolver, made by A. Henckell & Co in Germany, had been carefully hidden.

It was a pocket-model weapon, a small silver handgun made around 1884. On its crown, the letters R*C could be seen, and if you didn't know your weapons, you might have believed that it was an insignia from the Royal Constabulary, but it was actually a proof mark.

Delicately scratched into the pistol grip were swirling letters, an incriminating K.K. In the same way that Ned had affectionately inscribed a simple 'K' on his favourite rifle, which he dubbed 'Betty', Kate's pistol bore her initials, although written with an elegance absent in Ned's crude filings.

Wrapped in soft cloth and leather strapping, the gun was tucked away, and the farmer was convinced that no one would ever have a clue that it was under his steps, including Kate.

The revolver had been given to Kate by her employers when she worked at Cadow Station, and she was thrilled with it. Once an outlaw's sister, always an outlaw's sister; she felt naked without a gun. She held on to it and had it stashed away in various hiding holes from place to place as she changed jobs or moved homes.

When she met Bricky and started her life with him, the revolver came with her. Why wouldn't it? Kate had showed it to him in the early days and he didn't worry so much then, but as their relationship deteriorated, Bricky became nervous about what she might do with the gun. As the couple fought, Bricky wondered if one day maybe she would shoot him. And as Bricky heard Kate talk more of suicide, he thought maybe she might shoot herself.

He took the gun when she was out with the children one day, and all hell had broken loose when she'd noticed it missing a few weeks later. But it was too late. Bricky had concealed it in a parcel and asked Mr Hurley, who was a coach driver, to deliver it to his friend in Murga when he stopped there on the way to Orange. Mr Hurley knew enough to never ask questions, and the parcel was never spoken of again.

Kate was wild with Bricky about it. Her sense of self-protection had been removed with the gun, and she screamed at him, distressed and outraged.

'How dare yer take it! It wasn't yours to take. Did yer sell it? Is that what yer did? Give it back to me. I demand that you give it back to me. Where is it?' Kate was racing around the house, looking in tins and pulling up bedding trying to find where Bricky had put it.

'Who, wob, wob, knows what sap-skulled things you might have done with the thing. You don't need it anyway. You are safe. Stop making a, wob, wob, fuss.'

Kate stormed out of the house, swearing at Bricky and slamming the door as she went.

In Murga, the humble farmhouse hid the gun's presence well past the lives of Bricky and his friend until the old home became a demolition site nearly one hundred years after Kate's death.

FINDING THE GUN

Toiling away one day in the 1980s, the owner who was renovating the farmhouse in Murga gradually removed the materials that once comprised the home's character. Old wooden weatherboards and locally milled timbers were slowly pulled away with crowbars and hammers.

Dismantling the verandah frame and front steps, the home

owner noticed the dusty and dirty leather bundle, revealed as the wooden slats were smashed and removed. He scooped up the surprise package and placed it on a log nearby.

Wiping his face with the back of his forearm, the man quietly cleaned the parcel with a rag, spitting on the leather and cleaning it up, wondering excitedly what it was.

He slowly pulled back the hard strapping, stiff with age, strip by strip, and put it aside. He pulled away the cloth, corner by corner, enjoying the surprising adventure. Like a child on Christmas morning, he exclaimed aloud when the pistol materialised. What a gift it was.

So many bushranging stories had swirled around that patch of countryside that he had almost expected to find something as he worked away. He had hoped to, anyhow. How could a building be so old, in a place so full of history, and not have revealed some secrets as it was dismantled?

There was only one famous K.K. that he could think of. Only one woman with those initials who might have a shady history or a weapon that needed concealing. Whoever secreted the gun away didn't want it found, that's for sure. Who else could it belong to? The man wondered about the history and the age of the gun. He was curious about how it came to be stashed there, but he resigned himself to probably never knowing.

He eventually sold the gun to a friend and that friend did the same. But the fun of it all turned sour and friendships were lost when a family friend suggested to the latest owner of the gun that they let him put it to auction through someone he knew.

It was a time far removed from Kate's lifetime, and her memorabilia, including the gun, would collect a high fee. Some kind of Kelly charisma swam in Kate's blood, her magnetism reaching through time. And the general public's fascination with 'Kellyana' was still alive and well.

29

Memories of Kate

In the 1950s, Kate's memory was still warmly held in the hearts of those who had known her and lived long enough to tell some stories about her life. Her brother-in-law, Ted Foster, wrote many fond letters about her to the press, but never speculated about her death even though she passed him on the street not long before she was found drowned.

The sad question of the truth behind Kate's death lingered for some, while others were very sure that the travelling troupe of the Bohemian Lecturer had played a devastating role in their beloved Kate's demise.

Clara Rae, who was there the night that Kate was in the audience of the Bohemian Lecturer's show, contacted the local paper, the *Forbes Advocate*, on 12 August 1955 when she heard that someone was saying that it wasn't Ned Kelly's little sister who had lived in Forbes. In her old age, Clara Rae still felt the need to stick up for her friend and share her recollections.

'She was definitely "the Kate Kelly",' Clara was adamant.

'She told me that she used to ride out and give food to her brothers when they were being sought by the police. She went under the name Kate Hennessey. She did not want it known generally that she was a sister of the Kelly boys.'

Clara recalled the performance that had upset Kate so much. 'A terrible thing happened to her when a man came to town and put on a show called The Kelly Gang. When a girl came on stage in the part of Kate Kelly, the real Kate in the audience became hysterical and had to be escorted out. I was at the show, and I knew why she was hysterical.'

Another woman, Mrs E. Markwort, was motivated to write to *The Truth* newspaper in July 1954 after reading a story on Ned Kelly. Mrs Markwort wrote that she, too, had lived on Browne Street in Forbes, the same street as 'Mrs Bill Foster', who she recalled was 'found drowned'.

> In my opinion her death was caused by a play that came to Forbes called The Kelly Gang. I went to see the play; it was the best I had ever seen.
>
> A friend of mine who lived close to Mrs Foster told me that Mrs Foster sat with her head in her hands while the play was at Forbes . . . I have heard my mother say the Kellys did not do half of what they were blamed for and that they were hounded down.

In 1970 or thereabouts, Jack Cavanagh travelled to Forbes on a road trip from Victoria with an old army mate. He stood next to the tall, white headstone of Kate Kelly's grave, feeling the western sun on his back, while his friend snapped a keepsake for the bookmaker.

He was sixty years old and had promised himself he would get a new photo of his grandmother's grave after he'd lost the only one he had. All of the stories his mother Gertrude and great-grandmother

Ellen had told him through the years sang in his ears while the emotion of his family history swelled in his heart.

'It was never proved that she committed suicide,' he told his friend.

'That's true, Jack, very true.'

Kate was drowned at Forbes

I was very interested to read your account of the life of Ned Kelly.

Years ago, when I was about 19 or 20, I lived in Brown St., Forbes, the same street as Kate Kelly, or, I should say, Mrs. Bill Foster, lived.

Mrs. Foster was found drowned. 'In my opinion her death was caused by a play that came to Forbes called The Kelly Gang. I went to see the play: it was the best I had ever seen.

A friend of mine who lived close to Mrs. Foster told me that Mrs. Foster sat with her head in her hands while the play was at Forbes.

When it left she was reported missing, then found drowned.

Shortly after her death her brother Jim Kelly came to Forbes from Victoria in a waggonette and took her three children—two girls and a boy—back with him. The girls were very pretty like their mother.

I have heard my mother say the Kellys did not do half of what they were blamed for and that they were hounded down.

MRS. E. MARKWORT,
30 Woolesly St., Fairfield.

'Her death was caused by a play . . .' was something alluded to in folklore by many locals in Forbes who recalled the play Life and Adventures of the Kelly Gang, *performed by the Bohemian Medical Co.*

30

Kate's Lament

With her toes in the water, the rest of Kate's body is jealous of the cool relief. Craving the cool liquid, she bends over and palms it from her forehead down. It is divine. Crouching now, she cups her hands together, letting it cascade over her head, over and over again.

Kate has seen out the daylight. She has made it through the suffering and torment of the day. Her decision is final. She wants permanent relief, and she simply doesn't think anyone will care about her absence. Perhaps they will be grateful that she is gone.

Kate walks on her tippy-toes further in. It is cold to her fevered body but irresistible at the same time. The muddied blackness of her dress shines as the stain from the water creeps, extending itself up the fabric. As her hands drift out to her sides, the softness of the water is soothing, and she can feel the water ballooning her dress and climbing up her legs. Further and further into the water she slides, gasping a little as the colder water meets her skin.

She is a little frightened here in the dark, alone, but mostly she is too drunk to care. Her sickly body is trembling, vibrating with the fever and the chill of the water. Confusing signals in her brain are making her at once cold and hot and numb. Her feet feel the sticky mud until it slips away, her legs rising gently as she floats on her back. Underneath her is a mystery of reeds. It is heavenly to float, and there is a heaven above her. It is almost as if she is suspended in the safety of her mother's womb.

Her dress is saturated and is becoming heavier. Gazing into the blackness around her and up to the moon and the stars, she sees how bright they are, brighter than she has ever noticed before. She can see the answers to every question she has ever asked.

The stars absorb her suffering. Kate's mind takes her to another place. It is a place that brings her great comfort, even if it will only ever make sense in another realm. She can let go.

The reeds are licking at Kate's feet, entwining her body. Her dress feels heavy. As if the reeds had a secret plan all the while, they entangle her. This is her place now, and she will remain. Her struggle is a feeble one, a moment of weak jolting. Her body is ill, and her spirit is worn-out. Her lungs let the water in as if she is breathing air. Every struggle she has ever known is over. There is the peacefulness of surrender and then nothingness.

Author's Note

I believe Kate Kelly's story is important to Australian history. I have tried to tell it compassionately and as accurately and completely as the records available permit.

I have researched contemporary and later documents and newspaper reports, as well as other accounts of the Kelly story; consulted Kelly experts, community and family historians, and experts in women's health; and visited key locations. Details of my sources are in the references at the end of this book. Wherever possible, I have relied on a contemporary primary source, as the myth-making about the Kelly Gang that continues to this day can obscure the facts.

In 2016 and 2017, I spent much of my time fighting for my life. With pulmonary embolisms and medical complications throughout that period, I endured multiple operations and a blood transfusion. Each time I seemed to be getting better, the next medical complication would occur. It was exhausting and frightening.

During all of this, I decided to compile my years of research on Kate Kelly's life to try to do her story justice. Having this project to focus on kept me going in between every disheartening medical hiccup. The experience taught me a lot about myself and the human condition, and about how lucky I had been to be healthy for so long. It also made me consider how Kate's health might have been a factor in her demise.

My research has uncovered a sticky residue of less than flattering opinions of Kate that still circulate today. For example, when I visited a family history group in New South Wales, a man made a point of telling me that his town was about much more than a bushranger's drunk sister. And when I was researching in the heart of Kelly country in the towns of Glenrowan and Greta in Victoria, a woman told me bluntly that Kate was 'nothing but a drunk', as if there was nothing more to be said.

I was quite shocked at the one-dimensionality of some perceptions about Kate, all these years after her death, and it made me wonder about the way we are remembered, if we are remembered at all, and how we have no control over how people perceive us.

Kate was 'Kardashian' famous in her day, so much so that a wax figure was made of her and displayed to the masses in Melbourne in 1882 alongside the male Kelly Gang figures. Her name appeared in the press almost as frequently as the Kelly Gang.

The circumstances of her life were absolutely unique, distressing, harsh and often tragic. Many things happened to Kate that were beyond her control. The intense events she lived through caused her deep suffering, and I believe that untreated medical conditions played a big part in her decline and ultimate demise.

It is reasonable and highly possible, given the facts we know about Kate, that she suffered from conditions such as post-traumatic stress disorder (PTSD), perinatal depression and anxiety (PNDA), possibly alcoholism and perhaps even an untreated infection after giving birth to her last child. Kate's brother Jim refers to 'milk fever' and describes her as having 'gone mad', while her mother refers to Kate suffering a 'delirium' in a newspaper interview in 1911.

A medical expert I spoke to about Kate provided these comments about trauma and PNDA:

One of the biggest background issues for women with PNDA is previous trauma. Childhood trauma, child sexual abuse, even sexual abuse as an adult, but certainly childhood trauma overwhelmingly shows up in the data as a number one risk factor for PND.

In relation to the 'delirium' and 'milk fever' references from Kate's family:

That raises a flag for me. Far more acute and deadly than PNDA is postpartum psychosis. That's not only depression; they [mothers with the condition] become psychotic, they can genuinely believe something bizarre, like voices telling the mother that the baby is the devil for example. It is absolutely not based in reality. For her [Kate's] mum to use the word 'delirium' makes me wonder if maybe Kate had a postpartum psychosis. Alternatively, if retained product [such as part of the placenta] doesn't get expelled after the birth of the baby you can get a fever from that too. Infection from that can kill a recently delivered mother. Perhaps though, 'milk fever' is used as a euphemism for inexplicable postpartum behaviour. Obviously, no true diagnosis was possible back then, sadly.

In relation to Kate giving her baby to her neighbour before she disappeared, telling her that the baby was on the bottle and offering to give her money to look after the infant:

The fact that Kate said, 'the baby's on the bottle' and asked the neighbour to take the baby tells me there is still an element of Kate wanting to make sure the kids were all right. I think she possibly had a plan [for suicide] that seems likely given the eventual outcome. Offering to pay for the baby's care indicates a perceived requirement for ongoing care.

The Edinburgh Postnatal Depression Scale (EPDS) is a set of ten questions used today as a diagnostic tool to assess women for symptoms of emotional distress during pregnancy and the postnatal period. Child and family health nurses use this screening tool with every client at risk of depression.

Suicide is still a problem with postnatal depression. It's why we ask the last question on EPDS: 'Have you ever had any thoughts of harming yourself?' A common response is that they think the baby will be better off without them. That's the depression talking, that's not their real self-worth. I personally have never actually had someone say 'Yes' when I have asked them if they have a plan [for suicide] but I know it sometimes happens that they do. If depressed mothers get that critical, they rarely talk about a plan, they feel unable to tell anyone about it. A lot of people, when they do commit suicide, get as drunk as they can to do the act. That's very common with suicide—you get as blind drunk as you can afford to be.

Kate had her last baby alone and unsupported, and she had trouble breastfeeding—possibly caused by mastitis. There is a record of verbal abuse from her husband, so there were marital issues. Clearly, she was having a situational crisis and living with little meaningful support around her. She was probably self-medicating with alcohol as well. These circumstances collided with the debilitating and devastating factors in her personal history, not to mention the era she was born in, her gender and her class. Additionally, she had been publicly humiliated during an already distressing time.

Kate's story is a powerful reminder of the injustice of gender- and economic-based disadvantage and how these limitations can impact on women's health. All these issues are still relevant today.

In addition to examining for the first time these important issues in her life, this book includes new details about Kate, important events and key people connected with her story.

Many important characters in Kate's life have not been identified or fully examined before, and it has been my goal to paint a reliable and insightful picture of these people. They include: Kate's husband, Bricky Foster; Kate's neighbours, Susan and Edward Hurley; Mr Sullivan, who found Kate's body and failed to testify about what he knew of Kate's death; Hugh McDougall, who gave Kate an opportunity to change her life; the Collits family descendants at Cadow Station, who were the first family Kate worked for when she went to the Forbes region; Senior Constable Garstang, whose less than impressive job investigating Kate's disappearance meant that she was not found for many days; Flash Jack Donovan, the agent who toured and promoted Kate; Robert Fitzallan Long, who brought Kate to Adelaide; the Bohemian Lecturer, aka Mr Cole, who exposed and humiliated Kate days before her death; the pivotal and controversial figure Constable Alexander Fitzpatrick, who ended up in gaol himself later in life; and, of course, Kate Kelly herself.

Following are some points regarding some of my research.

KATE AND FITZPATRICK

We can be confident that there was an affair between Kate and Fitzpatrick, based on oral history from family and friends who contributed to other books. The suggestion that Kate bore Fitzpatrick's child has been circulating since the late 1870s.

In Dagmar Balcarek and Gary Dean's 2012 edition of their book *Ellen Kelly: An historical novel as told by Ellen Kelly*, Dagmar thanks Mrs L.H. Earp for sharing intimate knowledge of Ellen's life with her. In the foreword, Gary Dean describes his great, great-grandmother as a close friend of Ellen's. He also states that information was supplied by Kelly family descendants and that they gave their permission to share those stories because particular Kelly relatives had passed away and that Gary has more stories to reveal as time moves on.

Balcarek and Dean's book contains many references to Ellen's response to Kate's unfolding affair with Fitzpatrick:

- Kate is seen 'taking (horse) rides' and 'arriving home late', and offering 'no explanation' (page 145).
- Ellen sees 'Kate sneaking out without explanation'. She confronts her daughter and tells her she that cannot see Fitzpatrick anymore (page 146).
- Then Ellen finds out 'definitely that it was Fitzpatrick whom Kate had been secretly meeting' (page 147).

Joseph Ashmead's 1922 manuscript, *The Thorns and the Briars*, also refers to an affair between Fitzpatrick and Kate. Ashmead was reportedly a local lad and Kelly peer, around the same age as Jim Kelly.

We also know that Fitzpatrick got other young women pregnant and that he tried very hard to shirk any responsibility for those women and children. In Justin Corfield's *Ned Kelly Encyclopaedia* (page 163), it is recorded that Jessie McKay had a child to Fitzpatrick in Meredith and that he paid her maintenance until he left town. My research suggests that the child was possibly put up for adoption when he stopped paying maintenance and died not long after, but I cannot be one hundred per cent certain that it is the same child.

Corfield writes (and it is recorded elsewhere) that Anna Savage found herself pregnant to Fitzpatrick at the age of fifteen, and that he refused to marry her. This prompted a letter from her father to the police about Fitzpatrick's lack of accountability. He eventually forced Fitzpatrick's hand, and it is recorded that Fitzpatrick 'married her (Anna), 10 July 1878' (page 165).

An article published in the *South Australian Chronicle and Weekly Mail*, 15 February 1879, says:

Miss Kelly did not hesitate to state that on the occasion Trooper Fitzpatrick visited their house in the beginning of last year, he did not do so for the purpose of executing a warrant.

If he was not there on police business, it is possible that he was there only to see Kate and their new baby, Alice, who was a matter of days old. Indeed, in Balcarek and Dean's *Ellen Kelly*, the character Ellen says of the court case where she has been charged for attempting to murder Fitzpatrick:

'... it was probably a mistake not to allow Kate to testify as Ned and I had forbidden her to take part, lest her relationship with Constable Fitzpatrick came out' (page 165).

Fitzpatrick seemed to have a feeling of entitlement and recklessness when it came to women, given what we know about the stories of at least two other women (there may have been more) and his conduct with a housemaid during his posting in Sydney.

The scenario at the Kelly homestead takes on new possibilities if we consider that perhaps Fitzpatrick was still Kate's lover; the father of her child; and possibly refusing to take accountability, as he would later attempt with Anna Savage and had already done with Jessie McKay.

Ellen always claimed that Alice was her child, but mothers have covered for their daughters in this regard in many circumstances to prevent public humiliation. We know that George King (Ellen's husband) had been absent from Ellen Kelly's bed and her life for a very long time before Alice King was born. By Ned's own accounts, George was off with him stealing horses prior to Alice's birth, and then George disappeared from Ellen's life altogether.

It is accepted that Alice was breastfed by Ellen Kelly and that is why the child was taken with her to prison. It is possible that Ellen Kelly was still breastfeeding toddler Jack (Ellen's youngest child) when Alice was born and thus was able to accommodate Alice as well, or that she relactated for Alice (this is when a woman who has had previous pregnancies produces breastmilk on demand, even if she hasn't recently given birth, which was a common practice in the past for mothers living in the same home as their pregnant daughters).

On page 162 of Balcarek and Dean's book *Ellen Kelly*, Ellen's character declares, 'I have a baby girl only three days old and I breastfeed her.' Generally speaking, most published Kelly material that relates to Ellen Kelly acknowledges that she breastfed Alice.

Ellen Kelly's charge sheet no. 3520 indicates that she had an 'infant child with her,' so we know that baby Alice was taken to Beechworth Gaol along with Ellen from April to June 1878, when Ellen was bailed. Ellen's trial was heard in Beechworth in October, and from there she went to Melbourne Gaol. The entry on her charge sheet describing her incarceration in Melbourne Gaol makes no mention of a child. There are reports that Alice was returned to the Kelly homestead from Beechworth Gaol after Ellen's sentencing, and other reports that Alice was returned from Melbourne Gaol, so it is unclear exactly, but I have taken the return of Alice to have been from Beechworth Gaol in October 1878.

The whole situation between Fitzpatrick and Kate is a controversial and pivotal one in the wider Kelly story.

HORSESHOES

A Forbes family generously shared their stories about how their grandfather who had a blacksmith business in Daysdale was 'often ordered out of bed at night at gunpoint to shoe Ned and Kate's horses. He was ordered to shoe Kate's horses back to front as she was a messenger for her brothers and the troopers thought that Kate would lead them to her brothers.'

Daysdale is located in the Riverina region of New South Wales and is these days only about an hour's drive from Greta in Victoria. The Riverina was a region through which Ned and the gang traversed regularly, shifting stolen horses and committing robberies at Euroa and Jerilderie.

Horse experts have advised me that this technique of shodding horses is possible but would be uncomfortable for the horse for anything other than short periods.

KATE'S RIDING ADVENTURES AND ESCAPADES

Jim Kelly is on record admitting that Kate helped her brothers as much as she could and that she fooled the police many times. The media often wrote of how Kate had baffled and tricked the police and that she had played tormenting games with them. The press also documented how Kate lost the police in Melbourne and how Maggie and Tom had fooled gun-shop staff (and others). But, of course, many specific details were not going to be revealed by the Kellys, who were all tight-lipped about many things for very good reason, so I have had to fill in the gaps to take the reader on Kate's wild rides based on what evidence I could find.

Ted Foster, Kate's brother-in-law, wrote many letters to the *Forbes Advocate* in which he stated that Kate had told him about taking a bullet in her hip from her horseriding escapades. In the *Forbes Advocate*, 19 July 1960, in an article called 'Last Link With Kelly Gang: Ted Foster's Story', there is a subheading entitled 'Shot in the Leg' with text that reads as follows: 'On one occasion, said Mr Foster, police had shot Kate in her leg when she returned to their farm from Ned's bush hideout.'

He also wrote about how mostly only people within the Foster family and selected close friends knew who Kate really was. He confirmed that Kate used the pseudonym 'Ada', but others have speculated that she also used other false names including Kate Ambrose, Ada Hennessey and Kate Hennessey. An article appeared in the *Freeman's Journal*, 1892, outlining how, after a successful equestrian display in Bathurst, a Mrs Ambrose was dogged by rumours that she was Kate Kelly's sister, and how she wanted these unfounded reports to stop.

Kate's visits and performances in Sydney, Adelaide and Melbourne were all documented in the press with details of dates, the descriptions of the crowds who attended and the attitude of the police towards the Kellys, but only minor details were recorded about the actual performances and displays.

NED KELLY

I have placed an emphasis on Ned's intention to create an uprising at Glenrowan to form 'The Republic of North-Eastern Victoria'. The late Ian Jones, well-known and respected Ned Kelly expert and author of *Ned Kelly: A short life*, appears to have been a strong believer in Ned as a political figure and that is how I see him, too. There are many clues in newspaper articles, police testimony and oral history from Kelly or other family descendants that I believe make it a very feasible proposition.

On a different note, at Ned's trial he had many female admirers, and there is speculation that it was not Ettie Hart whom he was blowing kisses to but another woman. The mystery woman remains just that, and for me the only evidence we do have points to Ettie and Ned being an item. In particular, the keepsakes and sad poems of loss that were discovered by the O'Keefe family in recent years that belonged to Ettie. Her time in Melbourne and her attendance at Ned's court case was documented in the press, and this adds to my belief that it was Ned she was there for.

STEVE HART AND DAN KELLY

There are many theories about how Steve and Dan died at Glenrowan. Some believe that the pair escaped and lived their lives out in anonymity. Others believe that the two of them committed suicide by ingesting poison at Ann Jones' Hotel, and others believe that they were shot dead. I have gone with the last theory because, for me, that is the most predictable outcome for men who were engaged in a shootout with police.

CROSS-DRESSING

My focus has always been on Kate, but to tell her story I needed to research the wider Kelly story, particularly about Ned and the gang. In recent times, there have been suggestions that Ned and his gang members were gay or that they cross-dressed to create the impression of madness as a fear tactic, which I don't think is correct. It is my belief that it was most likely Steve Hart who used a woman's veil and hat as a disguise, as he reportedly left those items behind after the Euroa robbery. There were reports from the public at the time that a 'woman' who looked a lot like Steve Hart had been seen in that disguise with a packhorse. The only other report I found was from a man in Beechworth who made a comment to a journalist, but would not give his name. He said that he had been stopped in the street and asked directions by two men on horses who had women's clothes on. In all of the documents I have examined, I found only these two references to this form of disguise. It is my belief that this was in no way an expression of sexuality or a tactic to suggest insanity. It was most likely just a clever tool to preserve their lives.

THE ENGLISH CIRCUS

I strongly suspect that Kate met the English Circus manager (T. King) and performers that toured in South Australia while she was in Adelaide in January 1881, as both Kate and the English Circus troupe were mentioned in an article, along with the touring waxworks that included many Kelly effigies and relics. The English Circus also travelled through Victoria and New South Wales, and I have been told by locals that Kate spent time on a property near Grenfell around the time the troupe was travelling through that region, so it fits. Some people say that she worked in Albury as well, and that would also fit with the dates of the tour through there in 1881. The comment in the *Burrangong Argus* article about 'an important addition to the horses and riding staff' of the circus makes me think that it was referring to Kate. The English Circus had a strong equestrian element, so it would be a natural fit. There has been speculation in the past that Kate toured with Wirths Circus and also with a troupe run by Lance Skuthorpe; however, Skuthorpe's troupe was touring in a different period of time and could not have involved Kate. It was Kate's younger brother Jack who performed with both Lance Skuthorpe's troupe and Wirths Circus.

THE PERIOD 1883–85

Between Kate's 1883 stint in hospital with consumption and 1885, when she went to Cadow Station in Forbes, I lose track of Kate. There is some speculation that she went to New Zealand to perform, but her youngest brother, Jack Kelly, is on the record as saying that Kate did not leave Australia. Maybe with the increased digitising of records more will be revealed in the future about this part of her life. However, it's likely she started using different names around this time.

KATE WORKING IN FORBES

It has been reported that Kate worked at Cadow Station for twelve months, but in *The Forbes History Book*, 1997, it is recalled by Jeanette Hildred and Graham Williams that she remained at Cadow Station for two years before heading into the township.

It is also recorded that Judy Girot remembered stories about Kate working for Mr Prow in his home in Forbes, and that Mrs Prow died in 1884, leaving ten children in his care.

SULLIVAN

The only details we have about Sullivan, the man listed in the newspaper account of the inquest into Kate's death, is that he supposedly found Kate's body and told the police about it. We also know that he showed up for the inquest but left without testifying.

I have done my best to find out which of the Sullivans of the district is the most likely to have been the absent witness. Because of Thomas's criminal record (he was gaoled for stealing and killing a horse) and his threatening behaviour towards witnesses in his own case, I have unanswered questions about his possible involvement in Kate's death. However, unless some revealing evidence comes to light, we will never have definitive answers to my suspicions about him and what he really knew about Kate's death.

These days, failure to answer questions fully or truthfully when giving evidence at an inquest can result in up to five years' imprisonment.

KATE'S LAST BABY

In relation to Kate's youngest child, Catherine, her brother Jim and mother Ellen both offered different versions of what happened to that child after Kate died. As part of the Cookson interviews for *The Sun* newspaper, Jim said, 'The baby did not live. Both [Kate and the infant] were dead and buried when I got there.'

In *Ellen Kelly*, Balcarek and Dean suggest, through Ellen's character, that baby Catherine was left behind with relatives of Bricky Foster because she was too young to make the long journey and survive.

Records indicate that Kate's neighbour Susan Hurley lived at no. 1 Browne Street. Susan had a child, Ethel Alma Hurley, in July 1898. Records also indicate that the death of baby Catherine was reported in December of the same year. It seems likely to me that Susan would have tried to keep baby Catherine alive after the other children had gone with Jim back to Victoria. Susan is the only one we know for sure was caring for Kate's children after her death because of her testimony at Kate's inquest.

THE NOTE

The note that Kate asked Susan to write for her is referred to in Susan Hurley's testimony yet it was completely under-investigated at the time of Kate's death or at least under-reported in the newspaper record that remains. Kate could read and write. She could have written her own note. It has been portrayed in fiction as a suicide note, but that is probably the one thing we know it is not. In Susan Hurley's recorded testimony, she is adamant that Kate did not mention suicide to her.

POLICE INVESTIGATION

We cannot ignore the fact that some suspicious circumstances exist around Kate's death. Sullivan provided no evidence at the inquest and was never held to account. There are questions that were never really answered by Bricky either. This points to potential scenarios other than suicide. Today police are quick to suspect a husband or partner in the case of a woman's suspicious disappearance or death. Bricky's whereabouts could easily have been traced, if the police had investigated Kate's disappearance thoroughly, but we will never know if they did that work. Bricky's record of abuse against Kate does not mean that he murdered her, even though it would appear that circumstances were dire between the couple. How could Bricky ever really understand the torment his wife was suffering? Overall, there are many questions that seem to have been ignored by the police at the time.

KATE'S GUN

It is claimed that the Henckell & Co gun that possibly belonged to Kate Kelly was found in Forbes, which is a different story to the accounts shared with me. I was advised that a man discovered the weapon during farmhouse renovations during the 1980s in the township of Murga. Mr N (name withheld) from Bedgerebong purchased the weapon from his Murga friend, and then Mr A (name withheld) bought it from him in the 1990s. From there, a friend got involved and it ended up at auction.

Relatives of Mr A very kindly shared what they knew of the weapon's history and how it had ended up at auction.

In an article for *The Age*, 14 November 2007, Carolyn Webb and Daniella Miletic wrote:

> The gun, a .32 calibre revolver, was sold for $72,870 to an absentee bidder at Mossgreen auction house in South Yarra. [Someone] representing the anonymous owners had told *The Age* that the gun was found in a house or shed as it was demolished in the western NSW town of Forbes in the 1980s.

At the time of auction, the journalists writing the story asked for proof of provenance, but none was provided:

> Neither [of the men involved in the auction of the gun] was this week able to provide *The Age* with evidence of the gun's provenance or authenticity.

According to newspaper reports, a heritage weapon like the .32 calibre revolver sold at auction most likely would be valued at around four hundred dollars if there were no connection to a famous figure like Kate.

A newspaper article reported that a team of experts from the University of NSW had identified that the gun sold at auction was probably from around 1870–80 and that the initials K.K. were engraved before 1900.

However, another gun expert, supported by two others of the same opinion, contacted *The Age* and was reported as suggesting that the gun was not manufactured before 1884. Additionally, they suggested that the weapons most commonly provided to constables in Victoria were Webley revolvers from a Melbourne distributor, whereas this was a Henckell, a kind of copy of the popular Webley. So, it is unlikely to have been Fitzpatrick's weapon and probably had nothing to do with the Kelly Gang, despite speculation that it was the gun that had been removed from Fitzpatrick in 1878 at the Kelly homestead.

It was also documented that the gun had an insignia from the Royal Constabulary, and in the article referred to earlier, it was reported that Ian Jones, author of *Ned Kelly: A short life*, suggested this was not a usual police-gun marking for that period. Further commentary suggests that it was actually a simple proof mark, not a royal insignia.

My theory about how the gun came to be in Murga in the first place and how Kate may have acquired it is in the book.

PHOTOS OF KATE KELLY

The photos that are believed to be of Kate Kelly are reproduced in this book:

1. A cameo photograph of Kate Kelly, described as a 'carte de visite', 10.4 cm × 6.3 cm, is held in the State Library of New South Wales (P1/873). Entitled 'Kate Kelly?' (this is written on the back in ink), it has been credited to the Adelaide photographer 'E.G. Tims, Australian Photographic Co.' (in pencil on

the reverse). In the catalogue listing, it is proposed that the photo was taken between 1873 and 1878. The earlier date is simply too early because Kate would have been ten years old and is clearly older in the photo. I think that it would be more likely to have been taken between 1878 and 1880.

2. Almost immediately after the sensational siege at Glenrowan, an illustration based directly on E.G. Tims' photo was published in the *Illustrated Adelaide News*, 1 July 1880, and was captioned as being Kate Kelly. This unattributed sketch has not been reproduced in any other published material on Kate Kelly. I located an article in *The Evening News*, 25 June 1879, indicating that Kate and others had been invited to have their portraits taken by a well-known photographer in Melbourne but have been unable to confirm who that was. It is possible that E.G. Tims (who was based in Adelaide) went to Melbourne specifically to take Kate's photo.

3. Two studio photographs of Kate in a black mourning outfit with a riding crop. Most likely these were taken at a Melbourne studio at the time of Kate's public appearances after Ned's execution in 1880. One of these images was published in an unidentified newspaper (c. 1914–41) with the caption 'This old picture of the eighties looks impressive. It portrays Kate Kelly, sister of Ned and Dan, and has been for many years in the possession of Mr A. Skinner.' Held in the SLV, Accession No: H23557, the image is attributed to A.C. Dreier postcard collection.

One version of these *carte de visites* was listed for sale in the catalogue of the Melbourne-based auctioneers Mossgreen, 2007, and was expected to sell from $5,000–8,000. Inscribed on the back is the text: 'Kate Kelly' and 'Bought at the waxwork exhibition (signature) N.Z. April 13 1881 H.H.'

I have uncovered an advertisement in the *Newcastle Morning Herald and Miner's Advocate* Saturday, 5 November 1881, promoting 'The Great Waxworks Exhibition', which reveals that the waxworks exhibit had toured New Zealand and that it had included two groupings of Kelly Gang displays as well as Ned Kelly's armour. This shows the international appeal of the Kelly story and verifies that a Kelly-related waxworks exhibit was in New Zealand in 1881. It is likely that Kate Kelly souvenirs were being sold as part of the exhibit. In Brisbane's *Telegraph*, 11 July 1881, an article on the Great Waxworks Exhibition whose description matched the details provided in the *Newcastle Morning Herald* attributed the waxworks to Mr Cristofani & Co. In March 1882, a wax figure of Kate Kelly became part of the Kelly Gang display in Kreitmayer's waxworks in Melbourne.

4. A head-and-shoulders cameo of Kate is believed to have been given to bushranger expert Edgar Penzig in the 1970s by an American family with connections in the Glenrowan region. (Thanks to Gary Dean for this information.)

BOHEMIAN LECTURER

Oral historian Rob Willis shared recordings of interviews that he conducted with Dave Mathias and Beryl McNamara. These Forbes locals were neighbours to the Foster family and heard stories from Ted and Arthur Foster about Kate and Bricky. The brother and sister interacted with their neighbour Bricky when they were young, and their mother would read documents and letters for Bricky when he needed assistance, sometimes cooking him a meal. These recordings provided a lot of detail about Bricky, but also a lot of other stories about Jim Kelly coming to Forbes, Ted having seen Kate on her way to the lagoon and the Bohemian Lecturer coming to town. The belief that the travelling show had played a part in Kate's demise has lingered in folklore, and Dave believed this, too. Rob Willis also shared some important newspaper articles that helped to confirm so much of what had been recalled in oral history about the Bohemian Medical Company.

CLOSING THOUGHTS

If suicide was the true cause of Kate's death, there should be no shame for Kate or her family. We live in a time when we can recognise the effects of mental health issues such as depression and PNDA. We can acknowledge the depth of despair Kate must have been feeling, plus the sadness that losing her would have brought to her loved ones, both those alive at the time of her death and the generations of her family since then.

Bereavement by suicide is a particular type of trauma. For Fred, Gertrude and Elsie to have lost their mother and then be removed from the care of their father could have left them feeling unlovable or unwanted, despite the love they may have received from the Kelly family who raised them. It would most likely have left them with many unanswered questions and possibly shame about their mother's mysterious death, too.

I feel that Kate Kelly ought to be respectfully remembered for all her complexities, triumphs, strengths, weaknesses and tragedies, all the assets and flaws of the human condition that make us who we are.

Kate's story is a valuable opportunity to remind ourselves of how women have suffered from PNDA through the ages and to acknowledge the impact of PTSD and other untreated medical conditions in women. Kate's story also reminds us that it is the combination of our successes and failures that truly defines us, not simply one or the other.

Parts of Kate's short life were extraordinary and extreme, drawing out from her the qualities of bravery, strength, resourcefulness, resilience, craftiness and great physical skill, even when she was still a child. But the losses and traumatic experiences of her life caused deep and everlasting pain and suffering.

Regardless of my feelings and any conclusions I might draw from my research, the official record is that Kate drowned without an explanation, and so it remains.

Acknowledgements

Elizabeth Weiss—thank you for your professionalism, insight, support and encouragement, and for making my dream come true!

The Allen & Unwin team and editors—you have all been wonderful to work with, and I thank each of you for everything you have contributed in making this book the best it could be.

Special thanks to Paul Terry, Professor Graham Seal, Rob Willis OAM and Kerry Negara for your support and feedback. It is greatly appreciated.

Dr Alison Lyssa—you are an amazing and generous teacher, writer, editor and mentor. Thank you for everything you have taught me and all that you have contributed in helping me make my dream come true.

Special thanks to Jacqueline McGrath for all your generous and specialised support, information and advice.

David Thompson; Lindy Davis; Janine Wilson; Jake Wilson; Wid George; Mick, Dan and Gail McGrath; Tracey Callinan, Executive

Director of Arts OutWest; Sarah Gurich, Director of Bathurst Regional Art Gallery; Jonathan Turner, curator, arts critic and writer; Elizabeth Rogers, CEO of Regional Arts NSW; Margot Jolly, President of River Arts Festival; Carly Brown and Weddin Shire Council; Claire McCann and Grenfell Art Gallery team; John McRae Photography & Studio; Amie Zar, Coordinator Community History and Heritage Inner West Council, and the Leichhardt Library team; Kathryn Bancroft and Jenny Barry at BooksPlus Bathurst; Ana Young, Gary Rush, Rosemary Valadon; the Kimm family; and the many other friends, relatives and supporters who have been there for me along the way and who have contributed so much—thank you for your support, advice, feedback, research material, information, contacts and other contributions over the many years of this project.

Mel Pearce and the team at ABC Central West NSW; Neil Gill at Southern Cross Austereo; Diana Plater, writer and journalist; Robyne Young, writer; Frank Canu, producer—thank you for your commitment to sharing stories and promoting regional and rural artists and storytellers.

Special thanks to Ian and Janene for your kind assistance and information; also Mark and Sheryl at the Collits Inn for your generosity and willingness to help; Frances Higgins for your images of and information about Cadow Station, also Michelle and Will for your important expertise in your individual fields and to Pat Wright and Noreen McDonald for sharing your stories with me.

Very big thanks to Rob Willis, OAM, folklorist, oral historian, and Folklore and Social History Interviewer at the National Library of Australia. Thanks for sharing your recordings from the National Library of Australia's Willis Collection—thank you for your encouragement, generosity of spirit and all the helpful information you shared and the important work that you do.

Thanks also to Gary Dean for your interesting perspectives and information about Edgar Penzig's photo of Kate Kelly (black and white cameo image).

Many thanks to all the kind volunteer staff at Forbes Family History Group and Canowindra Historical Society and Museum for all your help.

Special acknowledgement of the great library staff and online services at the State Library of New South Wales, National Library of Australia, the State Library of Victoria, and the State Library of South Australia.

Selected Bibliography

PRIMARY SOURCES, UNPUBLISHED

Archives

Australian Military Forces Records
Australian Military Forces, Australian Imperial Force, Attestation Paper of
Persons Enlisted for Service Abroad, Foster, Frederick Arthur, Joined
29 June 1915, Next of Kin WH Foster, Father, Contact c/Mrs D Scott,
Thirroul, ancestry.com.au

Bathurst Library
Family and local history records

Beechworth Courthouse
Beechworth Court, Charge Sheet 3520, p. 197, 9 October 1878: Ellen
Kelly, Wounding with intent to prevent lawful apprehension,
Read or write, neither, date of birth 1836, Native place Antrim,
Particular marks, cut on right hand, scar top of forehead and left
cheek, Beechworth Gaol 9.10.78, Melbourne Gaol 24.10.78, Freedom

Revision (January 1881) 7 February 1881 (Mother of Edward Kelly, Daniel Kelly and James Kelly)

Benalla Costume and Kelly Museum

Benalla and District Historical Society (compilations), photographs and text re Ned Kelly's cummerbund, acquired by Dr Nicolson at Glenrowan when treating Ned's wounds, 28 June 1880

Canowindra Historical Society and Museum, 1879–83

Collits Family Collection: historical documents and records related to Collits and pioneer settlers

Items relating to James Collits: land grants (c. 1830s); family tree; property ownership in Canowindra in 1800s; photographs of Collits Inn (c. 1900s)

Forbes Family History Group Collection (FFHG)

Cavanagh, Jack (Kate Kelly's grandson), letter to Forbes Shire Council, 3 July 1996, informing them that Hugh McDougall had paid for Kate's headstone

County Map of Gipps, Diagram 58, Forbes, Grenfell, Hillston, showing Lake Cowal, Cadow and Warroo Stations

Death certificate, unnumbered: Kate Foster, DOD 15 October 1898; witnesses: George Thomson, Richard Stone and Walter Foster

Family Group Worksheet, unnumbered: Edward Jones, Elizabeth Strickland (nee Scott), Cadow Station

Family Group Worksheet, unnumbered: Scott–Strickland–Jones' connections

Family Group Worksheet 104: William (Bricky) Foster and Catherine Kelly

Family Group Worksheet 124: James Foster and Mary Anne Pass (Bricky Foster's grandparents)

Foster, Edward (Kate Kelly's brother-in-law), typewritten letter, 'Ned Kelly's Sister Kate', undated

Hollow, Ellen, letter to Curator, 'Kelly House', Beveridge, 22 June 1996, requesting copies of the photographic Kelly family tree; the letter confirms that Ellen Hollow is the daughter of Ruby Cavanagh, whose mother Gertrude Foster (married to Douglas Cavanagh) was Kate Kelly's daughter, and that Jim Kelly lived with the Griffiths family in his last years

McDougall, Hugh, handwritten letter on Warroo letterhead, to Arthur Foster, Kate Kelly's brother-in-law, 6 December 1925, thanking him for undertaking to care for Kate Kelly's headstone, letting him know that he will send photographs of the headstone to Kate's surviving brother Jim Kelly and her grandson Jack Cavanagh, and offering to send Arthur a photograph, too

Parish Map, 1977: Environs of Forbes, showing Ah Foo Lots 351, 352, 1210, 183

Parish Map of Forbes County of Ashburnham, 1893

Forbes Museum

The Forbes History Book, Forbes, NSW: Forbes Historical Society, 1997

Photographs of Burrawang Station, late 1890s

Woman's side saddle, 1800s

National Library of Australia, Trove <www.trove.nla.gov.au>, accessed 2011–20

The New South Wales Government Gazette, Sydney, NSW: Government Printer, 1832–1900, Tuesday 20 September 1864 (No. 185), information about the mail run, Murga, New South Wales

New South Wales Police Gazette, 16 March 1904 and 6 July 1904, Thomas Sullivan, Return Record, showing how his cases for trial were disposed of at quarter sessions, Forbes, New South Wales: 30 June 1904—Bail; 3 November 1904—Thomas Sullivan, Guilty, Imprisonment, Bathurst, three years hard labour

NSW Registry of Births, Deaths and Marriages

Birth Cert. 13762 Arthur Bertram Foster, DOB 15 March 1889 (Frederick Arthur)

Birth Cert. 30404, Catherine Foster, DOB 7 September 1898

Death Cert. 05006 William Henry Foster, DOD 10 March 1894

Death Cert. 11617 Ruby Ethel Foster, DOD 9 November 1897

Death Cert. 13762, Catherine Foster (infant), DOD 15 December 1898

Death Cert. 2062, Gertrude Eileen Cavanagh, DOD 24 January 1925

Marriage Cert. 04514, William Foster, Ada Kelly, 25 November 1888

State Library of South Australia

The Manning Index of South Australian History, <https://manning.collections.slsa.sa.gov.au/>

The State Archives and Records Authority of New South Wales

SRNSW: NRS 906 (temporary ref: NUA 262, May 2003). Parkes, Henry, NSW Premier, handwritten draft of letter to Graham Berry, Chief Secretary of Victoria, 14 February 1879, suggesting united action by the NSW and Victorian governments in relation to the Kelly Gang including the offer of a joint reward for their capture, <www.records.nsw.gov.au/archives/collections-and-research/guides-and-indexes/stories/the-ned-kelly-papers>, accessed 2015–20

Wangaratta Tourist Information Centre

Maps of the local area, information about the Kelly family and descendants and sites related to the Kelly Gang and miners' rights in the area.

Correspondence

MacDonald, Noreen, letter, 11 July 2015, describing the friendship between Noreen's grandmother, Henrietta Irving, and Kate Kelly, and the social implications when Henrietta, a Protestant, married an Irish Catholic policeman, Michael McEnerny, who supposedly was involved in hunting the Kellys. Noreen's great-grandparents, James and Henrietta Irving, were School Master and Assistant at Avenel, Victoria, where their daughter Henrietta was at school with some of the Kellys.

Wright, Pat, letter, April 2015, telling stories of her husband David's forebears, blacksmiths in Daysdale woken at night by Ned Kelly and commanded to shoe the Kellys' horses, and Kate's horse back to front.

Government publications

'Aboriginal Blue Mountains: Aboriginal people, services, culture and heritage in the Blue Mountains', booklet, Katoomba, NSW: Blue Mountains City Council, on behalf of the Aboriginal and Torres Strait Islander community, undated, <www.bmcc.nsw.gov.au>, accessed 8 December 2016

Kate Kelly, leaflet, Forbes, NSW: Forbes Shire Council, c. 2014

Interviews

English, Senior Constable William, personal interview, in Hill End, 25 November 2019, about his twenty years with the NSW Police Service: ten years in Macquarie Fields and ten in regional NSW, missing persons cases in modern policing, suicide cases, persons of interest in investigations

Higgins, Frances, personal interview, 2020. As a former owner of Cadow Station, Higgins shared her knowledge and photographs

Jeffery, M. J., personal interviews, 2018–20. A Master of Health Science, Sydney University, a dedicated nurse since the mid-1980s, a midwife since 1990, and a qualified Sexual Assault Forensic Examiner, Jeffrey specialises in neo-natal intensive care, child and family health nursing

Names withheld, personal interview, 2015. Former owners of Kate Kelly's antique gun

Thompson, David, personal interviews, 2011–20. Former endurance horserider, all-round bushman, proud Wiradyuri man

Oral histories

David Mathias, Beryl McNamara, interviewed by Rob Willis at Forbes, NSW, 14 May 1990, National Library of Australia: Rob and Olya Willis folklore collection, sound tape reel (c. 33 min.)

Reports

Parliamentary Statutes

The *Destitute Person's Act 1881*: An Act to repeal 'The Destitute Persons Relief and Industrial and Reformatory Schools Act, 1872,' and to make other provisions in lieu thereof', 18 November 1881 (Act 210/1881). *Find and Connect*, <www.findandconnect.gov.au/guide/sa/SE00260>, accessed 2016

The *Felons Apprehension Act* (Act 612), <http://kellygang.asn.au/wiki/Felons_Apprehension_Act>, accessed 2012–20

Royal Commission Report

Royal Commission on the Police Force of Victoria, 1881, Facsimile Reprint, 1968, Registry Number Aus 68-1548, *National Library of Australia*, <https://ironicon.com.au/the-royal-commission-kelly-outbreak.html>, accessed 2020

PRIMARY SOURCES, PUBLISHED

Books

Ashmead, Joseph W., (1922) (ed. Gary Dean) *The Thorns and the Briars: A true story of the Kelly Gang*, Glenrowan, Vic.: Glen Rowen Cobb & Co, c. 1980

Miscellaneous

'McGrath family reunion', Gooloogong, NSW, 5 October 1996, showing links to Collits and Cadow Station, McGrath family papers, copy provided by Mick McGrath, author unknown

Newspaper articles

* Note that the modern spelling of Kreitmayer has been used in the text of this book while the original spelling (Kreitmeyer) has been used in all contemporary references.

Adelaide Observer (SA: 1843–1904), Saturday 9 August 1879, p. 6, re prostitutes and disorderly persons at Galatea Hotel, Adelaide; Robert Fitzallan Long charged

Adelaide Observer (SA: 1843–1904), Saturday 25 June 1881, p. 34, 'Baby Show and Athletic Sports', re Robert Fitzallan Long's exhibition of Kate Kelly in person

The Age (Melbourne, Vic.: 1854–1954), Friday 21 June 1878, p. 3, 'The Victorian Commissioner at the Paris Exhibition', re Kreitmayer's wax figure Digger

Albury Banner and Wodonga Express (NSW: 1871–1938), Friday 26 August 1881, p. 12, advertisement for the 'English Circus' performed Monday in Albury

Areas' Express (Booyoolee, SA: 1877–1948), Saturday 4 December 1880, p. 5, descriptions of crowd, Kate Kelly's performance in Sydney, police intervention, performance moving to Victoria Theatre, stopped by police, agents arrested and bail given

The Argus (Melbourne, Vic.: 1848–1957), Friday 28 October 1870, p. 7, 'Covent of the Good Shepherd Bazaar', re Kreitmayer's wax figures of Mary Queen of Scots and Mary Magdalene

The Argus (Melbourne, Vic.: 1848–1957), Monday 5 February 1872, p. 6, 'The Australian and South Sea Islands Museum', re Kreitmayer's touring of Aboriginal busts and casts

The Argus (Melbourne, Vic.: 1848–1957), Tuesday 5 October 1875, p. 7, 'Execution of Howard', re Kreitmayer's requests for a cast of a hanged man

The Argus (Melbourne, Vic.: 1848–1957), Wednesday 12 February 1879, p. 6, 'The Kelly Gang at Jerilderie', re Ned Kelly and Joe Byrne destroying the telegraph wires, Jerilderie

The Argus (Melbourne, Vic.: 1848–1957), Saturday 30 October 1880, p. 8, 'Trial and Conviction of Edward Kelly'

The Argus (Melbourne, Vic.: 1848–1957), Saturday 6 November 1880, p. 8, 'The Condemned Bushranger', reporting speeches and crowd, Melbourne

The Argus (Melbourne, Vic.: 1848–1957), Monday 8 November 1880, pp. 4–5, 'To our Correspondents', critical of David Gaunson for 'abusing his position' with his appeal for a reprieve for Ned Kelly and his support for the petition, the article argued that there was 'no reason for mercy'

The Argus (Melbourne, Vic.: 1848–1957), Monday 8 November 1880, p. 7, 'The Condemned Bushranger', re Kate Kelly meeting the Governor and falling on her knees, Melbourne

The Argus (Melbourne, Vic.: 1848–1957), Tuesday 9 November 1880, p. 7, 'Country News', re fear of retribution if people do not sign petition to spare Ned Kelly, north-east Victoria

The Argus (Melbourne, Vic.: 1848–1957), Wednesday 10 November 1880, p. 6, 'The Condemned Bushranger', describing public meeting on the Reserve

The Argus (Melbourne, Vic.: 1848–1957), Thursday 11 November 1880, p. 5, 'The Condemned Bushranger', re reprieve committee and Patrick Quinn story

The Argus (Melbourne, Vic.: 1848–1957), Friday 12 November 1880, p. 6, 'The Execution of Edward Kelly', re history of the gang, details of execution

The Argus (Melbourne, Vic.: 1848–1957), Saturday 13 November 1880, p. 6, refers to Georgia Minstrels interrupted, and Kate and Jim Kelly banned from appearing at the Apollo again following their 11 November appearance

The Argus (Melbourne, Vic.: 1848–1957), Saturday 13 November 1880, p. 21, Kate and Jim Kelly's appearance at Apollo Theatre cancelled

The Argus (Melbourne, Vic.: 1848–1957), Wednesday 17 November 1880, p. 1, re Katoomba ship departs Melbourne at 2 p.m. for Sydney

The Argus (Melbourne, Vic.: 1848–1957), Tuesday 26 November 1935, p. 10,

'Obituary', Samuel Wilson of Mansfield, Lake Cowal and Victorian properties

The Argus (Melbourne, Vic.: 1848–1957), Saturday 10 June 1939, p. 3, 'Thrills and Chills in the Waxworks: Kate Kelly and Kelly relatives frequent visitors of waxworks in 1800s'

The Armidale Express and New England General Advertiser (Armidale, NSW: 1856–1861; 1863–1889; 1891–1954), Friday 17 December 1880, p. 3, 'Epitome of News', re Kate Kelly in Sydney

Australian Star (Sydney, NSW: 1887–1909), Friday 21 August 1896, p. 5, re shearing commenced at reduced rate for shearers, Warroo

Australian Town and Country Journal (Sydney, NSW: 1870–1907), Saturday 10 July 1880, p. 8, 'Kate Kelly', attributing her with great natural intelligence, which gave immunity to the Kelly Gang

Australian Town and Country Journal (Sydney, NSW: 1870–1907), Saturday 27 November 1880, p. 13, 'The Kelly Show Stopped', description of the crowds in Sydney, mentioning Pringle, Tompkins, Anderson and Det. Williams

Australian Town and Country Journal (Sydney, NSW: 1870–1907), Saturday 11 May 1901, p. 15, re trial of Mary and brother John in Cowra, attempted murder and accessory before the fact

Ballarat Courier (Vic.: 1869–1883; 1914–1918), Monday 17 January 1881, p. 2, 'Kate weary, Ettie at RB Hotel' re Kate Kelly in Melbourne

Ballarat Star (Vic.: 1865–1924), Wednesday 3 November 1880, p. 2, 'The Close of the Kelly Trial'

Ballarat Star (Vic.: 1865–1924), Friday 5 November 1880, p. 3, re Kate Kelly visits Ned and Ellen in gaol with Jim, Melbourne

The Bega Gazette and Eden District or Southern Coast Advertiser (NSW: 1865–1899), Saturday 30 December 1899, 'Daughters of Eve', re Kate Kelly suicide

Bendigo Advertiser (Vic.: 1855–1918), Thursday 22 March 1877, p. 1, re Kreitmayer's waxworks exhibition of Hastings, Duff and other criminals

Bendigo Advertiser (Vic.: 1855–1918), Thursday 20 March 1879, p. 2, 'The Border Police' re four armed men matching description of the Kelly outlaws seen at Kerang near Gunbower

Bendigo Advertiser (Vic.: 1855–1918), Wednesday 21 January 1880, p. 2, re Kreitmayer's display at Easter Fair: Kelly Gang and Captain Moonlite

Bendigo Advertiser (Vic.: 1855–1918), Friday 2 July 1880, p. 3, 'Glenrowan Tragedy', with details of Kreitmayer's Chamber of Horrors, his casting of Joe Byrne's body, and purchasing his riding boots

Bendigo Advertiser (Vic.: 1855–1918), Tuesday 2 November 1880, p. 2, 'The convict Kelly', re David Gaunson calling a public meeting for Monday to request a Ned Kelly reprieve

Bendigo Advertiser (Vic.: 1855–1918), Tuesday 13 November 1883, p. 2, re letter from a secretary to say that Kate Kelly had never been in Beechworth Hospital

Brisbane Courier (Qld: 1864–1933), Tuesday 2 November 1880, p. 2, 'Melbourne: Procession to Govt. House'

Brisbane Courier (Qld: 1864–1933), Thursday 4 January 1900, p. 4, Mr Cole (Bohemian Lecturer) in Brisbane, Wild West Dramatic Company, Kelly production called 'Hands Up!', Bohemian Lecturer

The Bulletin (Sydney, NSW: 1880–1984), Saturday 4 December 1880, p. 4, 'Kate Kelly has invested in a fashionable riding habit at a leading house . . . While Kate Kelly was holding a reception the other evening the footpath became so crowded that a number of respectable citizens took to the road.' (Seen at www.KateKelly.biz)

The Bulletin (Sydney, NSW: 1880–1984), Saturday 11 December 1880, p. 3, Jane Fitzpatrick visits Kate and Jim Kelly asking for money. 'The sister of Fitzpatrick—the constable who had the first dispute with the Kellys; resulting as they say, in their taking to the bush—called on Kate Kelly, while in this city. She asked for assistance, but it was not given her.'

The Bulletin (Sydney, NSW: 1880–1984), Saturday 18 December 1880, p. 9, 'When people say the Kelly troupe were solely patronised by

the larrikin class they live like the special correspondent of a daily
sausage wrapper. As a proof of this I may mention that one of the
most influential men in this city was met the last night of the show
by Frank Warden, who asked if he had been in to see the Kellys.'
(Seen at www.KateKelly.biz)

The Burrangong Argus (NSW: 1865–1913), Wednesday 31 August 1881, p. 2,
'Circus', re important additions to the English Circus's horses and
riding staff

The Burrangong Argus (NSW: 1865–1913), Saturday 3 September 1881, p. 3,
advertisement, 'Last Night of the Season' re English Circus's performance at Young that night, their last night before Grenfell

The Burrangong Argus (NSW: 1865–1913), Saturday 1 October 1881, p. 3,
'Brevities'

The Burrowa News (NSW: 1874–1951), Friday 16 September 1881, 'The
Great English Circus', re performance in Burrowa

Camperdown Chronicle (Vic.: 1877–1954), Friday 14 February 1879, p. 2,
re Euroa robbery

The Cootamundra Herald (NSW: 1877–1954), Saturday 27 November 1880,
p. 4, 'Crumbs', re Kate Kelly and Jim making money out of showing a
bay horse, Sydney

The Cootamundra Herald (NSW: 1877–1954), Saturday 3 September 1881,
p. 4, re English Circus introducing well-known clown Benhamo;
trapeze and several specialties

Corowa Free Press (NSW: 1875–1954), Friday 2 July 1880, p. 2, 'Another
Kelly Outrage', Glenrowan

Corowa Free Press (NSW: 1875–1954), Friday 29 October 1880, p. 2, 'Latest
Telegrams'; 'Ned Kelly's Trial', Melbourne

Devon Herald (Latrobe, Tas.: 1877–1889), Saturday 3 July 1880, p. 2, Kate
Kelly, Glenrowan

Evening News (Sydney, NSW: 1869–1931), Wednesday 25 June 1879,
p. 3, 'More Kelly Rumours', 'Kate Kelly, Maggie, Wild Wright and

Tom Lloyd invited to Melbourne photographer for a good sum of money to sit for portraits.' They consented and sitting was to take place that day.

Evening News (Sydney, NSW: 1869–1931), Friday 29 October 1880, p. 2, 'Ned Kelly's Trial', Melbourne

Evening News (Sydney, NSW: 1869–1931), Saturday 20 November 1880, p. 4, 'Kate Kelly in Sydney', arriving from Melbourne with agent, staying at Freshwater's Packhorse Inn

Evening News (Sydney, NSW: 1869–1931), Friday 26 November 1880, p. 2, 'The Kelly Show Moved On', re marquee in Bathurst Street

Evening News (Sydney, NSW: 1869–1931), Monday 22 March 1897, p. 7, 'Drought in the Country', Warroo

Express and Telegraph (Adelaide, SA: 1867–1922), Friday 11 July 1879, p. 2, 'Police Court', Robert Fitzallan Long charges patron who stole from lodger

Express and Telegraph (Adelaide, SA: 1867–1922), Saturday 7 August 1880, p. 2, 'The Trial of Ned Kelly', re details of Stringybark Creek

Forbes Advocate (NSW: 1911–1954), no date, 'Here to Photograph Famous Grave', provided to FFHG by Arthur Willis

Forbes Advocate (NSW: 1911–1954), Friday 16 September 1921, p. 7, Forbes reflections

Forbes Advocate (NSW: 1911–1954), Friday 25 August 1922, 'Early Forbes. In the Mining and Bushranging Days. Old Memories Recalled.' Yellow Dick, German Harry, Coobang Mick, Ben Hall's first gold, ref. Strickland & Rawsthorne families, Forbes

Forbes Advocate (NSW: 1911–1954), Friday 9 August 1946, p. 4, 'Obituary: Mr. Wm. Henry Foster'

Forbes Advocate, Friday 12 August 1955, 'Right Kate Came Here'. Clara Rae says it was 'the Kate Kelly' in Forbes, talks about going to dances with Kate Kelly, Kate Kelly dating, a square frame show, Kate Kelly becoming hysterical, Kate Hennessey alias.

Forbes Advocate, Friday 21 October 1955, 'True Story of Kate Kelly', re Edward R. Foster, aka Ted Foster (Bricky's brother); Kate Kelly's bullet wounds

Forbes Advocate, Tuesday 19 July 1960, 'Last Link with Kelly Gang', re Edward, aka Ted Foster; Kate Kelly travelling show, FFHG

Forbes Advocate, Saturday 9 May 1998, re Jack Cavanagh, grandson of Kate Kelly, raised by Ellen Kelly, FFHG

Forbes Advocate (NSW: 1911–1954), Saturday 10 October 2015, volume 3625, 'A Piece in Historic Puzzle', pp. 1, 3, re Willis discovers Bohemian Medical Company advertisement and article

Forbes and Parkes Gazette (NSW: 1872–1899), Tuesday 18 October 1898, 'Found Drowned', re Report on the Magisterial Inquiry into the Death of Kate Kelly (Foster), FFHG

Forbes Times (NSW: 1912–1920), Friday 2 January 1914, p. 3, Forbes Gaol opened 1889, also Burrawang reference, Forbes

Forbes Times (NSW: 1912–1920), Tuesday 10 March 1914, 'A Shocking Tragedy at Cadow Station'

Forbes Times (NSW: 1912–1920), Tuesday 11 July 1916, p. 2, 'Valedictory. Sergeant John Garstang'

Freeman's Journal (Sydney, NSW: 1850–1932), Saturday 23 April 1892, p. 9, 'Not Kate Kelly', re Mrs Ambrose

Freeman's Journal (Sydney, NSW: 1850–1932), Saturday 14 May 1892, p. 21, wild boar attack, Warroo

Freeman's Journal (Sydney, NSW: 1850–1932), Thursday 9 July 1925, p. 15, 'Puffs, Pars and Personals': Kate Kelly performance site was where the Star and Garter Hotel was subsequently rebuilt, Sydney

Geelong Advertiser (Vic.: 1859–1929), Saturday 4 August 1877, p. 2, re David Gaunson

Geelong Advertiser (Vic.: 1859–1929), Saturday 7 August 1880, p. 3, 'Ned Kelly's Trial', Beechworth

Geelong Advertiser (Vic.: 1859–1929), Tuesday 23 November 1880, p. 2, re Fitzpatrick

Geelong Advertiser (Vic.: 1859–1929), Saturday 27 November 1880, p. 2, 'Town Talk', re tent erected on Bathurst Street

Gippsland Times (Vic.: 1861–1954), Friday 4 June 1880, p. 3, 'The Kelly Gang', re Kate Kelly in Benalla, supplies for gang, 'cut your ears off', sympathisers, 'feminine attire', referring to a woman's hat and veil left at Younghusband's Station, Steve Hart

Goulburn Herald (NSW: 1881–1907), Thursday 22 September 1881, p. 3, advertisement, 'English Circus: Favourite equestrian company, Best circus now travelling, Bourke St near Montague Street, Manager T. King'

Goulburn Herald (NSW: 1881–1907), Thursday 22 September 1881, p. 3, 'English Circus: Favourite equestrian company', re its performance in Goulburn

Goulburn Herald (NSW: 1881–1907), Saturday 24 September 1881, p. 2, advertisement re English Circus performing that night, Argyle Inn, Bourke Street, Goulburn

Goulburn Herald (NSW: 1881–1907), Saturday 24 September 1881, p. 4, 'Circus', describing English Circus horses as 'a good deal worn and fatigued'

Goulburn Herald and Chronicle (NSW: 1864–1881), Wednesday 17 November 1880, p. 4, 'Disgraceful Proceedings', re Apollo Theatre Appearance, Kate and Jim Kelly

Grenfell Record and Lachlan District Advertiser (NSW: 1876–1951), Monday 24 May 1926, p. 2, 'Mr Hugh McDougall'

Gundagai Times and Tumut, Adelong and Murrumbidgee District Advertiser (NSW: 1868–1931), Tuesday 30 August 1881, p. 2, reporting on English Circus: 'Gundagai last night . . . large crowds . . . steel teeth lady . . . perform in Coolac tonight'

Herald (Melbourne, Vic.: 1861–1954), Monday 2 August 1880, p. 3, 'Ned Kelly's Removal', re Kelly being taken to Beechworth for trial

Herald (Melbourne, Vic.: 1861–1954), Friday 6 August 1880, p. 3, 'Ned Kelly's Trial', Beechworth

Herald (Melbourne, Vic.: 1861–1954), Wednesday 11 August 1880, p. 3, 'Ned Kelly's Trial'

Illustrated Adelaide News, (SA: 1875–1880), Thursday 1 July 1880, p. 8, 'The Kelly Gang', illustration of Kate Kelly based on E.G. Tims' photograph, no artist attributed

Illustrated Adelaide News (SA: 1875–1880), Sunday 1 August 1880, p. 3, 'Kate Kelly': 'Fine specimen native born bush girl ... most skilful horsewoman ... wonder she hasn't been arrested as the most prominent sympathiser ... great pluck and endurance'

Illustrated Australian News (Melbourne, Vic.: 1876–1889), Saturday 6 November 1880, p. 203, 'Trial of Edward Kelly', summary of trial, Ned's banter with Judge Barry

Illustrated Sydney News and New South Wales Agriculturalist and Grazier (NSW: 1872–1881), Saturday 10 July 1880, p. 1, 'The Kelly Gang. The capture of the Kelly Gang. The murder of Sherritt.'

Kalgoorlie Miner (WA: 1895–1950), Thursday 30 July 1931, p. 7, 'Sideshows and Freaks of Other Days', stories of Flash Jack Donovan

Kalgoorlie Western Argus (WA: 1896–1916), Tuesday 12 December 1905, p. 25, 'The Kelly Gang', re Kate Kelly travelling

Kapunda Herald (SA: 1878–1951), Tuesday 16 November 1880, p. 3, re Kate Kelly offered five pounds a week to perform in Adelaide

Kapunda Herald (SA: 1878–1951), Friday 7 January 1881, p. 3, 'Late Telegrams'

Kapunda Herald (SA: 1878–1951), Tuesday 11 January 1881, p. 3, 'Robert Fitzallan Long confirms Kate Kelly still at his hotel ... difficulty has arisen in connection with her appearance in public.'

Kerang Times and Swan Hill Gazette (Vic.: 1877–1889), Friday 20 June 1879, p. 4, re Kate Kelly and Maggie in Melbourne, Carlton, Sandridge, and police complaints to the press

Kyneton Guardian (Vic.: 1870–1880; 1914–1918), Saturday 7 August 1880, p. 2, 'Ned Kelly's Trial', Beechworth

Kyneton Observer (Vic.: 1856–1900), Saturday 14 August 1880, p. 2, 'Trial of Kelly at Beechworth'

Lachlander and Condobolin and Western Districts Recorder (NSW: 1899–1952), Friday 31 March 1899, p. 8, 'Typhoid outbreak, Forbes'

Lachlander and Condobolin and Western Districts Recorder (NSW: 1899–1952), Wednesday 26 May 1926, 'Obituary Mr Hugh McDougall'

Launceston Examiner (Tas.: 1842–1899), Thursday 29 December 1870, p. 3, 'Victoria', Kreitmayer's drunken sailor patron kicked out

Launceston Examiner (Tas.: 1842–1899), Monday 15 November 1880, p. 3, 'Execution of Ned Kelly'

Launceston Examiner (Tas.: 1842–1899), Saturday 4 March 1882, p. 3, 'Waxworks Exhibition', re Kelly Gang wax figures, Stringybark Creek incident; Kate Kelly also a figure

Leader (Melbourne, Vic.: 1862–1918, 1935), Saturday 13 November 1880, p. 17, 'The Kelly and Gaunson Scandal'

Leader (Melbourne, Vic.: 1862–1918, 1935), Saturday 9 January 1909, p. 30, 'Obituary Flash Jack'

Lithgow Mercury (NSW: 1898–1954), Friday 19 December 1952, p. 4, 'Collits of Collits Inn'

Lorgnette (Melbourne, Vic.: 1878–1898), Tuesday 11 January 1881, p. 2, 'The Last of the Kellys', a play performed in the Royal Theatre, Nelson

The Maitland Daily Mercury (NSW: 1894–1939), Thursday 5 December 1895, p. 2, 'Local and General Items', re E. J. Cole, better known as the Bohemian Lecturer

Maitland Mercury and Hunter River General Advertiser (NSW: 1843–1893), Thursday 11 November 1880, p. 5, 'Melbourne', re Ann Jones arrested, feloniously harbouring Ned Kelly; attempted train wreck at Lancefield, night before Ned hanged

Maitland Mercury and Hunter River General Advertiser (NSW: 1843–1893), Tuesday 23 November 1880, p. 4, 'Special Telegrams', re Kate Kelly and Jim arriving in Sydney

Maitland Weekly Mercury (NSW: 1894–1931), Saturday 22 October 1898, p. 10, 'News of the Week', re Mrs Wm Foster, Kate Kelly suicide

Manaro Mercury, and Cooma and Bombala Advertiser (NSW: 1862–1931), Wednesday 10 November 1880, p. 3, 'Ned Kelly Sympathy', re Hippodrome meeting, Melbourne

The Mercury (Hobart, Tas.: 1860–1954), Saturday 8 March 1879, p. 1, 'Victoria', Kate Kelly, Benalla

The Mercury (Hobart, Tas.: 1860–1954), Monday 12 July 1880, p. 3, 'The Kelly Gang', re Kelly Gang display waxworks, visited by Kellys, Kate Kelly in town, Melbourne

The Mercury (Hobart, Tas.: 1860–1954), Saturday 13 November 1880, p. 2, 'The carnival in Melbourne had a most unhappy ending', Kate Kelly kneeling for Governor's mercy described as 'Claptrap and theatrical effect'

The Mercury (Hobart, Tas.: 1860–1954), Monday 11 April 1881, p. 3, 'The Kelly Enquiry'

The Mercury (Hobart, Tas.: 1860–1954), Saturday 30 April 1881, p. 3, 'Victoria', re Kate and Maggie restoring Ellen's selection, Melbourne

Mirror (Perth, WA: 1921–1956), Saturday 5 September 1953, p. 9, 'The Real Story of NED KELLY'

Molong Argus (NSW: 1896–1921), Friday 28 October 1898, p. 4, re Bohemian Lecturer

Molong Argus (NSW: 1896–1921), Friday 27 October 1905, p. 5, 'Bushranging Episodes', re Kate Kelly exhibition in back lane off King Street, Sydney

Morning Bulletin (Rockhampton, Qld: 1878–1954), Friday 26 November 1880, p. 2, 'New South Wales', re Kate and Jim Kelly charged with creating a nuisance, Sydney

Morning Bulletin (Rockhampton, Qld: 1878–1954), Friday 26 November 1880, p. 2, Kate Kelly, Sydney

Mount Alexander Mail (Vic.: 1854–1917), Tuesday 17 June 1879, p. 3,

'Kate Kelly in Melbourne', re Kellys visiting Sandridge twice, Kate disappearing despite being watched by police

Mount Alexander Mail (Vic.: 1854–1917), Monday 22 December 1879, p. 2, re David Gaunson's public meeting, Ararat

Mount Alexander Mail (Vic.: 1854–1917), Tuesday 10 August 1880, p. 3, 'Ned Kelly's trial', re David Gaunson cross-examines witnesses; opossum rug for Ned

Mount Alexander Mail (Vic.: 1854–1917), Saturday 13 November 1880, p. 2, 'Items of News', re Apollo Theatre Appearance, Kate and Jim Kelly

Mount Alexander Mail (Vic.: 1854–1917), Wednesday 22 December 1880, p. 2, 'Items of News', re Kate Kelly returning to Melbourne

Mount Alexander Mail (Vic.: 1854–1917), Thursday 5 May 1881, p. 2, 'Items of News,' re Kate getting photos of Ned printed, Melbourne

Mount Alexander Mail (Vic.: 1854–1917), Monday 22 August 1881, p. 2, re Wild Wright and Jim Kelly at Wangaratta; the English Circus; Wright drunk, fined and released

Narracoorte Herald (SA: 1875–1954), Tuesday 27 January 1880, p. 2, re rumours that Kate Kelly intended to petition the government for the release of her mother Ellen

National Advocate (Bathurst, NSW: 1889–1954), Monday 7 November 1904, p. 4, re Ned Kelly sentenced to gaol

National Advocate (Bathurst, NSW: 1889–1954), Wednesday 24 July 1907, p. 4, 'Potato Stealing', Warroo

National Advocate (Bathurst, NSW: 1889–1954), Thursday 16 December 1915, p. 2, 'Personal', re Hasemer Brickyards Diprotodon, Forbes

Newcastle Morning Herald and Miners' Advocate (NSW: 1876–1954), Monday 20 September 1880, p. 2, 'Trial of Ned Kelly', re summons to change venue to Melbourne

Newcastle Morning Herald and Miners' Advocate (NSW: 1876–1954), Saturday 5 November 1881, p. 1, advertisement for The Great Waxworks Exhibition

The North Eastern Ensign (Benalla, Vic.: 1872–1938), Tuesday 17 April 1883, p. 2, re Kate Kelly sick, in Wangaratta Hospital

The North Eastern Ensign (Benalla, Vic.: 1872–1938), Friday 7 April 1899, p. 4, re Bohemian Lecturer's bushranger play

Northern Argus (Clare, SA: 1869–1954), Friday 3 September 1880, p. 2, 'Kapunda', Kreitmayer's waxworks at Kapunda

Northern Argus (Clare, SA: 1869–1954), Tuesday 11 January 1881, p. 2, 'Northern Jottings', Kate Kelly in Adelaide

Northern Argus (Clare, SA: 1869–1954), Tuesday 2 August 1881, p. 3, re Benhamo of the English Circus being sued for wages, Ballarat

Northern Miner (Qld: 1874–1954), Thursday 4 November 1880, pp. 205, 215, 'Ned Kelly', 'Devil dodgers' and 'Gospel grinders', 'rid of such a monster', David Gaunson and 'criminal classes', 'too good a fate for Devil's spawn' (205); 'The Verdict', saving 'scoundrelism', (215) The Governor and Kate Kelly in Melbourne

Northern Territory Times and Gazette (Darwin, NT: 1873–1927), Saturday 15 January 1881, p. 2, 'Our Melbourne Letter', re Long employing Kate Kelly in Sydney

Northern Territory Times and Gazette (Darwin, NT: 1873–1927), Saturday 14 May 1881, p. 3, 'Our Melbourne Letter', re Ned Kelly's body and Ellen Kelly's selection forfeited

Port Adelaide News (SA: 1878–1883), Friday 24 December 1880, p. 1, criticism of Kate Kelly in Adelaide

Protestant Standard (Sydney, NSW: 1869–1895), Saturday 8 September 1877, p. 10, 'General Post Office', re mail routes, Murga, NSW

Queanbeyan Age (NSW: 1867–1904), Wednesday 5 June 1895, p. 2, re shots fired at coach on way to Forbes

Queensland Times, Ipswich Herald and General Advertiser (Qld: 1861–1908), Tuesday 16 November 1880, petition for Ned Kelly reprieve

Queenslander (Brisbane, Qld: 1866–1939), Saturday 10 July 1880, p. 55, 'The Kelly Gang', Glenrowan

Queenslander (Brisbane, Qld: 1866–1939), Saturday 8 January 1881, p. 54, 'Intercolonial News in Brief', re Kate Kelly in Adelaide

Riverine Herald (Echuca, Vic.: Moama, NSW: 1869–1954), Tuesday 11 April 1876, p. 2, 'Echuca', re Madame Tussaud and Kreitmayer

Singleton Argus (NSW: 1880–1954), Monday 24 August 1942, p. 4, 'Constable Fitzpatrick of Kelly Fame'

South Australian Advertiser (Adelaide, SA: 1858–1889), Friday 7 December 1877, p. 2, 'Public Notices: Robert Fitzallan Long Insolvency'

South Australian Advertiser (Adelaide, SA: 1858–1889), Tuesday 29 June 1880, p. 4, summary of Glenrowan siege

South Australian Advertiser (Adelaide, SA: 1858–1889), Thursday 1 July 1880, p. 5, 'The Kelly Bushrangers'; 'The Shooting of Sherritt'; 'Inquest into the Body of Byrne'; 'The State of Ned Kelly'; 'The Rumour that Kate Kelly had shot Sergeant Steele'

South Australian Advertiser (Adelaide, SA: 1858–1889), Monday 31 October 1881, p. 4, re commission into the Victorian Police and their conduct towards the Kellys

South Australian Chronicle and Weekly Mail (Adelaide, SA: 1868–1881), Saturday 15 February 1879, p. 21, re visitors to Kate Kelly, comments that Fitzpatrick was intimate with family, and not there to serve warrant

South Australian Register (Adelaide, SA: 1839–1900), Thursday 27 February 1879, p. 5, 'Colonial Telegrams. Victoria.', Mrs Smith sues Kreitmayer; Ned Kelly sympathisers detained in Beechworth

South Australian Register (Adelaide, SA: 1839–1900), Saturday 10 July 1880, p. 1, 'Ned Kelly in Gaol', re Ellen's visit to her son Ned

South Australian Register (Adelaide, SA: 1839–1900), Tuesday 21 December 1880, p. 4, 'Arrivals Monday 20 December on the South Australian Steamer: A. King'

The Sun (Sydney, NSW: 1910–1954), Thursday 7 September 1911, p. 9, B.W. Cookson Interviews, 'The Kelly Gang From Within'

Sydney Daily Telegraph (NSW: 1879–1883), Saturday 23 April 1881, p. 7, 'The Victorian Police Commission'

The Sydney Morning Herald (NSW: 1842–1954), Saturday 11 September 1880, p. 2, re Ned's armour and Kreitmayer

The Sydney Morning Herald (NSW: 1842–1954), Friday 26 November 1880, p. 3, re Kate Kelly attempting two exhibitions, Wednesday, Sydney

The Sydney Morning Herald (NSW: 1842–1954), Thursday 2 December 1880, p. 7, 'Accidents and Offences', re Kate and Jim Kelly. 'The brother and sister of notorious bushranger Ned Kelly have paid a visit in Sydney for the purpose of exhibiting themselves and some of the relics of the bushranging conflicts; but the police interfered, and the exhibition has been stopped.'

The Sydney Morning Herald (NSW: 1842–1954), Saturday 15 October 1898, p. 10, 'Suicide of a Woman', re Kate Kelly suicide

The Sydney Morning Herald (NSW: 1842–1954), Monday 9 March 1914, p. 9, 'Station Tragedy', re Cadow Station

The Sydney Morning Herald (NSW: 1842–1954), Saturday 6 August 1932, p. 9, 'The Collits Family Passing of the Pioneers'; Surveyor Mitchell meets James Collits

The Sydney Morning Herald (NSW: 1842–1954), Tuesday 11 February 1936, p. 9, 'Cadow Station Sold'

The Sydney Morning Herald: Good Weekend, Saturday 3 September 2011, pp. 16–21, Chandler, Jo, 'A Question of Identity,' Ned Kelly article, skull stolen, historical research and forensic medicine to identify Ned's skull

Sydney Sportsman (Surry Hills, NSW: 1900–1954), Wednesday 13 March 1907, p. 7, 'Kate Kelly's Lament'

Sydney Stock and Station Journal (NSW: 1896–1924), Friday 28 January 1898, p. 5, 'The Lachlan', State of the Lachlan River 1898, re 'liquid mud', 'large fish kills', Forbes

Telegraph (Brisbane, Qld: 1872–1947), Thursday 25 November 1880, p. 2, re Kate and Jim Kelly arrested in Sydney, their performance officially prohibited, their appearance in court, bail granted on condition that they did not perform again; Pringle and Tompkins also arrested.

Telegraph (Brisbane, Qld: 1872–1947), Monday 11 July 1881, p. 2, 'The Waxworks'

Telegraph (Brisbane, Qld: 1872–1947), Monday 9 March 1914, p. 7, re Sidney Jones, Cadow Station

Telegraph (Brisbane, Qld: 1872–1947), Tuesday 8 April 1930, p. 8, 'The Kelly Gang', reprint of article from 8 April 1880, re Kate and Dan at the races; Kate on guard

Town and Country Journal (Sydney, NSW: 1870–1907), Wednesday 5 October 1910, p. 26, 'The Lachlan's Early Settlers—Links with the Past', re Edward Jones, Elizabeth Scott, Strickland, Jones, Pierce Collits and others; Cadow Station

Truth (Perth, WA: 1903–1931), Saturday 20 May 1911, p. 14, a report from a witness in the crowd re Kate Kelly on horseback arriving for the show, the crowd gathering, Sydney

Truth (Brisbane, Qld: 1900–1954), Sunday 15 May 1927, p. 23, 'Ned Kelly's Sister', re Kate Kelly performing with Flash Jack Donovan

Truth (Sydney, NSW: 1894–1954), Sunday 24 September 1950, p. 36, 'Flash Jack Donovan. King of the Spielers', re Flash Jack's exploitation of Kate, description of their tour

Truth (Sydney, NSW: 1894–1954), Sunday 25 July 1954, p. 60, 'Kate was drowned at Forbes'; 'Mrs Markwort says play killed Kate', FFHG

Victorian Express (Geraldton, WA: 1878–1894), Wednesday 15 December 1880, p. 3, 'New South Wales', re Kate Kelly exhibitions stopped

Wagga Wagga Advertiser (NSW: 1875–1910), Tuesday 9 November 1880, p. 4, 'Ned Kelly Sympathised With', Melbourne

Wagga Wagga Advertiser (NSW: 1875–1910), Thursday 4 August 1892, p. 2 (2), Gnalta Station

Wagga Wagga Advertiser (NSW: 1875–1910), Saturday 15 October 1898, p. 2, re Kate Kelly suicide

Warragul Guardian and Buln Buln and Narracan Shire Advocate (Warragul, Vic.: 1879–1894), Thursday 11 November 1880, p. 3, 'Ned Kelly's Relations and Friends'

Weekly Times (Melbourne, Vic.: 1869–1954), Saturday 30 December 1871, p. 7, 'The Waxworks', re 'breathing soldier', Kreitmayer

Weekly Times (Melbourne, Vic.: 1869–1954), Saturday 6 November 1880, p. 19, 'Convict Kelly', re Kate Kelly in Melbourne; Executive Council Meeting

Weekly Times (Melbourne, Vic.: 1869–1954), Saturday 27 December 1902, p. 37, 'Notes and Comments', Burrawang Station

The West Australian (Perth, WA: 1879–1954), Tuesday 6 September 1898, p. 6, reporting that Highlander, a thoroughbred prize-winning horse, trained by Kate Kelly, died shortly after Kate

Western Champion (Blackall/Barcaldine, Qld: 1879–1891), Friday 28 October 1881, p. 3, 'Letter from Adelaide says Kate Kelly was killed while riding a horse'

Western Champion (Parkes, NSW: 1898–1934), Friday 23 September 1898, p. 9, 'Forbes', re Bohemian Medical Company Cycloramic Exhibition, Bohemian Lecturer

Western Champion (Parkes, NSW: 1898–1934), Friday 30 September 1898, p. 8, re Bohemian Lecturer

Western Champion (Parkes, NSW: 1898–1934), Friday 30 September 1898, p. 8, 'Forbes', re Bohemian Medical Company Drama, *Queens' Pardon* and Bushrangers of Australia, Bohemian Lecturer

Western Champion (Parkes, NSW: 1898–1934), Friday 21 October 1898, p. 8, 'Forbes', re Mrs Foster's body 'floating in the lagoon'

Western Champion (Parkes, NSW: 1898–1934), Friday 24 November 1899, p. 5, 'Maliciously Wounding', re William 'Bricky' Foster

Western Champion (Parkes, NSW: 1898–1934), Friday 20 November 1903, p. 5, 'Police Court'

Western Champion (Parkes, NSW: 1898–1934), Friday 27 November 1903, p. 17, 'District Notes', Murga, NSW

Western Champion (Parkes, NSW: 1898–1934), Friday 11 November 1904, p. 6, 'Maliciously Killing a Horse'

Western Champion (Parkes, NSW: 1898–1934), Friday 17 March 1905, p. 11, 'District Court', re Canfell (Sullivan's tent neighbour), Andrew Shean landowner

Western Champion (Parkes, NSW: 1898–1934), Thursday 19 March 1914, p. 8, 'Thirty Years', Senior Constable Garstang, Forbes

Wodonga and Towong Sentinel (Vic.: 1885–1954), Friday 8 December 1899, p. 2, re Kate Kelly suicide

Wyalong Star and Temora and Barmedman Advertiser (West Wyalong, NSW: 1894–1895; 1899), Tuesday 13 August 1895, p. 2, 'A Trip to Lake Cowal'

Yorke's Peninsula Advertiser (SA: 1878–1922), Tuesday 21 December 1880, p. 3, 'Kate Kelly arrived in Adelaide today'

Young Witness (NSW: 1915–1923), Tuesday 14 November 1916, p. 2, 'Swagman Suicides', Forbes

Song lyrics

Dion Boucicault, 'The Wearing of the Green,' song lyrics, in *Arraghna Pogue* [*The Wicked Wedding*], 1864, *University of South Florida: Scholar Commons*, <https://scholarcommons.usf.edu/cgi/viewcontent.cgi?article=1000&context=artstud_pub>, accessed 2020

SECONDARY SOURCES

Articles

'The Australian Magistracy: from Justices of the Peace to Judges and Beyond', Lowndes Paper, <http://jca.asn.au/wp-content/uploads/2013/11/LowndesPaper.pdf>

Dawson, Stuart E., 'Redeeming Fitzpatrick', *Eras Journal*, vol. 17, no. 1, <www.monash.edu/__data/assets/pdf_file/0011/1675919/eras-171-4-stuart-dawson-final.pdf >

Flood, Joe Doctor, 'Urban Slums Report: The Case of Sydney, Australia', Sydney 1788–2001

Gall, Jennifer, 'Kate Kelly in Story and Song', *National Library of Australia Magazine*, June 2015, pp. 24–7

Gelder, Ken, 'The case for Ned Kelly's Jerilderie Letter', The Conversation, 5 May 2014, <https://theconversation.com/the-case-for-ned-kellys-jerilderie-letter-25898>, accessed 2020

James, Marianne, Anderson, Jessica, and Putt, Judy, 'Missing Persons in Australia', Trends and issues in crime and criminal justice, no. 353, Canberra: Australian Institute of Criminology, <www.aic.gov.au/publications/tandi/tandi353>

Jowett, Stephanie, Carpenter, Belinda, and Tait, Gordon, 'Determining a suicide under Australian Law: A comparative study of coronial practice', *University of New South Wales Law Journal*, 2018, vol. 41, no. 2, pp. 355–79, <www.unswlawjournal.unsw.edu.au/wp-content/uploads/2018/05/Jowett-Carpenter-and-Tait.pdf>, accessed 2015–20

Kass, Terry, 'A Thematic History of the Central West: Comprising the NSW Historical Regions of Lachlan and Central Tablelands', Parramatta, NSW: Heritage Office, 2003, <https://trove.nla.gov.au/work/19346236>

Kronborg, Jamie, 'Ned and Ettie's love story', *Wangaratta Chronicle*, 4 July 2014, <https://wangarattachronicle.com.au/2014/07/04/ned-and-etties-love-story/>, accessed 2020

Liston, Carol, 'Convict Women in the Female Factories of New South Wales', <www.rahs.org.au/wp-content/uploads/2015/08/Convict-Women-in-the-Female-Factories-of-New-South-Wales.pdf>

Morgan, Danny, 'Letter detailing Ned Kelly's last stand to go on public display [at the State Library of Victoria]', *ABC News*, 9 October 2013, <www.abc.net.au/news/2013-10-09/letter-ned-kelly-last-stand-public-display/5010526?nw=0>, accessed 2013; the letter from Donald Sutherland to his parents in Scotland, 1880, bears witness to the final stages of the Kelly Gang's last stand at Glenrowan, with Kate holding the wounded Ned's neck, and Grace and Maggie wailing

Romeo, Lisa, review of Brouwer, Xavier, writer/director, *Ned Kelly My Love—The Untold Story of Ettie Hart*, first performed Metanoia Theatre, Mechanics Institute, Brunswick, Vic., 9 November 2016, *Stage Whispers*, <www.stagewhispers.com.au/reviews/ned-kelly-my-love>, accessed 2020

Rosenberg, Sebastian, Mendoza, John, Lifeline Australia and Suicide Prevention Australia (Organisation), 'Suicide and suicide prevention in Australia: Breaking the silence', Lifeline Australia: Suicide Prevention Australia, [Australia] 2010, <https://trove.nla.gov.au/work/38234144>

Sontag, Susan, 'Illness as Metaphor', *The New York Review of Books*, 26 January 1978, <www.nybooks.com/articles/1978/01/26/illness-as-metaphor/>, accessed 2019–20

Sydney Criminal Lawyers, 'What is the law on suicide in Australia?', *FindLaw Australia*, <www.findlaw.com.au/articles/5556/what-is-the-law-on-suicide-in-australia.aspx>, accessed 2015–20

Webb, Carolyn and Miletic, Daniella, 'Kelly Gang gun goes for $70,000, but is it the real thing?', *The Age*, 14 November 2007, <www.theage.com.au/national/kelly-gang-gun-goes-for-70-000-but-is-it-the-real-thing-20071114-ge6arm.html>, accessed 2015

Youssef, N.A., Lockwood, L., Su, S., Hao, G. and Rutten, B., 'The Effects of Trauma, with or without PTSD, on the Transgenerational DNA Methylation Alterations in Human Offsprings', *Brain Sciences*, 2018, vol. 8, no. 5, p. 83, <https://doi.org/10.3390/brainsci8050083>, accessed 2015–20

Books

Balcarek, Dagmar and Dean, Gary, *Women and Bushrangers*, Glenrowan, Vic: Glen Rowen Cobb & Co, 2002

Balcarek, Dagmar and Dean, Gary, *Ellen Kelly*, revised edition, Glenrowan, Vic: Glen Rowen Cobb & Co, 2012

Birmingham, John, *Leviathan*, North Sydney, NSW: Random House, 1999

Boxall, George, *Australian Bushrangers: An illustrated history*, Adelaide, SA: Rigby, 1975

Burke, Colleen Z. and Woods, Vincent (eds.), *The Turning Wave: Poems and songs of Irish Australia*, Armidale, NSW: Kardoorair Press, 2001

Clune, Frank, *Frank Clune's Ned Kelly*, North Ryde, NSW: Angus & Robertson, 1954, reprinted 1980

Corfield, Justin J., *The Ned Kelly Encyclopaedia*, Melbourne: Lothian, 2003

Jones, Ian, *Ned Kelly: A short life*, Port Melbourne: Lothian, 1995

Kelson, Brendon and McQuilton, John, *Kelly Country: A photographic journey*, St Lucia, Qld: University of Queensland Press, 2001

Oakley, Barry, *The House Under the Hill: A brief history of Collits' Inn*, Hartley Vale, NSW: Collits' Inn, 2001

Mossgreen Auctions, *Important Australian and International Art*, vol. 13 November 2007, Melbourne, Victoria: 2007

Scott, Bill, *Australian Bushrangers*, Frenchs Forest, NSW: New Holland, 2000

Shaw, Ian W., *Glenrowan: The legend of Ned Kelly and the siege that shaped a nation*, Sydney: Pan Macmillan, 2012

Wilson, Rebecca, story and images, *Kate Kelly: Sister of an Outlaw*, Hill End, NSW: 2015

Websites

Ancestry.com.au, family tree research, <www.ancestry.com.au>, accessed 2011–20

Australian Dictionary of Biography, <adb.anu.edu.au/>, accessed 2011–20

Australian War Memorial, Roll of Honour: Frederick Arthur Foster, Private, 17th Australian Infantry Battalion, First World War, Date of death 15 April 1917, Killed in Action, 28 years, Villers-Bretonneux

Memorial, Villers-Bretonneux, Picardie, France, <www.awm.gov.au/collection/R1730440>, accessed 2020

Beyond Blue, <www.beyondblue.org.au>, accessed 2015–20

Canowindra Visitors Centre, <www. nswvisitorguide.com.au/canowindra/>, accessed 2020

Gidget Foundation Australia, information, resources and support for Perinatal Depression and Anxiety (PNDA), <www.gidgetfoundation. org.au>, accessed 2019

Hollow, Ellen, 'Catherine Kelly: In Defence Of My Great Grand Mother', *IronOutlaw.com*, 25 August 2001, <www.ironoutlaw.com/writings/catherine-kelly-in-defence-of-my-great-grand-mother/>, accessed 2015–20

The Institute of Australian Culture, 'The Cameron letter [by Ned Kelly, 1878]', Edward Kelly, letter, posted at Glenrowan, 14 December 1878, to Victorian Member of Parliament Donald Cameron; source: Public Record Office Victoria: 'Edward Kelly gives statement of his murders of Sergeant Kennedy and others and makes other threats', <www.australianculture.org/the-cameron-letter-ned-kelly-1878>, accessed 2020

Kelly, Edward, letter to the Legislative Assembly, February 1879, *National Museum of Australia Online Features: Ned Kelly's Jerilderie Letter*, <www.nma.gov.au/explore/features/ned-kelly-jerilderie-letter>, accessed 2015–20

Kelly, Kate website, <www.katekelly.biz>, *Lachlan Valley Gold Journal* 73, FFHG 2004, p. 7, Kate Kelly working in Forbes oral history, accessed 2010–15

National Trust of Australia (Victoria), <www.nationaltrust.org.au/vic>, accessed 2014–20

NSW Government Spatial Services: *SIX MAPS*, <https://maps.six.nsw.gov.au/>, NSW land divisions, accessed 2013–20

Old Melbourne Gaol, <www.oldmelbournegaol.com.au/>, accessed 2015–20

Rawsthorne, David, researcher, Collits, Lees, Morris and Field family histories, <www.davidrawsthorne.com>, accessed 2011–15

State Library of New South Wales, <www.sl.nsw.gov.au>, accessed 2010–20

'Sydney Harbour, New South Wales, 1880s–1890s', *Art Gallery of NSW*, <www.artgallery.nsw.gov.au/collection/works/118.1988/>, accessed 2020

www.trove.nla.gov.au

HISTORIC SITES

Beechworth, Victoria

Benalla, Victoria

Canowindra, NSW

Chiltern, Victoria

Eugowra, NSW

Forbes, NSW

    Bedgerabong Road; Sherriff and Browne Streets; Camp Street Bridge; Forbes Hospital; Forbes Courthouse; Forbes Police Station; Victoria Park; Forbes Lake and Lagoon; Forbes Racecourse; Forbes Town Hall; Forbes School of Arts; Lachlan River, various other regional sites

Glenrowan, Victoria

    Glenrowan Railway Station; Ann Jones' Hotel site

Greta, Victoria

King Valley, Victoria

Murga, NSW

Rutherglen, Victoria

Wangaratta, Victoria

Woolshed, Victoria

Illustration Sources

Photo section in order of appearance

Kate Kelly cameo: State Library of New South Wales

Kate Kelly illustration: The National Library of Australia

Ellen Kelly: State Library of Victoria

Maggie Kelly: State Library of Victoria

Young Ned Kelly: National Museum of Australia

Jim Kelly: source unknown

Dan Kelly: State Library of Victoria

Alexander Fitzpatrick: The Victoria Police Museum

Kelly Hunters: State Library of Victoria

Kelly Gang: State Library of Victoria

French illustration of Kate: State Library Victoria

Ned Kelly illustration: State Library Victoria

Kate on horseback: National Library of Australia

Ned Kelly: State Library Victoria

Kelly homestead: State Library of Victoria

Waxworks: Getty Images

Kate postcards: State Library of Victoria (top); Mossgreen Auctions catalogue, November 2007 (bottom)

Apollo Hall: Public Record Office Victoria

Ticket: *The Winter 2007 Newsletter of Victoria Theatres Trust*

Cadow Station: Frances Higgins

Kate Kelly: source unknown

Young Bricky: source unknown

Old Bricky: Forbes Historical Museum

Warroo Station: Forbes Historical Museum

Burrawang Station: Forbes Historical Museum

Prow's General Store: Forbes Historical Museum

Forbes street: Forbes Historical Museum

Forbes lagoon: Rebecca Wilson

Forbes Courthouse: New South Wales State Archives and Records

Fred Foster: Forbes Historical Museum

Kate's grave: State Library of Victoria

Kate's gun: Mossgreen Auctions catalogue, November 2007

In-text illustrations in order of appearance

Page 23: 'Capture of the Kelly Gang,' *Illustrated Sydney News and New South Wales Agriculturalist and Grazier* (NSW: 1872–1881) 10 July 1880: 11.

Page 70: 'Forbes,' *Western Champion* (Parkes, NSW: 1898–1934) 30 September 1898: 8; Advertising, *Western Champion* (Parkes, NSW: 1898–1934) 21 October 1898: 7.

Page 107: 'More Kelly Rumours,' *Evening News* (Sydney, NSW: 1869–1931) 25 June 1879: 3.

Page 139: Advertising, *Newcastle Morning Herald and Miners' Advocate* (NSW: 1876–1954) 8 November 1881: 3.

Page 218: Kelly Historical Collection, Part 2, Crown Law Department, VPRS 4966, P0000, 3.

Page 247: 'Kate Kelly's Troupe,' originally published in *The Bulletin*, 27 November 1880. Reprinted in *The Bulletin*, 26 November 1966.

Page 261: 'Latest Telegrams,' *The Telegraph* (Brisbane, Qld.: 1872–1947) 25 November 1880: 2.

Page 280: Advertising, *Goulburn Herald* (NSW: 1881–1907) 22 September 1881: 3.

Page 283: 'Kate Kelly,' *The Illustrated Adelaide News* (SA: 1875–1880) 1 August 1880: 4.

Page 334: 'Kate Was drowned at Forbes,' *Truth* (Sydney, NSW: 1894–1954) 25 July 1954: 60.